PUBLIC CITY / PUBLIC SEX

Andrew Israel Ross

PUBLIC CITY / PUBLIC SEX

Homosexuality, Prostitution, and Urban Culture in Nineteenth-Century Paris

TEMPLE UNIVERSITY PRESS
Philadelphia • Rome • Tokyo

TEMPLE UNIVERSITY PRESS
Philadelphia, Pennsylvania 19122
tupress.temple.edu

Portions of Chapters 2, 3, and 6 were reprinted from the following sources:
Chapter 2: Andrew Israel Ross, "Dirty Desire: The Uses and Misuses of Public Urinals in
   Nineteenth-Century Paris," *Berkeley Journal of Sociology* 53 (2009): 62–88.
Chapter 3: Andrew Israel Ross, "Sex in the Archives: Homosexuality, Prostitution, and the
   Archives de la Préfecture de Police de Paris," *French Historical Studies* 40, no. 2 (2017):
   267–290. Copyright 2017, the Society of French Historical Studies. All rights reserved.
   Republished by permission of the copyright holder and the present publisher, Duke
   University Press, www.dukeupress.edu.
Chapter 6: Andrew Israel Ross, "Serving Sex: Playing with Prostitution in the *Brasseries à
   femmes* of Late Nineteenth-Century Paris," *Journal of the History of Sexuality* 24, no. 2
   (2015): 288–313. Copyright © 2015 by the University of Texas Press. All rights reserved.

Library of Congress Cataloging-in-Publication Data

Names: Ross, Andrew Israel, 1983– author.
Title: Public city/public sex : homosexuality, prostitution, and urban
   culture in nineteenth-century Paris / Andrew Israel Ross.
Description: Philadelphia : Temple University Press, 2019. | Series:
   Sexuality studies | Includes bibliographical references and index. |
Identifiers: LCCN 2018054722 (print) | LCCN 2019001918 (ebook) |
   ISBN 9781439914908 (E-book) | ISBN 9781439914885 (cloth : alk. paper) |
   ISBN 9781439914892 (pbk : alk. paper)
Subjects: LCSH: Male homosexuality—France—Paris—History—19th century. |
   Prostitution—France—Paris—History—19th century. | Public sex—France—
   Paris—History—19th century. | City and town life—France—Paris—History—
   19th century. | City planning—France—Paris—History—19th century. |
   Social control—France—Paris—History—19th century. | Paris (France)—
   Social conditions—19th century. | Paris (France)—Social policy.
Classification: LCC HQ76.2.F82 (ebook) | LCC HQ76.2.F82 R67 2019 (print) |
   DDC 306.76/620944361—dc23
LC record available at https://lccn.loc.gov/2018054722

Printed in the United States of America

9 8 7 6 5 4 3 2 1

In memory of Erin Berman

CONTENTS

ACKNOWLEDGMENTS

I write these acknowledgments at a moment of professional transition, having just moved to a new city to begin the fall semester at a new institution. I therefore find it especially gratifying to think back now on all the people who helped make this book possible.

I have benefited from constant mentorship. Steven Hause introduced me to the city of Paris and to French history. It is thanks to him and his work that I developed into a historian of sexuality in the first place. Dena Goodman's seminar on cultural history helped crystallize my own approach. David Caron graciously agreed to serve on my dissertation committee and provided immensely useful comments that made this a better book. Éric Fassin graciously sponsored me as I applied for research funding and invited me to attend his sexuality studies seminar in Paris. Michael Sibalis oriented me to the archives. Without his pathbreaking work, my own would not have been possible. He also introduced me to Régis Revenin, who graciously shared some of his own research notes with me. Malika Rahal was my landlord and roommate in Paris, and she helped me find my bearings there as well. Kathleen Canning and Scott Spector shaped this project both formally and informally; their continued assistance and encouragement have been essential to my success. Finally, Joshua Cole has been central to my development as a scholar. As mentor, colleague, and friend, Josh has provided the advice, critique, and conversation necessary to complete this book. It is impossible to express how much his faith in me and my work has meant over the years.

This work also could not have come to fruition without the support of the Departments of History at Kenyon College and the University of Southern Mississippi. I am especially grateful to my department chairs for their advice and professional support: Glenn McNair and Wendy Singer at Kenyon and Kyle Zelner at Southern Miss. My new colleagues at Loyola University Maryland provided a warm welcome as I finished this project.

Friends and colleagues all over the globe shaped this book. Special thanks go to Lucy Biederman, Patrick Bottiger, Hanno Burmeister, Catherine Clark, Kristyna Comer, Ela Gezen, Kirsten Leng, Kithika St. John, Kathleen Tipler, David Trout, Oslec Villegas, Alexia Yates, and everyone in London for their companionship both at home and abroad. Minayo Nasiali and Peter Soppelsa remain both friends and mentors. Jessica Fripp was and continues to be my favorite Paris buddy, an amazing scholar who helps me think about art in new ways. I owe special thanks to Rosemary O'Neil, always ready with insightful advice, both professional and personal. Jill Abney, Allison Abra, Courtney Luckhardt, and Alexandra Valint made Hattiesburg a special place.

Too many people read parts of this book to mention them all, but I am grateful to Catherine Clark, Jessica Fripp, David Halperin, Jessie Hewitt, Brian Jacobson, Bruce Kinzer, Kirsten Leng, Tyson Leuchter, Sun-Young Park, Carolyn Purnell, Peter Soppelsa, Alexandra Valint, and Alexia Yates, all of whom provided valuable feedback at various points. At Southern Miss, Jill Abney, Matt Casey, Joshua Haynes, Courtney Luckhardt, and Rebecca Tuuri formed a faculty writing group whose members commented on several chapters. Allison Abra also participated in that group and by the end of the process had read the entire book. It is so much improved for her insight. I owe special thanks as well to Nina Kushner, who provided invaluable input on an initial draft. Holly Grout read the entire manuscript with a great deal of attention several times. The value of her comments cannot be overstated; anyone would be lucky to have a reader as conscientious and insightful as she proved to be. It was a privilege to work with Sara Jo Cohen at Temple University Press, who guided this work to completion. This book also benefited from comments offered at many conferences, but especially at those sponsored by the Society for French Historical Studies and the Western Society for French History.

Without the assistance of the staffs at the Archives de Paris, the Archives Nationales de France, the Bibliothèque Nationale de France, and especially the Archives de la Préfecture de Police de Paris, this project could not have become a reality. I am especially grateful to Isabelle Tarisca at the Paris Police Archives, who helped me locate files and organize my notes as an important series of documents was being reclassified.

This project was supported by funding from several organizations. The University of Michigan History Department and Rackham Graduate School provided travel funds for initial research trips to Paris. The Georges Lurcy Charitable and Educational Trust enabled me to stay. Revisions to the manuscript were made possible by funds from the Institut Français d'Amérique, Kenyon College, and the Aubrey Keith Lucas and Ella Ginn Lucas Endowment at the University of Southern Mississippi. The cost of obtaining permissions was covered by the Orazio A. Ciccarelli Faculty Research Endowment of the Department of History at the University of Southern Mississippi. The Center for the Humanities at Loyola University Maryland provided funds that supported the preparation of the final manuscript.

Finally, and most importantly, I owe thanks to my family. My aunt Sandy is also a historian, and we both know my interest in history came from her. My grandparents passed away as I began my academic career, but they continue to inspire me. My cat, Meika, must be credited for lap time. I am fortunate to have a small, loving extended family: Aunt Rikki and Uncle Marc, Uncle Ozzie, Uncle Ed, Annie, Parker, Andy, Will, and Sam. My sister, Michelle, has always encouraged me as I pursued my goals, even when they took me to unexpected places. Last, my mom and dad have always supported me in my choices and have seen me through this process with constant love. As I finish these acknowledgments, my small extended family has unexpectedly become smaller with my cousin Erin's sudden passing. I dedicate this book to her.

PUBLIC CITY / PUBLIC SEX

INTRODUCTION

On March 28, 1874, the minister of public works of the young French Third Republic (1870–1940) wrote a short note to the prefect of police of Paris, alerting him to a problem at the Palais-Royal in the center of the French capital. Onetime residence of the Orléans branch of the French royal family, the Palais-Royal was by then a well-established arena of public sociability, with a garden, arcades, and small shops. It was also a long-standing haunt of women who sold sex and men who sought sex with other men.[1] As the letter explained, "The tenants of the Galerie d'Orléans [an arcade situated between the palace itself and the garden] of the Palais-Royal complain that this gallery serves every day, particularly in the evening, as the rendezvous of individuals of both sexes with depraved morals, whose presence keeps away honest people and which causes real harm to commerce."[2] About a month and a half later, the police responded to the minister's concern by affirming that this area remained under near-constant surveillance, which resulted in the "daily arrest of prostitutes and pederasts," as men who sought

---

1. Michael Sibalis, "The Palais-Royal and the Homosexual Subculture of Nineteenth-Century Paris," *Journal of Homosexuality* 41, nos. 3–4 (2001): 117–129; Andrew J. Counter, *The Amorous Restoration: Love, Sex, and Politics in Early Nineteenth-Century France* (Oxford: Oxford University Press, 2016), chap. 3; Clyde Plumauzille, *Prostitution et révolution: Les femmes publiques dans la cité républicaine (1789–1804)* (Ceyzérieu, France: Champ Vallon, 2016), 94–114.

2. Ministre des Travaux publics to Préfet de Police de Paris, March 28, 1874, "Palais-Royal. Dossier général," JC 33, formerly BM2 32, Archives de la Préfecture de Police de Paris (henceforth APP).

sex with other men were commonly called in the nineteenth century.[3] At the same time, the police noted their concern that this surveillance in such a busy part of the city might also "keep away those taking a promenade without producing the desired results and that it could bring, to the contrary, grave harm to the commerce of the arcade."[4]

These letters place sexual solicitation as a central administrative issue and underscore its significance to wandering the Palais-Royal, especially in the evening.[5] Though brief, the exchange reveals themes that were central to discussions of the security, safety, health, and morality of Paris among the police, moral commentators, and other administrators during the nineteenth century. The call for the police to manage who could and could not access public space, often in the name of commerce, and in light of an apparent distinction between "honest" and "dishonest" Parisians, threaded their way through attempts to manage the life of a city undergoing rapid and large-scale change. And yet the police's fear that their own intervention would only exacerbate the problem highlights a simple fact: sex could not so easily be hidden from public view, nor could the distinction between the proper and improper users of urban space be easily sustained. Indeed, the very attempt to control those seeking sex in public may have only perpetuated the problem.

This book traces the struggle between those who tried to control evidence of sex in public and those who provided it, sought it out, and otherwise encountered it in transforming urban spaces. In doing so, it posits the central importance of women who sold sex and men who sought sex with other men to what we now consider characteristically "modern" forms of urban culture.[6] Through the course of the century, Paris provided the setting for the development of new models of urban renewal that remade the capital into the city of broad boulevards, department stores, cafés, restaurants, and dance halls that we know today. State administrators, expert moralists, police authorities, and

---

3. On the term "pederast," see Jean-Claude Féray, *Grecques, les mœurs du hanneton? Histoire du mot* pédérastie *et de ses dérivés en langue française* (Paris: Quintes-Feuilles, 2004).

4. Préfet de Police de Paris to Ministre des Travaux publics, May 19, 1874, "Palais-Royal. Dossier général," JC 33, formerly BM2 32, APP.

5. On the difference between the Palais-Royal during the day and at night, see Simone Delattre, *Les douzes heures noires: La nuit à Paris au XIXe siècle* (Paris: Albin Michel, 2003), 222–227.

6. On nineteenth-century Paris as a site of "modernity," see, for example, T. J. Clark, *The Painting of Modern Life: Paris in the Art of Manet and His Followers,* rev. ed. (Princeton, N.J.: Princeton University Press, 1999); David Harvey, *Paris, Capital of Modernity* (New York: Routledge, 2006); H. Hazel Hahn, *Scenes of Parisian Modernity: Culture and Consumption in the Nineteenth Century* (New York: Palgrave Macmillan, 2009); Hollis Clayson and André Dombrowski, eds., *Is Paris Still the Capital of the Nineteenth Century? Essays on Art and Modernity, 1850–1900* (London: Routledge, 2016).

private entrepreneurs struggled to redesign, redevelop, and redeploy city space in ways that opened Paris to new modes of social control, circulation, and consumption. The destruction of slums and other crowded spaces to make room for new apartment buildings and streets encouraged upwardly mobile Parisians to use the public spaces of the city, which in turn propelled the growth of a mature consumer culture.[7] At the same time, the apparent embourgeoisement of the city during the second half of the nineteenth century entailed greater efforts on the part of the authorities to manage its working-class and poor populations. Housing segregation complemented continuing police efforts to monitor working-class establishments and the streets of the city.[8] These efforts to keep distinct the "respectable" and "disreputable" populations of the city, however, had paradoxical effects: attempts to prevent certain kinds of social interactions actually created novel opportunities for them to thrive. The provision of avenues for public enjoyment—pleasure— also provided opportunities for locating public sex.

Although the idea of Paris as a "capital of pleasure" already rose to the level of cliché in the nineteenth century, sex has often stood at the margins of histories of the city.[9] This book reinscribes sex at the center of the history of nineteenth-century Parisian culture by arguing that the very effort to

---

7. On nineteenth-century Parisian consumer culture, see Michael B. Miller, *The Bon Marché: Bourgeois Culture and the Department Store, 1869–1920* (Princeton, N.J.: Princeton University Press, 1981); Rosalind H. Williams, *Dream Worlds: Mass Consumption in Late Nineteenth-Century France* (Berkeley: University of California Press, 1982); Charles Rearick, *Pleasures of the Belle Époque: Entertainment and Festivity in Turn-of-the-Century France* (New Haven, Conn.: Yale University Press, 1985); Vanessa R. Schwartz, *Spectacular Realities: Early Mass Culture in Fin-de-Siècle Paris* (Berkeley: University of California Press, 1998); Victoria E. Thompson, *The Virtuous Marketplace: Women and Men, Money and Politics in Paris, 1830–1870* (Baltimore: Johns Hopkins University Press, 2000); Lisa Tiersten, *Marianne in the Market: Envisioning Consumer Society in Fin-de-Siècle France* (Berkeley: University of California Press, 2001); Ruth E. Iskin, *Modern Women and Parisian Consumer Culture in Impressionist Painting* (Cambridge: Cambridge University Press, 2007).

8. On class segregation in Paris, see Tyler Stovall, *The Rise of the Paris Red Belt* (Berkeley: University of California Press, 1990), esp. chap. 1; Colin Jones, *Paris: Biography of a City* (New York: Penguin, 2004), 318–320, 357–360, 364–367; James Cannon, *The Paris Zone: A Cultural History, 1840–1944* (Farnham, U.K.: Ashgate, 2015). On the policing of working-class spaces, see esp. Susanna Barrows, "'Parliaments of the People': The Political Culture of Cafés in the Early Third Republic," in *Drinking: Behavior and Belief in Modern History,* ed. Susanna Barrows and Robin Room (Berkeley: University of California Press, 1991), 87–97; W. Scott Haine, *The World of the Paris Café: Sociability among the French Working Class, 1789–1914* (Baltimore: Johns Hopkins University Press, 1996), chap. 1. On street policing in nineteenth-century Paris, see Clive Emsley, "Policing the Streets of Early Nineteenth-Century Paris," *French History* 1, no. 2 (1987), 257–282; Quentin Deluermoz, *Policiers dans la ville: La construction d'un ordre public à Paris (1854–1914)* (Paris: Publications de la Sorbonne, 2012).

9. Rearick, *Pleasures of the Belle Époque,* 39–42; H. Hahn, *Scenes of Parisian Modernity,* 45–46.

police the city created new opportunities for women who sold sex and men who sought sex with other men. These opportunities became clear to passing Parisians by way of ephemeral signs: an older woman standing at the door of a brothel, a discreet glance between two men outside a public urinal, a shout across a street between a woman and a passer-by. The ability to locate sex in public, made more possible by urban renovations and new police practices, implicated anyone who became aware of it. Therefore, the appropriation of the city by women who sold sex and men who sought sex with other men not only entailed the growth of two discrete sexual subcultures but also highlights the appearance of a much more diffuse sexual culture to which anyone could—temporarily, perhaps—belong. The story told here, therefore, does not revolve around the emergence of particular sexual identities as women and men sought sexual pleasure outside the family. Rather, it shows how the uses of public space encouraged various kinds of relationships between strangers that gave rise to desires that may or may not have been linked to a particular kind of identity, whether homosexual or heterosexual. The city, in this sense, incited sexual desire among the populace in an effort at controlling its effects, but sex ultimately exceeded the control of those who designed, observed, and policed it.

Histories of Paris, Histories of Sex

Stretching from the late Restoration (1815–1830) through successive regimes of the July Monarchy (1830–1848), Second Republic (1848–1851), Second Empire (1852–1870), Commune (1871), and first decades of the Third Republic, the story told here does not always align with major political changes. Slower and less related to singular events, the ongoing development of the city and the emergence of sexual publics relied on discourses, institutions, and practices that crossed political boundaries.[10] That said, the basic periodization of the story told here follows trends laid out by other historians of sexuality, urban culture, and Parisian governance.

Recent histories of Paris have revised once-common temporal boundaries by emphasizing the significance of early nineteenth-century innovations in urban design and policing. Drawing on then-novel notions of urban development that reconceptualized the city on a grand scale in order to harmonize its constituent parts, urbanists and urban thinkers envisioned an

---

10. As Dagmar Herzog has explained, "The shapes of daily life activities . . . transform in response to events and pressures that may not always be clearly linked to what political regime happened to be in power." Dagmar Herzog, *Sex after Fascism: Memory and Morality in Twentieth-Century Germany* (Princeton, N.J.: Princeton University Press, 2005), 18–19. See also Laure Adler, *Les maisons closes, 1830–1930* (Paris: Fayard/Pluriel, 2010), 17.

urban plan that "would elevate the moral and physical condition of all its inhabitants" in order to manage a rapidly growing population, especially of the working class.[11] Intervention into the city's infrastructure was fairly limited until the Second Empire, but urbanist discourse complemented studies that linked housing conditions to disease and emphasized the risk posed by urban slums, even as local urban works foreshadowed the grand projects of Georges-Eugène Haussmann and a form of advertising laid the groundwork for the consumer culture of the latter period.[12]

Public City/Public Sex brings this story into dialogue with the history of sexuality by showcasing how early nineteenth-century attempts to manage the city complemented and were shaped by police efforts to control public sex. Historians of prostitution have shown that the early decades of the century were essential to the emergence of comprehensive attempts to manage and police female prostitution.[13] Historians of male homosexuality, meanwhile, have emphasized the public evidence of men who sought sex with other men in the same period.[14] These developments complemented emerging hygienic discourse and practice.[15] The construction of a "regulated" system to control female prostitution entailed the use of physical spaces—*maisons de tolérance* (tolerated brothels)—to facilitate the provision of "seminal drains" for a growing working-class population in order to ensure public health and safety.[16] At the same time, the city began constructing public urinals that quickly served

11. Nicholas Papayanis, *Planning Paris before Haussmann* (Baltimore: Johns Hopkins University Press, 2004), 247.

12. Ann-Louise Shapiro, *Housing the Poor of Paris, 1850–1902* (Madison: University of Wisconsin Press, 1985), chap. 1; Andrew R. Aisenberg, *Contagion: Disease, Government, and the "Social Question" in Nineteenth-Century France* (Stanford, Calif.: Stanford University Press, 1999), chaps. 1 and 2; H. Hahn, *Scenes of Parisian Modernity*, pt. 1; Ralph Kingston, "Capitalism in the Streets: Paris Shopkeepers, *Passages Couverts,* and the Production of the Early Nineteenth-Century City," *Radical History Review* 2012, no. 114 (2012): 39–65. On the social question more generally in early nineteenth-century Paris, see esp. Giovanna Procacci, *Gouverner la misère: La question sociale en France, 1789–1848* (Paris: Seuil, 1993).

13. Alain Corbin, *Les filles de noce: Misère sexuelle et prostitution au XIXe siècle* (Paris: Flammarion, 1982), esp. pt. 1; Jill Harsin, *Policing Prostitution in Nineteenth-Century Paris* (Princeton, N.J.: Princeton University Press, 1985), pt. 1.

14. Sibalis, "Palais-Royal," 121–123.

15. On this theme, see, for instance, Charles Bernheimer, *Figures of Ill Repute: Representing Prostitution in Nineteenth-Century France* (Cambridge, Mass: Harvard University Press, 1989), chap. 1; Donald Reid, *Paris Sewers and Sewermen: Realities and Representations* (Cambridge, Mass: Harvard University Press, 1991), 23; Briana Lewis, "The Sewer and the Prostitute in *Les Misérables*: From Regulation to Redemption," *Nineteenth-Century French Studies* 44, nos. 3–4 (2016): 266–278. See also Frank Mort, *Dangerous Sexualities: Medico-moral Politics in England since 1830,* 2nd ed. (London: Routledge, 2000).

16. Louis Fiaux, *La police des mœurs devant la Commission Extraparlementaire du Régime des Mœurs* (Paris: Félix Alcan, 1907), 1:212. See also Corbin, *Les filles de noce,* 84.

men seeking sex with other men in public.[17] These "drains"—physical and metaphorical, hygienic and sexual—linked early Paris urbanism directly to the management of public sex.

The coincidence of new urbanist ideas and forms, novel police practices around female prostitution, and increasing public visibility of men who sought sex with other men was no accident. Rather, these elements were brought together by broader changes in urban governance, as state officials, expert commentators, and builders began to bring environment and society into "a common frame."[18] The groundwork laid during the first half of the century coalesced during the process known as Haussmannization, which has dominated discussion of French urban history generally and Parisian history in particular.[19] Haussmann drew on an existing urbanism that emphasized the need to see the city "as a whole" and strove to ensure that its interlocking parts—its sewers and water systems, streets and public transport, train lines and train stations—worked together in order to facilitate the circulation of people, goods, and capital.[20]

Haussmann's feats have, by now, been well rehearsed: the demolition of slums, the building of new boulevards, the creation of new sewer lines displaced hundreds of thousands in an effort to open the "medieval" city to circulation.[21] "Boulevards," as T. J. Clark put it, "were the heart of the matter."[22]

---

17. William A. Peniston, *Pederasts and Others: Urban Culture and Sexual Identity in Nineteenth-Century Paris* (New York: Harrington Park Press, 2004), 140–141; Régis Revenin, *Homosexualité et prostitution masculines à Paris, 1870–1918* (Paris: L'Harmattan, 2005), 36–41; Andrew Israel Ross, "Dirty Desire: The Uses and Misuses of Public Urinals in Nineteenth-Century Paris," *Berkeley Journal of Sociology* 53 (2009): 62–88.

18. Paul Rabinow, *French Modern: Norms and Forms of the Social Environment* (Chicago: University of Chicago Press, 1995), 11.

19. The literature on Haussmannization is vast. See esp. David H. Pinkney, *Napoleon III and the Rebuilding of Paris* (Princeton, N.J.: Princeton University Press, 1958); François Loyer, *Paris Nineteenth Century: Architecture and Urbanism,* trans. Charles Lynn Clark (New York: Abbeville Press, 1988); David P. Jordan, *Transforming Paris: The Life and Labors of Baron Haussmann* (New York: Free Press, 1995); Michel Carmona, *Haussmann: His Life and Times, and the Making of Modern Paris,* trans. Patrick Camiller (Chicago: Ivan R. Dee, 2002); D. Harvey, *Paris, Capital of Modernity*; Eric Fournier, *Paris en ruines: Du Paris haussmannien au Paris communard* (Paris: Éditions Imago, 2008); Stephane Kirkland, *Paris Reborn: Napoléon III, Baron Haussmann, and the Quest to Build a Modern City* (New York: St. Martin's Press, 2013).

20. On the origins of these ideas, see esp. Papayanis, *Planning Paris before Haussmann.* On nineteenth-century urbanism before Haussmann more broadly, see esp. Karen Bowie, ed., *La modernité avant Haussmann: Formes de l'espace urbain à Paris, 1801–1853* (Paris: Éditions Recherches, 2001).

21. Haussmann himself claimed to have displaced about 350,000 people (or 117,552 families). Shapiro, *Housing the Poor of Paris,* 34–35.

22. Clark, *Painting of Modern Life,* 37.

The emphasis on movement further cemented public space as the central axis around which the city revolved as public display took on greater importance in an emerging society of consumption.[23] As those who once characterized the public life of the city—the working class and poor—were supposedly pushed to the side (though not, as we shall see, totally removed), a rising middle and upper-middle class increasingly emphasized their own public life.[24] The streets became, by some lights, a place to display one's life rather than actually live.[25]

Haussmannization, then, contributed to the development of new forms of consumption that drew on preexisting associations of certain areas of the city with the pursuit of "pleasure." However, although some historians have acknowledged the use of sex to sell goods, few have integrated sex qua sex into their definitions of pleasure.[26] Public sex, it seems, was one of those objects

---

23. Marshall Berman, *All That Is Solid Melts into Air: The Experience of Modernity* (New York: Penguin, 1988), 151–152; D. Harvey, *Paris, Capital of Modernity,* 216; Greg M. Thomas, "Women in Public: The Display of Femininity in the Parks of Paris," in *The Invisible* Flâneuse? *Gender, Public Space, and Visual Culture in Nineteenth-Century Paris,* ed. Aruna D'Souza and Tom McDonough (Manchester, U.K.: Manchester University Press, 2006), 32–48.

24. Philip G. Nord, *Paris Shopkeepers and the Politics of Resentment* (Princeton, N.J.: Princeton University Press, 1986), chap. 3; Victoria E. Thompson, "Urban Renovation, Moral Regeneration: Domesticating the Halles in Second-Empire Paris," *French Historical Studies* 20, no. 1 (1997): 87–109. Temma Balducci has recently emphasized the continuing presence of men and women of all classes on the boulevards of post-Haussmann Paris. See Temma Balducci, *Gender, Space, and the Gaze in Post-Haussmann Visual Culture: Beyond the Flâneur* (London: Routledge, 2017), esp. chap. 1. On working-class life in Paris during and after Haussmannization, see, for instance, Shapiro, *Housing the Poor of Paris*; Eliza Ferguson, "The Cosmos of the Paris Apartment: Working-Class Family Life in the Nineteenth Century," *Journal of Urban History* 37, no. 1 (2011): 59–67.

25. Clark, *Painting of Modern Life,* 36; D. Harvey, *Paris, Capital of Modernity,* chap. 12. On one representation of the relationship between rich and poor during Haussmannization, see Berman, *All That Is Solid Melts into Air,* 152–155; Edward J. Ahearn, "A Café in the High Time of Haussmannization: Baudelaire's Confrontation with the Eyes of the Poor," in *The Thinking Space: The Café as a Cultural Institution in Paris, Italy, and Vienna,* ed. Leona Rittner, W. Scott Haine, and Jeffrey H. Jackson (Farnham, U.K.: Ashgate, 2013), 93–100.

26. Considerations of the relationship between sexuality and consumer culture include Ruth E. Iskin, "Selling, Seduction, and Soliciting the Eye: Manet's Bar at the Folies-Bergère," *Art Bulletin* 77, no. 1 (1995): 25–44; Karen L. Carter, "Unfit for Public Display: Female Sexuality and the Censorship of Fin-de-Siècle Publicity Posters," *Early Popular Visual Culture* 8, no. 2 (2010): 107–124; Lela F. Kerley, *Uncovering Paris: Scandals and Nude Spectacles in the Belle Époque* (Baton Rouge: Louisiana State University Press, 2017). Historians and art historians of prostitution, on the other hand, have more readily integrated histories of consumption with that of sex and sexual activity. See, for example, Theresa Ann Gronberg, "Femmes de Brasserie," *Art History* 7, no. 3 (1984): 329–344; Hollis Clayson, *Painted Love: Prostitution in French Art of the Impressionist Era* (Los Angeles: Getty Publications, 2003), chap. 4; Lola Gonzalez-Quijano, *Capitale de l'amour: Filles et lieux de plaisir à Paris aux XIXe siècle* (Paris: Vendémiaire, 2015).

effaced by the new regime, referenced and imagined, but not really practiced. The introduction to a recent volume bringing together essays on Parisian modernity, for instance, describes "the image of Paris as a world headquarters of beauty and pleasure" and references the various entertainments and spectacles that so enamored its residents and visitors during the second half of the nineteenth century—cafés, the Eiffel Tower, even its sewers—but fails to mention sex as one of the pleasures on offer.[27] Studies of the transformation of Paris before, during, and after the process of Haussmannization have similarly had relatively little to say about sex and sexuality.[28] Making sex available—both for sale and not—however, provided one avenue for working-class and other marginalized individuals to continue to participate in the shaping of urban life.

Sex stood as a major focus of debates around the changing city for politicians, the police, and Parisians. The attempt to manage the ways that prostitutes, pederasts, and other Parisians sought out sexual pleasure formed an important component in broader efforts to police the city while also providing the grounds on which urban space could and would be appropriated by supposedly marginal individuals. Indeed, sex forms but one avenue for witnessing the significance of the socially marginalized to the emergence of modern Paris more broadly. Understanding the relationship between the city and its citizens necessitates attention to the dynamic relationship between police attempts to manage sex and those who practiced sexual solicitation in public spaces, because this relationship implicated not only those two groups but also all Parisians and visitors to Paris. Whether addressing the commercialization of sex and the creation of sex districts for prostitution, the emergence of commercial venues for men and women to meet, or the development of gay and lesbian subcultures, scholars of sexuality have long recognized that the transformation of urban space shaped the sexual economies of the city.[29]

---

27. Hollis Clayson and André Dombrowski, "Introduction," in *Is Paris Still the Capital?*, 1–2. This is all the more surprising considering that one of the editors of the volume once declared, "The existence of prostitution on a scale so widespread and obvious that it alarmed contemporaries was a distinctive and distinguishing feature of nineteenth-century Parisian culture." Clayson, *Painted Love*, 1. This claim closely echoes one made in Richard J. Evans, "Prostitution, State, and Society in Imperial Germany," *Past and Present* no. 70 (1976): 106.

28. Although Colin Jones's *Paris: Biography of a City*, for instance, does occasionally mention prostitution; it references homosexuality only twice and does not address sex or sexual behavior more broadly. See Jones, *Paris: Biography of a City*.

29. To name just a few examples that have informed my own thinking, see John d'Emilio, "Capitalism and Gay Identity," in *Powers of Desire: The Politics of Sexuality*, ed. Ann Snitow, Christine Stansell, and Sharon Thompson (New York: Monthly Review Press, 1983), 100–113; Lawrence Knopp, "Sexuality and the Spatial Dynamics of Capitalism," *Environment and Planning D: Society and Space* 10, no. 6 (1992): 651–669; Timothy J. Gilfoyle, *City of Eros: New York City, Prostitution, and the Commercialization of Sex, 1790–1920* (New York: W. W. Norton,

Historians of sexuality in Paris have taken up these themes, showing how urban transformation, the emergence of public spaces such as urinals and parks, and the development of commercial entertainments reshaped the business of prostitution while also providing new opportunities for men to meet other men and women to meet other women.[30] In general, however, these insights have not been addressed by historians in their efforts to understand the transformation of Paris more broadly.

This lacuna remains despite important recent work that has shifted our attention away from the timing and extent of an urban development that emerged from the top down to interpretations that emphasize a more multi-layered process involving administrators, workers, residents, financiers, and entrepreneurs acting against and alongside one another in diverse ways to reconstruct the city.[31] One exception is Richard Hopkins's recent *Planning the Greenspaces of Nineteenth-Century Paris,* which explores the relationship between the design and the actual use of parks and gardens. Hopkins traces the conflicts and debates that shaped urban space as Parisians took up the built environment to their own ends. In an all-too-brief discussion, Hopkins

---

1992); Judith R. Walkowitz, *City of Dreadful Delight: Narratives of Sexual Danger in Late-Victorian London* (Chicago: University of Chicago Press, 1992); George Chauncey, *Gay New York: Gender, Urban Culture, and the Making of the Gay Male World, 1890–1940* (New York: Basic Books, 1994); Henning Bech, *When Men Meet: Homosexuality and Modernity,* trans. Teresa Mesquit and Tim Davies (Chicago: University of Chicago Press, 1997); Kevin J. Mumford, *Interzones: Black/White Sex Districts in Chicago and New York in the Early Twentieth Century* (New York: Columbia University Press, 1997); Lynda Nead, *Victorian Babylon: People, Streets, and Images in Nineteenth-Century London* (New Haven, Conn.: Yale University Press, 2000); Moira Rachel Kenney, *Mapping Gay L.A.: The Intersection of Place and Politics* (Philadelphia: Temple University Press, 2001); Michael Sibalis, "Urban Space and Homosexuality: The Example of the Marais, Paris' 'Gay Ghetto,'" *Urban Studies* 41, no. 9 (2004): 1739–1758; Matt Houlbrook, *Queer London: Perils and Pleasures in the Sexual Metropolis, 1918–1957* (Chicago: University of Chicago Press, 2005). More recently, a turn to rural spaces has complicated the emphasis on the city. See John Howard, *Men Like That: A Southern Queer History* (Chicago: University of Chicago Press, 1999); Scott Herring, *Another Country: Queer Anti-Urbanism* (New York: New York University Press, 2010); Colin R. Johnson, *Just Queer Folks: Gender and Sexuality in Rural America* (Philadelphia: Temple University Press, 2013).

30. Corbin, *Les filles de noce,* 87–89; Revenin, *Homosexualité et prostitution masculines,* pt. 1; Gonzalez-Quijano, *Capitale de l'amour*; Leslie Choquette, "Gay Paree: The Origins of Lesbian and Gay Commercial Culture in the French Third Republic," *Contemporary French Civilization* 41, no. 1 (2016): 1–24.

31. Rosemary Wakeman, *The Heroic City: Paris, 1945–1958* (Chicago: University of Chicago Press, 2009); Allan Potofsky, *Constructing Paris in the Age of Revolution* (New York: Palgrave Macmillan, 2009); Kingston, "Capitalism in the Streets"; Julian Brigstocke, *The Life of the City: Space, Humour, and the Experience of Truth in Fin-de-Siècle Montmartre* (Farnham, U.K.: Ashgate, 2014); Alexia M. Yates, *Selling Paris: Property and Commercial Culture in the Fin-de-Siècle Capital* (Cambridge, Mass: Harvard University Press, 2015); Sun-Young Park, *Ideals of the Body: Architecture, Urbanism, and Hygiene in Postrevolutionary Paris* (Pittsburgh: University of Pittsburgh Press, 2018).

argues that this interaction also involved marginalized groups within the population, including female prostitutes and men who sought sex with other men, both of whom participated in the creation of communities based on the common use of public space.[32]

In this study I explore the dynamic relationship between those who built and those who used the city, but I argue that the sexual uses of space were more significant than has generally been recognized.[33] In order to do so, I deemphasize the relative weight historians of sexuality have placed on the "marginalization" or "enclosed world" of prostitution and the development of subcultures among men who sought sex with other men.[34] In both instances, historians have emphasized a certain separateness of both groups from the broader social and cultural milieu of which they were also a part, even as some have acknowledged their sheer visibility.[35] Indeed, the very insistence on writing a "history of prostitution" or a "history of homosexuality" orients the project around specific identities that may or may not have even operated at the time. In contrast, my approach refuses to take "identity" as my analytical center. Instead of tracing the ways specific individuals, defined in large measure by modern sexual categories, responded to repressive police forces intent on maintaining strict distinctions between "honest" Parisians and "indecent" women and "depraved" men, therefore, I question these categories.

If "respectable" heterosexual complementarity seems missing here, it is because it was always simultaneously assumed *and* implicated in these other forms of public sexual activity. Just as Laure Murat has troubled gender difference in nineteenth-century France through her analysis of the "third sex," I trouble

---

32. Richard S. Hopkins, *Planning the Greenspaces of Nineteenth-Century Paris* (Baton Rouge: Louisiana State University Press, 2015), 125–129.

33. In this sense, I share with recent work in the history of prostitution a concern to capture how individuals and groups who were marginalized because of their sexual behavior shaped the systems of regulation and management that sought to constrain them as they participated in the broader community. See, for instance, Nina Kushner, *Erotic Exchanges: The World of Elite Prostitution in Eighteenth-Century France* (Ithaca, N.Y.: Cornell University Press, 2013), 6–10; Keely Stauter-Halsted, *The Devil's Chain: Prostitution and Social Control in Partitioned Poland* (Ithaca, N.Y.: Cornell University Press, 2015), esp. chap. 3.

34. Corbin, *Les filles de noce,* pt. 1, chap. 2; Harsin, *Policing Prostitution,* 206; Peniston, *Pederasts and Others,* 67–69. Scholars in the fields of literary criticism, queer studies, and social theory have been more apt to highlight the centrality of these figures—even if often only as symbols—to modern urban life. See, for instance, Susan Buck-Morss, "The Flâneur, the Sandwichman, and the Whore: The Politics of Loitering," *New German Critique* 39 (1986): 104; Rita Felski, *The Gender of Modernity* (Cambridge, Mass: Harvard University Press, 1995), 19–20; Bech, *When Men Meet,* 154; Julie Abraham, *Metropolitan Lovers: The Homosexuality of Cities* (Minneapolis: University of Minnesota Press, 2009), 30.

35. Corbin, *Les filles de noce,* 302; Sibalis, "Palais-Royal," 117; Revenin, *Homosexualité et prostitution masculines à Paris,* 19–21; Gonzalez-Quijano, *Capitale de l'amour,* 69.

the too often assumed distinction between "normal" and "abnormal" sexuality. In doing so, I question whether it is true, as she argues, that during the long nineteenth century "the 'third sex' will always be the other, the stranger, the incongruous, and, between 1835 and 1939, no matter their sexuality, the 'feminine' man and the 'masculine' woman remain 'displaced' figures, provoking more often malaise than enthusiasm."[36] By opening up the categories of the prostitute and the homosexual and refusing to project contemporary categories backward into the past, I show that neither person remained fixed by virtue of their sexual behavior.[37] The archival traces of female prostitution and same-sex sexual attraction and their relation to other kinds of urban subjectivities emerge instead as a key analytic question. By taking "public sex," rather than "the female prostitute" or "the homosexual," as the frame of reference, I show how the story of Paris and Parisians remains incomplete without the story of sex as well.

The Logic of Regulationism

Public City/Public Sex integrates histories of sexuality with histories of Paris by emphasizing the mutually constitutive nature of space, sex, and identity. In this regard, I remain indebted to Michel Foucault's interpretation of the history of sexuality. Rejecting what he termed the "repressive hypothesis," Foucault claimed that the eighteenth and especially nineteenth centuries witnessed an "apparatus for producing an ever greater quantity of discourse about sex, capable of functioning and taking effect in its very economy."[38] The constitution of a particular relationship between desire, pleasure, the body, and the self emerged out of various practices that demanded new ways of speaking of sex. As sex became a key avenue through which populations would be managed and the body regimented, new sexualities themselves emerged. If I avoid here Foucault's famous declaration that this process turned the ho-

---

36. Laure Murat, *La loi du genre: Une histoire culturelle du "troisième sexe"* (Paris: Fayard, 2006), 25.

37. In doing so, I follow recent work in queer studies and queer history. See Scott Bravmann, *Queer Fictions of the Past: History, Culture, and Difference* (Cambridge: Cambridge University Press, 1997); Howard, *Men Like That*; Scott Herring, *Queering the Underworld: Slumming, Literature, and the Undoing of Lesbian and Gay History* (Chicago: University of Chicago Press, 2007); Laura Doan, *Disturbing Practices: History, Sexuality, and Women's Experience of Modern War* (Chicago: University of Chicago Press, 2013); Johnson, *Just Queer Folks*; Peter Coviello, *Tomorrow's Parties: Sex and the Untimely in Nineteenth-Century America* (New York: New York University Press, 2013); Andrew E. Clark-Huckstep, "*The History of Sexuality* and Historical Methodology," *Cultural History* 5, no. 2 (2016): 179–199. (Note: I use the plural pronoun to refer to subjects whose gender remains unclear or was indeterminate from the historical record in order to avoid ascribing a gender identity that may or may not accurately reflect the person's sense of self.)

38. Michel Foucault, *The History of Sexuality*, vol. 1, *An Introduction*, trans. Robert Hurley (New York: Vintage, 1990), 23.

mosexual, for example, into a "species," it is because I am more interested in the multiplicities and indeterminacies implied by his argument.[39] As Andrew Clark-Huckstep has argued in light of Foucault's claims, following Laura Doan, "identity should be a contingent space, one held open enough to allow for ambiguity, disidentification and perhaps the lack of sexual identity to be found in historical sources."[40] I therefore follow Foucault's recommendation to "reverse the direction of our analysis: rather than assuming a generally acknowledged repression[,] . . . we must begin with these positive mechanisms, insofar as they produce knowledge, multiply discourse, induce pleasure, and generate power."[41] This approach assumes that discourses, institutions, and practices that struggled to control people, their desires, and their activities actually made new kinds of social relationships, identities, and desires that may or may not be familiar to those we live with today. Processes of urban management were thus always at one and the same time processes of urban creation as well.

In particular, I reorient Foucault's description of the "incitement to discourse" in *The History of Sexuality* around the questions of space that he addressed more fully elsewhere.[42] For Foucault, modern society "incites" people to speak of their sex and sexuality as a way of producing it as an object of examination, regulation, and subjecthood.[43] In *Discipline and Punish*, Foucault also addresses the ways that space "disciplines" the body by enforcing particular relations between individuals. While this feat often came in the guise of enclosure—placing people in prisons, asylums, even schools—it also necessitated particular bodily arrangements: "Power has its principle not so much in a person as in a certain concerted distribution of bodies, surfaces, lights, gazes; in an arrangement whose internal mechanisms produce the relation in which individuals are caught up."[44] According to Foucault, the arrangement of space simultaneously enforces and primes specific responses within the body. The attempt to regulate space does not repress certain kinds of experiences; rather, it creates them.

Public City/Public Sex takes up these ideas at the level of the city, arguing that sexual desire was produced through a logic of regulationism that captured various forms of sexual behavior, created common understandings

---

39. Ibid., 43.

40. Clark-Huckstep, "*History of Sexuality* and Historical Methodology," 182. See also Doan, *Disturbing Practices,* chap. 2.

41. Foucault, *History of Sexuality,* 73.

42. Michel Foucault, *Discipline and Punish: The Birth of the Prison,* trans. Alan Sheridan (New York: Vintage, 1979), esp. pt. 3, chap. 3. See also Michel Foucault, "Of Other Spaces," *Diacritics* 16, no. 1 (1986): 22–27.

43. Foucault, *History of Sexuality,* 17–35.

44. Foucault, *Discipline and Punish,* 202.

of the relationship between such behavior and urban sexual management, and thus became integral to the everyday life of nineteenth-century Paris. "Regulationism" in this context usually refers to state efforts to manage the business of female prostitution through a combination of medical and legal efforts to monitor women who sold sex. First put into practice in France, but then used throughout nineteenth-century Europe, regulationism involved police registration of prostitutes and licensing of brothels in order to track and enclose women who sold sex, combined with regular medical examinations to prevent the spread of venereal disease. Regulationism was premised on a specific understanding of male sexual desire. Understood as an almost uncontrollable force, male desire required suitable outlets. Especially directed at the city's growing working-class population, regulation was a "necessary" and "inevitable" evil that would ensure the moral and physical health of the city's residents by hiding away and monitoring prostitutes.[45]

Regulationism therefore refers to the state control over working-class women's bodies in the service of male heterosexual desire. But it also foregrounds a broader spatial politics—a logic of regulation—that united a wider range of relationships between space, desire, and publicity in the modern metropolis.[46] Premised on the provision of spaces for the fulfillment of male sexual urges, the logic of regulationism promoted a spatial organization that simultaneously acknowledged the sexual connotations of urban space and attempted to hide them away. In this sense, the entire city was designed to facilitate male heterosexual sexual pleasure. The logic of regulation organized space in ways that strove to control how sex appeared and to ensure that people—medical and state authorities, to be sure, but also residents and tourists—could recognize the city's sexual possibilities. This awareness and disavowal characterized an urban politics that revolved around managing the use of public space for seeking out sex and for eliciting sexual desire that

---

45. Corbin, *Les filles de noce,* 24–34. For discussions of nineteenth-century regulationism in other geographic contexts, see, for example, Evans, "Prostitution, State, and Society"; Judith R. Walkowitz, *Prostitution and Victorian Society: Women, Class, and the State* (Cambridge: Cambridge University Press, 1980), esp. chap 4; Mary Gibson, *Prostitution and the State in Italy, 1860–1915,* 2nd ed. (Columbus: Ohio State University Press, 1999), esp. chap. 1; Stauter-Halsted, *Devil's Chain,* 28–31.

46. The phrase "logic of regulation" is not original to my work, but it usually refers to regulationism more strictly defined. See, for example, Alain Corbin, *Women for Hire: Prostitution and Sexuality in France after 1850,* trans. Alan Sheridan (Cambridge, Mass: Harvard University Press, 1990), ix; Peter Baldwin, *Contagion and the State in Europe, 1830–1930* (Cambridge: Cambridge University Press, 1999), 357–367. Others have noted how the regulation of prostitution revolved around much more than just the seclusion of suspect women but was also wrapped up in an entire economy of moral and medical regulation. See, for instance, Aisenberg, *Contagion,* 59–60.

involved more than managing brothels. Rather, it implicated entire neighborhoods as people navigated a city increasingly devoted to managing public sex.

I draw on work by historians and geographers of sexuality to argue that regulationist thought implicated a wider range of hygienist and moralist thought and administrative and police practice than the management of female prostitution. Rather, the discourses and practices that undergirded tolerated sex work created broadly shared modes of understanding and using sexualized public spaces.[47] As administrators, moral commentators, and public hygienists sought to encourage and direct heterosexual desire, they provided new avenues for all Parisians, whether prostitutes, pederasts, their clients and partners, or passersby, to encounter one another in city spaces implicitly and explicitly associated with sexual desire. Those encounters, in turn, produced a sexualized city that often escaped the limits laid out by the authorities in the first place.

By centering everyday encounters in its analysis, *Public City/Public Sex* asserts that those who used public space played an important role in defining the city and urban culture. In doing so, it follows Michel de Certeau's claim that spatial meaning emerges out of a dialogue between those who envision urban space as a source of social control and those who use it.[48] Specifically, the very premise of regulationism—that men's sexual energies required outlets—necessitated the provision of sexual spaces and signifiers in public space that could never be completely under the control of those who described and built them. Once these spaces and signs were put into place, women who sold sex and men who sought sex with other men were able to rely on them and

---

47. Geographers of sexuality and historians of colonialism especially have long recognized the spatial implications of regulation at local, national, and transnational levels. See, for example, Phil Hubbard, *Sex and the City: Geographies of Prostitution in the Urban West* (Aldershot, U.K.: Ashgate, 1999); Philippa Levine, "Modernity, Medicine, and Colonialism: The Contagious Diseases Ordinances in Hong Kong and the Straits Settlements," in *Gender, Sexuality, and Colonial Modernities,* ed. Antoinette Burton (London: Routledge, 1999), 35–48; Philip Howell, "Prostitution and Racialised Sexuality: The Regulation of Prostitution in Britain and the British Empire before the Contagious Diseases Acts," *Environment and Planning D: Society and Space* 18, no. 3 (2000): 321–339; Alan Hunt, "Regulating Heterosocial Space: Sexual Politics in the Early Twentieth Century," *Journal of Historical Sociology* 15, no. 1 (2002): 1–34; Stephen Legg, *Prostitution and the Ends of Empire: Scale, Governmentalities, and Interwar India* (Durham, N.C.: Duke University Press, 2014).

48. Michel de Certeau, *The Practice of Everyday Life,* trans. Steven Rendall (Berkeley: University of California Press, 1984), chap. 7. If I am more influenced by de Certeau, I still keep in mind Henri Lefebvre's tripartite conceptualization of the production of space through spatial practice, representations of space, and representational space, as his work shapes any consideration of the socially constructed nature of space. Henri Lefebvre, *The Production of Space,* trans. Donald Nicholson-Smith (Oxford, U.K.: Blackwell, 1991). My own analysis is especially indebted to Phil Hubbard and Teela Sanders, "Making Space for Sex Work: Female Street Prostitution and the Production of Urban Space," *International Journal of Urban and Regional Research* 27, no. 1 (2003): 75–89.

deploy them to their own ends, muddying their disciplining effects at least for a time. In doing so, they actively participated in shaping the meaning of modern Paris by forcing all Parisians to reckon with the sexual uses of space.

I approach my archive of police records, letters from Parisians, and published work of police memoir, sociology, and early sexology through a lens indebted to queer histories that have decoupled the history of sexuality from that of identity. Laura Doan has recently argued that "history making framed by 'identity knowledge' constrains even as it illuminates, because it is mobilized by the epistemological and social structures of modern sexuality."[49] Doan emphasizes the essential difference between even the recent sexual past and today, arguing that we should engage with a kind of "unknowingness about the past to discover what is now 'unheard of.'"[50] Complementing the work of other historians, such as John Howard, Sharon Marcus, and Colin Johnson, these ideas encourage scholars to approach the recent past cautiously, without categorizing forms of sexual behavior along familiar or modern lines.[51] Therefore, I trace how certain categories—the female prostitute, the male homosexual, the "normal" Parisian—remained rather murky when approached through an analysis of space. Indeed, I argue that urban space brought the three groups together without necessarily defining them as different from one another. Sexual identity thus fails to capture the significance of their encounters. Indeed, even as individuals negotiated often constraining social hierarchies as they interacted with others, their shared participation in an urban sexual culture ultimately also highlights the rather blurry lines between supposedly distinct, class, gender, and sexual identities.

My approach therefore recognizes that individuals experienced their sexual desires differently on the basis of their biological sex, their gender identity, and their class position, but it rejects the assumption that those distinctions necessarily created, constituted, or denoted new identity categories. Instead, I follow the archives themselves, which put into dialogue a wide range of sexual behaviors with that of female prostitution, the main focus of the nineteenth-century police.[52] This association challenges the idea that the late eighteenth century witnessed a clear fracturing of categories of moral disorder along identitarian

---

49. Doan, *Disturbing Practices,* ix.

50. Ibid., 4.

51. Howard, *Men Like That,* xviii; Sharon Marcus, *Between Women: Friendship, Desire, and Marriage in Victorian England* (Princeton, N.J.: Princeton University Press, 2007), 13; Johnson, *Just Queer Folks,* 17–18.

52. I address this idea more fully in Andrew Israel Ross, "Sex in the Archives: Homosexuality, Prostitution, and the Archives de la Préfecture de Police de Paris," *French Historical Studies* 40, no. 2 (2017): 267–290.

and regulatory lines.[53] Indeed, the authorities maintained a broader interest in managing what I call public sex, meaning any act that occurred in view of some group of strangers—a public—that referenced the possibility of sexual desire, relationship, or enticement.[54] The recognition of the signs of sex, then, created a public sexual culture premised on the incitement to sexual desire. This public sexual culture was defined by the momentary inclusion of people, acting in public, as they recognized the possibility of sexual encounter. Here I abide by Michael Warner's "notion of a public [that] enables a reflexivity in the circulation of texts among strangers who become, by virtue of their reflexively circulating discourse, a social entity."[55] Warner understands a public—as opposed to the public—as a formation that emerges through the mutual recognition and understanding of a particular discourse. Broadening out the meaning of "text," I describe a process of sexual public making that involved the creation of a common understanding of the signs of sex, the incitement of (usually, though not exclusively, male) sexual desire, and the momentary recognition of such an encounter between two or more people through letters, gestures, touch, and conversation.[56]

Warner differentiates between "publics" and "counterpublics." The latter emerges through forms of address that are directed at particular strangers and "maintains at some level, conscious or not, an awareness of its subordinate status."[57] "Counter," however, is not the same thing as "sub." To speak of publics and counterpublics is not to likewise speak of majorities and minorities, of culture and subculture, but to speak of particular modes of address: "Counterpublics are 'counter' to the extent that they try to supply different ways of imagining stranger sociability and its reflexivity; as publics, they remain oriented to stranger circulation in a way that is not just strategic but constitutive of membership and its affects."[58] The formation of a counterpublic is thus predicated on the possibility of producing forms of interaction that only some people may recognize and that run askew from "dominant" social expecta-

---

53. Michel Rey, "Police et sodomie à Paris au XVIIIe siècle: Du péché au désordre," *Revue d'histoire moderne et contemporaine* 29, no. 1 (1982): 124; Plumauzille, *Prostitution et révolution,* 9. New sources on male same-sex sexual activity in the late eighteenth century are enabling historians to further question the relationship between sexual behavior and identity at the time. See Jeffrey Merrick, "New Sources and Questions for Research on Sexual Relations between Men in Eighteenth-Century France," *Gender and History* 30, no. 1 (2018): 20–25.

54. Michael Warner, *Publics and Counterpublics* (New York: Zone Books, 2002), 74–76.

55. Ibid., 11–12.

56. I am here inspired by Lauren Berlant and Michael Warner's discussion of queer "world making" in Lauren Berlant and Michael Warner, "Sex in Public," *Critical Inquiry* 24, no. 2 (1998): 558.

57. Warner, *Publics and Counterpublics,* 119.

58. Ibid., 121–122.

tions, but they nevertheless remain by definition directed at everyone and thus accessible to anyone "in the know." This combination of an awareness of difference predicated on universal address is what makes this approach to sexual solicitation so powerful. Even as it recognizes the existence of public sex as oppositional to certain social expectations, it also acknowledges the power of public sexual activity to constitute forms of belonging that coexist and shape how anyone could understand their own location in the city.

These ideas have reoriented my interpretation of regulationism around a broader range of public interactions between Parisians. While regulationism as strictly defined focused on the problem of female prostitution, its foundational assumption that male heterosexual desire could be managed through the proper administration of people and spaces expanded the reach of administrators and moralists concerned with public sex more broadly. Specifically, by the mid-nineteenth century, as the police struggled to address sexual assault, exhibitionism, and voyeurism, the authorities and other experts became especially drawn to public sexual activity between men.[59] Ostensibly freed of state interference by the decriminalization of sodomy during the French Revolution, male same-sex sexual activity was nonetheless actively policed, often under the rubric of "public offenses against decency."[60] Despite exercising wide latitude over men who sought sex with other men, the police lamented sodomy or pederasty's absence from the law code, even as they essentially applied a regulationist logic to managing the "problem." A public

---

59. Until the very end of the century, female-female sexual activity did not attract much police attention outside its relationship with prostitution. By the end of the 1800s, lesbian bars, cafés, and other spaces of same-sex sociability became increasingly prominent. On the rise of a lesbian public at the end of the nineteenth century, see Catherine Van Casselaer, *Lot's Wife: Lesbian Paris, 1890–1914* (Liverpool: Janus Press, 1986); Francesca Canadé Sautman, "Invisible Women: Lesbian Working-Class Culture in France, 1880–1930," in *Homosexuality in Modern France,* ed. Jeffrey Merrick and Bryant T. Ragan Jr. (New York: Oxford University Press, 1996), 177–201; Nicole G. Albert, "De la topographie invisible à l'espace public et littéraire: Les lieux de plaisir lesbien dans le Paris de la Belle Époque," *Revue d'histoire moderne et contemporaine* 4, nos. 53–54 (2006): 87–105; Choquette, "Gay Paree." On the relationship between prostitution and lesbianism in the nineteenth century, see Leslie Choquette, "Degenerate or Degendered? Images of Prostitution and Homosexuality in the French Third Republic," *Historical Reflections/Réflexions Historiques* 23, no. 2 (1997): 205–228.

60. Michael Sibalis, "The Regulation of Male Homosexuality in Revolutionary and Napoleonic France, 1789–1815," in *Homosexuality in Modern* France, ed. Jeffrey Merrick and Bryant T. Ragan Jr. (New York: Oxford University Press, 1996), 82–87. On the use of this law against men who sought sex with other men, see also Peniston, *Pederasts and Others,* 18–19. For the broader context of the law, see Marcela Iacub, *Through the Keyhole: A History of Sex, Space, and Public Modesty in Modern France,* trans. Vinay Swamy (Manchester, U.K.: Manchester University Press, 2016). On the decriminalization of sodomy, see Thierry Pastorello, "L'abolition du crime de sodomie en 1791: Un long processus social, répressif et penal," *Cahiers d'histoire: Revue d'histoire critique,* nos. 112–113 (2010): 197–208.

offense against decency was, after all, not simply a moral category defined by the improper appearance of sex, sexual behavior, or genitals but also a spatial one, establishing publicity as key to an offense.[61] While the police never licensed brothels for men who sought sex with other men, they did recognize that they could not completely eradicate same-sex sexual activity from the city. Asserting that male same-sex sexual activity was evidence of sickness and moral deformity, they attempted to manage evidence of its existence much as they did female prostitution. Trying to control the public signs of sex, the police united their concern over female prostitution and men who sought sex with other men into a common problematic of urban governance. In this way they helped produce a shared sexual culture that implicated anyone who felt sexual arousal or disgust on the street.

The logic of regulation shaped how the police, prostitutes, pederasts, and other Parisians encountered one another, recognized the sexual possibilities of the city, and ultimately forged a modern urban culture in dialogue with one another through the course of the nineteenth century. The logic of regulation required that the police put into practice a form of urban regulation that largely revolved around providing for men's sexual appetites. In the wake of working-class population growth during the early part of the century, the police began building an administrative structure through which they attempted to regulate and manage all sorts of sexual behavior in public until the end of the century. Because regulationism asserted the central importance of recognizing and misrecognizing the indications and availability of public sex, these efforts laid the groundwork for the mid-century emergence of a public sexual culture that depended on ensuring that Parisians recognized the signs of sex. In response, even as the logic of regulation still shaped administrative approaches to sex and the city, by the end of the century it was also put into play by Parisians themselves. Indeed, the police found themselves torn between a Republican citizenry who demanded a purified urban space and Parisians and visitors who sought out sexual pleasure in new commercial establishments that found great profit in selling the pleasures of a public sexual culture.

Overview

An analysis that emphasizes this logic of regulation demands a broad chronological scope that encompasses almost the entirety of the nineteenth century.

---

61. Maurice Laugier, "Du rôle de l'expertise médico-légale dans certains cas d'outrage public à la pudeur," *Annales d'hygiène publique et médecine légale* 2, no. 50 (1878): 165. See also Chapter 2 herein.

In this respect, I follow historians of female prostitution who have routinely taken a century-long perspective in ways that urban historians, with their focus on Haussmannization and its pre- and post-histories, and historians of homosexuality, with their emphasis on the Third Republic, have not. Part I examines the intersection of sexual management, public hygiene, and policing in the nineteenth century. Emphasizing the spatial implications of regulationism during the early nineteenth century, Chapter 1 argues that the attempt to sanction tolerated brothels made female prostitution a central sign of urban life during the late Restoration and July Monarchy. At the center of these efforts were the maisons de tolérance, where prostitutes were able to ply their trade while also being subjected to regular forced medical inspections. The police justified this toleration by arguing that they were enclosing prostitutes and hiding them away from the eyes of the "honest" public. However, by allowing brothel keepers to light their doorways, station a retired prostitute or servant, or use a larger than normal address to signal the type of business they offered, the police did not hide sex away so much as they constructed new public indicators of its availability. By regulating prostitution, the Paris police attempted to render the signs of prostitution into evidence of administrative authority. They replaced the body of the prostitute as a sign of sexual solicitation in favor of their own signals. In doing so, they made knowing the signs of prostitution a necessary precondition to successfully navigating urban space.

The effort to manage the spatial organization of female prostitution was accomplished piecemeal, neighborhood by neighborhood. Such approaches to the city became less prominent with the rise of the Second Empire in the 1850s, when a cohort of public hygienists, supported by a powerful prefect of the Seine, collaborated to reshape the city on a grand scale in order to facilitate men's movement on the streets. Chapter 2 addresses an underappreciated, but necessary, facility meant to open the city to men's public use: the public urinal. In particular, the chapter traces the sexual uses of public urinals by men seeking sex with other men and argues that the urinal confounded regulationism by producing forms of desire that had been left unaddressed and therefore uncontained within the system designed at the beginning of the century. Public urinals first appeared on the streets of Paris during the 1830s, but their growth accelerated in the 1850s, at precisely the moment when the maison de tolérance began its decline. Under the aegis of a discourse that associated physical health with bodily propriety, public hygienists emphasized the necessity of not only building a sufficient number of facilities to serve the male population but also doing so in a way that paralleled the spatial logic of the brothel itself: plentiful and recognizable, these facilities were also able to hide the activities they enabled from the general public. In laying down these requirements, however, these experts rendered such spaces ideal for discreet rendezvous.

By the 1870s the public urinal had become the most important meeting place for men who sought sex with other men. This appropriation proved problematic, because the authorities, caught between their prerogative to protect men's access to public space and to prevent "public offenses against decency," had to distinguish between men who were using the urinals as they were intended and those who were not. I argue that neither the police nor the medical authorities who contributed to this debate were ultimately able to make such distinctions accurately. This failure rendered the very signs of heterosexuality—and thus of regulation—rather arbitrary.

Part I showcases how urban planners, the police, and public hygienists attempted to mold the city to encourage particular kinds of behaviors and, indeed, sexual desires within the population. It emphasizes the dichotomy between recognition and misrecognition as it inflected police attention to particular public spaces. This theme became especially important with the arrival of the Second Empire, as a reinvigorated conservative politics intersected with the growing emphasis on the public life of the city. This intersection of moral conservatism and public life lasted until at least the 1880s, when the liberal Third Republic secured itself.[62] The provision of new spaces under Haussmann and the increasing importance of public space to middle- and upper-class social practice made it increasingly difficult to prevent knowledge of and interaction with an emerging public sexual culture predicated on the ability of female prostitutes and men who sought sex with other men to make known their existence as they incited sexual desire among those who witnessed them.

Part II addresses this concern through an analysis of the relationship between female prostitution and male homosexuality, first in discourse and then on the streets of Paris. As Chapter 3 argues, the crisis of regulation encouraged a new discourse on public sexual activity to emerge in the 1850s.[63] These texts struggled to define, in particular, men who sought sex with other men as objects of state control. Lacking a clear legal foundation for the persecution and arrest of men who sought sex with other men, the police, medical au-

---

62. Sharon Marcus, *Apartment Stories: City and Home in Nineteenth-Century Paris and London* (Berkeley: University of California Press, 1999), 136–138.

63. The most important of the period was Ambroise Tardieu, *Étude médico-légale sur les attentats aux mœurs* (Paris: J.-B. Baillière, 1857). On Tardieu, see esp. Vernon A. Rosario, "Pointy Penises, Fashion Crimes, and Hysterical Mollies: The Pederasts' Inversions," in *Homosexuality in Modern France,* ed. Jeffrey Merrick and Bryant T. Ragan Jr. (New York: Oxford University Press, 1996), 148–153.

thorities, and other moral commentators associated such men with an existing social problem, one that was already supposedly defined: female prostitution. A reading of medico-legal and popular urban commentary in dialogue with police records shows that prostitution structured the way experts understood non-procreative, especially public, sexual activity. This discourse strove to construct distinct figures, identified and identifiable on the streets of Paris. Not quite the homosexual, the pederast was defined by his physical appearance, even as few commentators could resist also describing him in terms of female prostitution. Thus constructed, the pederast effectively shook off his biology, and his gender became something indistinct, rendered less formidable than the fact of his sexual behavior. Prostitution in turn was revealed less as a legal category attached to the *fille publique* (literally, "public girl," used as a synonym for "prostitute") than as a symbol of sexual deviancy writ large. The prostitute and the pederast thus emerged less as actualized identities, taken up and realized by individuals and communities, and more as ways of understanding desires that could be experienced by anyone and everyone.

Chapter 4 addresses the mobility of these figures through city space during the Second Empire and early Third Republic by arguing that sexual solicitation by men and women on the streets of Paris created a "public sexual culture" that captured those who recognized the signs of sex. Evidence of solicitation drawn from the police archives and published sources shows that sex constituted a kind of language with the power to bring together new kinds of publics that extended beyond the subcultures we usually associate with non-normative sexual practices. Rather than a kind of "resistance," then, those who sought to sell sex or sought out sex with members of the same sex produced a sense of belonging that was more widely shared, more diffused, but also more tenuous than we have previously understood. The very precariousness and instability of this public—the way it came into existence through a momentary look or discreet touch and then faded away again—made it not only uniquely malleable but also an effective source of sexual experimentation insofar as it presumed no sex act or identity for participation. Instead, the investment in sexual signification by police authorities, expert commentators, and prostitutes and men who sought sex with other men had made the very possibility of sexual pleasure into a shared mode of urban participation. The democratic public culture that other historians have traced on the streets of late Second Empire and early Third Republic Paris was thus deeply embedded with practices of public sex.[64]

The spread of sex through the city made it a potent, but essentially

---

64. See Schwartz, *Spectacular Realities,* 6.

multivalent, symbol of Parisian culture. The Third Republic thus faced a problem as evidence of public sex and the inability of the government, even an authoritarian one, to control it seemed increasingly evident. Part III addresses how the early Third Republic wrestled with and attempted to manage these issues. Haussmannization effectuated not only an increasing valorization of public display but also an "interiorization" of urban space as architects struggled to find ways of separating domestic life from public life.[65] This process, however, was reflected not simply in spatial forms but also in the ways that Parisians understood their own interactions in public space. The apparent failure of interiorization—indicated by the presence of sex in public—made it increasingly important for "respectable" Parisians to distinguish themselves from the public sexual culture. Throughout the nineteenth century, Parisians recognized that public sex constituted a threat to forms of bodily integrity, hygiene, and propriety that the city was supposed to guarantee.

By the early Third Republic, as Chapter 5 shows, the police were inundated with complaints about their failure to sweep the streets clean of the public sexual culture. While public sphere theory traditionally demands the abstraction of the self in order to enter a "rational" public sphere evacuated of subjective, personal concerns, this chapter shows that the public sphere of the liberal democratic Republic was in part constituted through a discourse of public sex.[66] In other words, evidence of public sex became the means through which a set of Parisians constituted themselves as "the public," speaking in the name of a "normative" culture that existed only by virtue of the sexual culture in the first place. Close readings of these letters demonstrate the mutually constitutive nature of the public sexual culture and the public of the early Third Republic.

The circulation of sex about the city enabled the development of late nineteenth-century Parisian consumer culture as well. Chapter 6 shows how the democratization of public culture in the nineteenth century ultimately led to the commodification of the public sexual culture in new institutions such as dance halls and cafés.[67] These commercial spaces offered new opportunities for women and men to locate sexual clients and partners while also

---

65. Marcus, *Apartment Stories,* chap. 4.

66. On the relationship between abstraction, gender, and citizenship, see Joan Wallach Scott, *Only Paradoxes to Offer: French Feminists and the Rights of Man* (Cambridge, Mass: Harvard University Press, 1996), chap. 1. See also Charles Sowerwine, "The Sexual Contract(s) of the Third Republic," *French History and Civilization* 1 (2005): 245–253.

67. Lola Gonzalez-Quijano has recently emphasized the diffusion of prostitution into diverse "spaces of pleasure" after Haussmannization. While Gonzalez-Quijano argues that the

offering—for a price—both the kinds of sexual play that once took place on the streets and greater opportunities for surveillance by the police. A culture of public sex thus stands at the heart of early mass consumption, even as that very development illustrates some of the tensions that would prove to be its undoing. On the one hand, the deployment of sex by new leisure spaces demonstrates the attraction of sexual entertainments—the opportunities to cross-dress, to encounter men who sought sex with other men and prostitutes, to inhabit otherwise foreclosed subject positions—that rested on the kinds of unstable sexual desires described throughout *Public City/Public Sex*. On the other hand, control over the meaning of these encounters began to escape the grasp of the men and women who enunciated them on the streets and instead lay in the hands of entrepreneurs who priced them, cooperated with the police, and ensured, above all, that they made a profit on them.

The precise strategies the authorities undertook in order to manage the appearance of public sex in Paris may have changed over the course of the nineteenth century, but they remained premised on a common understanding of a male sexual desire that would always need to be fulfilled. The various spatial arrangements set up by the authorities, imagined by moralists and doctors, and constructed by private investors contributed to the emergence of a particular kind of urban male (hetero)sexuality. And yet such efforts only ever seemed partially successful, as they enabled the production of other kinds of desire as well. Conceptualized under the "logic of regulationism," the various kinds of pleasures that were simultaneously produced and managed by the city shaped how people encountered one another and their environment in the nineteenth century. But insofar as these pleasures failed to remain "proper," they reveal the real limits of any easy distinction between the heterosexual/homosexual and respectable/disreputable. The brothel, the urinal, the street, the neighborhood block, and the café all contributed to placing sex at the center of modern urban life, but they often did so in ways that evaded the expectations of those who designed and built them.

---

commercialization of female prostitution depended on increasing divisions between categories of "honest" and "venal" womanhood, as well as between "public" and "private," and further marginalized female prostitutes, I argue that it is precisely by striving to muddy those distinctions and placing women who sold sex at the center that commercial establishments tried to commodify public sex. See Gonzalez-Quijano, *Capitale de l'amour,* 211–212.

PART I

1

REGULATION, THE MAISON DE TOLÉRANCE, AND THE SIGNS OF SEX

On November 30, 1829, a lawyer within the Ministry of Justice named J. Coppeaux sent a brief letter to the prefect of police of Paris in order to offer his "observations" regarding the prostitutes who habitually solicited sex "openly and without constraint on the streets of Paris." Recognizing that "it was a necessity for the government to suffer houses of prostitution[,] . . . it does not seem to me that it should follow that prostitutes should be able to claim the privilege to publicly engage in their infamous profession." Referring to recent restrictions placed on prostitutes by the police, Coppeaux argued, "I cannot imagine that the powers of the police stop there and that beyond those limits, which they have themselves traced, they have to respect the recognized rights, whatever they may be, of individuals who have placed themselves outside all law."[1] Coppeaux's note arrived at the prefecture as the police debated precisely these issues. Indeed, his letter encapsulates the struggle of the late Restoration and July Monarchy police to find ways of "tolerating" female prostitution. They acknowledged that prostitution was, in some sense, "necessary," but the precise "limits" remained very much to be determined.

That this functionary regurgitated the basic tenets of sexual management back at the police demonstrates the power of the regulationist vision of urban sexual management during the second quarter of the century. As we shall see,

---

1. J. Coppeaux to Préfet de Police, November 30, 1829, "Répression: Voie publique. Décisions," DA 223, doc. 6, APP.

the precise form of regulation underwent revision throughout the period, but its basic contours already existed by the 1820s. Rules limited the ability of prostitutes to move about the city and required them to register with the police, submit to medical examination, and refrain from public solicitation. They designated the maison de tolérance, or tolerated brothel, as the only acceptable space in which prostitutes could ply their trade and marked other public spaces as out of bounds to prostitutes.[2] However, efforts to enclose prostitutes in brothels could not help but also shape other city spaces. This chapter argues that debates surrounding the place of the tolerance within regulationist discourse produced new ways of understanding and recognizing the sexual uses of urban space in the first half of the nineteenth century.

Regulationism formed one component of a broader spatial strategy enacted by the police, theorized by sociologists and moral commentators, and enunciated by urbanists and entrepreneurs who sought to manage the working-class population of the city while also opening the city to middle-class publicity. The early nineteenth century witnessed a swell of concern over the growth of the working-class and poor population as urban migration continued apace.[3] During this period, new hygienic movements took shape that emphasized a relationship between the poor and disease, especially cholera.[4] At the same time, this cohort of experts argued that female prostitutes risked spreading syphilis to the "respectable" classes.[5] Attention to this new "social question" thus revolved around the development of state processes of intervention into individual lives, social groups, and environments in an effort to ensure the physical and moral health of the population.[6]

At the same time, urbanist thought increasingly sought to maximize the circulation of people, goods, and even air in the city. During the early nineteenth century, urban planners saw new possibilities for a "rational form" of the city that would preserve "order, safety, health, and efficient means of

---

2. Jill Harsin, *Policing Prostitution in Nineteenth-Century Paris* (Princeton, N.J.: Princeton University Press, 1985), 6.

3. Although heavily disputed, if not discredited, Louis Chevalier's *Laboring Classes and Dangerous Classes* remains the most influential description of early nineteenth-century anxieties of urban population growth. Louis Chevalier, *Laboring Classes and Dangerous Classes in Paris during the First Half of the Nineteenth Century,* trans. Frank Jellinek (New York: H. Fertig, 1973). On the "Chevalier Thesis," see esp. Barrie M. Ratcliffe, "Classes laborieuses et classes dangereuses à Paris pendant la première moitié du XIXe siècle? The Chevalier Thesis Reexamined," *French Historical Studies* 17, no. 2 (1991): 542–574.

4. Catherine J. Kudlick, *Cholera in Post-Revolutionary Paris: A Cultural History* (Berkeley: University of California Press, 1996), 52–63.

5. Andrew R. Aisenberg, *Contagion: Disease, Government, and the 'Social Question' in Nineteenth-Century France* (Stanford, Calif.: Stanford University Press, 1999), 59–60.

6. Giovanna Procacci, *Gouverner la misère: La question sociale en France, 1789–1848* (Paris: Seuil, 1993), 190–192; Aisenberg, *Contagion,* 25–26.

circulation of its populace, its police and armies, its manufactured goods, and its commercial trade."[7] Although July Monarchy administrators like the prefect of the Seine, Claude-Philibert de Rambuteau, made significant changes to the city, this comprehensive urban design was not put into practice until Haussmannization during the Second Empire.[8] That said, elements can be witnessed at the local level. For example, Ralph Kingston has shown how, faced with a lack of state interest, a group of businessmen made their own investments in urban redevelopment in order to facilitate the movement of people through their neighborhood.[9] Although the grand schemes of Haussmann had yet to be realized, the July Monarchy nonetheless saw new attempts to deploy urban space to facilitate both social control and mobility in ways that favored the reconstruction of social codes and hierarchies after the French Revolution.[10]

Regulationism stands as an important example of the new urban philosophy that advocated a broader use of public space by a certain segment of the population while restricting the ability of the socially marginal to do so. It also represents continuing debates over how best to manage the city: to take on the city "as a whole" or to make more targeted interventions. This chapter places regulationism and one of its tools—the tolerated brothel—at the heart of debates over how best to manage the city. The ability of the maison de tolérance to both hide away and reveal female prostitution parallels the broader contradiction at the heart of early nineteenth-century urbanism as efforts to manage the venal sexual economy "as a whole" ran aground against actual police efforts within individual neighborhoods.

The maison de tolérance stands as a physical instantiation of a broader process whereby urban space produced heterosexual desire. Space itself came to be oriented around the availability of women, especially working-class women, to men. As Sharon Marcus points out, this trend demanded women's public presence rather than their enclosure in private space.[11] Similarly, for

---

7. Nicholas Papayanis, *Planning Paris before Haussmann* (Baltimore: Johns Hopkins University Press, 2004), 247.

8. Colin Jones, *Paris: Biography of a City* (New York: Penguin, 2004), 284–286.

9. Ralph Kingston, "Capitalism in the Streets: Paris Shopkeepers, *Passages Couverts,* and the Production of the Early Nineteenth-Century City," *Radical History Review* 2012, no. 114 (2012): 39–65.

10. These efforts followed an initial restructuring of social codes during the Restoration. See Denise Z. Davidson, *France after Revolution: Urban Life, Gender, and the New Social Order* (Cambridge, Mass.: Harvard University Press, 2007); Sun-Young Park, *Ideals of the Body: Architecture, Urbanism, and Hygiene in Postrevolutionary Paris* (Pittsburgh: University of Pittsburgh Press, 2018).

11. Sharon Marcus, *Apartment Stories: City and Home in Nineteenth-Century Paris and London* (Berkeley: University of California Press, 1999), 39–40.

all the talk about the scourge of prostitution, the police nevertheless sanctioned regular reminders of its availability. The brothel served an essential purpose to the emergence of modern Paris in that it facilitated men's access to sex, spread sexual knowledge, and marked the city with sexual nodes to be avoided (or not) as both women and men moved about. As an institution of social control, the maison de tolérance facilitated access to working-class women's bodies. As a physical structure, the maisons de tolérance also elicited various responses—revulsion, attraction, desire, incomprehension, or apathy—among those who saw them.

The tolerance system created the very problems it claimed to solve, as it stood as a constant reminder of the possibility of female prostitution. As Sara Ahmed reminds us, "Sexuality itself can be considered a spatial formation not only in the sense that bodies inhabit sexual spaces, but also in the sense that bodies are sexualized through how they inhabit space."[12] The act of witnessing—usually but not always visually—a brothel reshaped passing Parisians' relationship to their own bodies, because it elicited a response, whether positive or negative. Insofar as such responses were often sexual, the maison de tolérance not only channeled male desire, as public hygienists claimed, but also "incited" it.[13] By tolerating the existence of the brothel, then, authorities both relied on and actively produced a particular understanding of male desire. That desire was, on the one hand, oriented toward the opposite sex and, on the other hand, always both uncontrollable and manageable at the same time. In its ideal form, the maison de tolérance encouraged and produced male desire, pushing and pulling men toward it in order to police their sex, even as its existence was premised on a fear that men's desire could never be totally contained.

Under the imprimatur of the police, the maison de tolérance represented an urban symbolic order that revolved around the availability of heterosexual sex for sale that was, by definition, visible. Efforts to police female prostitution through the tolerated brothel highlight the tension between authorities' desire to make significant interventions into the city and their fear of doing so. The authorities seemed aware that by setting aside certain spaces as acceptable arenas for engaging in non-procreative sexual activity, they also contributed to the construction of a system of urban sexual signification that

---

12. Sara Ahmed, *Queer Phenomenology: Orientations, Objects, Others* (Durham, N.C.: Duke University Press, 2006), 67.

13. I use the term "incitement" in the Foucauldian sense not simply to indicate a "reminder" of the brothel's purpose but also to argue that the brothel created the desires it was meant to serve. Michel Foucault, *The History of Sexuality,* vol. 1, *An Introduction,* trans. Robert Hurley (New York: Vintage, 1990), 17–35.

pervaded the French capital. In other words, the strategies used by the police in order to enclose prostitutes in brothels revolved as much around the production of sexual space in Paris as it did around repression of female bodies. These strategies of sexual management rendered the signs of the availability of sex into an important component of nineteenth-century urban culture.

Directing the "Torrent" of Prostitution

Although French officials had made efforts to intervene in the business of prostitution before the late eighteenth century, they had not managed to sustain those attempts over the long term.[14] The effort to systematize the regulation of female prostitution paralleled the modernization of the police in Revolutionary and early nineteenth-century Paris. During his tenure as *lieutenant général de police* between the 1770s and 1785, Jean-Charles Lenoir laid down rules that "designated the places where prostitutes could live, those where they could not show themselves, and times for leaving and returning home."[15] During the Revolution, prostitution was, like sodomy, decriminalized by omission. Unlike sodomites, however, female prostitutes found themselves increasingly under the authority of an administrative apparatus set up by the police themselves.[16] The year 1800 marked the emergence of the modern Préfecture de Police de Paris, and power over the "supervision of the streets" was given to police agents—*commissaires de police* and *officiers de paix*—in the neighborhoods of Paris.[17] Five years later, the prefecture created a dispensary tasked with examining prostitutes for venereal disease.[18] Other ordinances and regulations followed in the early decades of the nineteenth century, all of which strove to place female prostitutes under the prerogative of the authorities by controlling their ability to access public space, forcing

---

14. Félix Carlier describes efforts to police prostitution prior to regulation in *Études de pathologie sociale: Les deux prostitutions (1860–1870)* (Paris: E. Dentu, 1887), chap. 1.

15. "Rapport," June 11, 1853, "Renseignements généraux: Projets de règlements émanés de l'administration," DA 222, doc. 32, 2, APP.

16. On the policing of prostitution during the revolutionary period, see esp. Clyde Plumauzille, *Prostitution et révolution: Les femmes publiques dans la cité républicaine (1789–1804)* (Ceyzérieu, France: Champ Vallon, 2016), pt. 2. See also Susan Conner, "Life in the Streets: Policing Prostitution in Revolutionary Paris, 1789–1794," *Proceedings of the Consortium on Revolutionary Europe, 1750–1850* 16 (1986): 156–167.

17. Clive Emsley, "Policing the Streets of Early Nineteenth-Century Paris," *French History* 1, no. 2 (1987): 258; Jean Tulard, "1800-1815, L'organisation de la police," in *Histoire et dictionnaire de la police: Du moyen âge à nos jours*, ed. Michel Aubouin, Arnaud Teyssier, and Jean Tulard (Paris: Robert Laffont, 2005), 270–278.

18. Harsin, *Policing Prostitution*, 7–8.

their registration with the police, and ensuring their availability for regular medical inspection. Responsibility for guaranteeing the success of the project was given over to the *police des mœurs,* the morals police.[19]

The emergence of these policies toward female prostitutes occurred in the context of the increasing centralization of the French state. Concerned primarily with stamping out political and social dissent, agents of the prefecture were often simply seen as spies by both upper- and lower-class Parisians as police agents strove to extend their power over those who used the city.[20] The regulation of female prostitution formed part of the prefecture's efforts to intervene into the Parisian working class and poor in the name of social peace. As Jill Harsin has argued, these developments had the effect of gradually endowing the prefecture with arbitrary authority over an entire class of people: working and poor women.[21]

Regulationists justified police intervention into the business of prostitution and the lives of prostitutes by arguing that doing so constituted a "necessary evil."[22] "Prostitution is considered a fact which the authorities are unable to wipe out," an 1823 police circular explains, and "the object of the regulations is nothing more than to decrease its abuses, its dangers, and its scandals."[23] Prostitution was "necessary" in order to provide sexual outlets for a growing male population; it was "evil" because it combined immorality and physical

---

19. Véronique Willemin, *La mondaine: Histoire et archives de la police des mœurs* (Paris: Éditions Hoëbeke, 2009), 31–32.

20. The police theoretically faced little institutionalized constraint both during this period and after, though they rarely fully exercised their full prerogatives. Howard Payne, *The Police State of Louis Napoleon Bonaparte, 1851–1860* (Seattle: University of Washington Press, 1966), 32–33. On political policing, see John Merriman, *Police Stories: Building the French State, 1815–1851* (Oxford: Oxford University Press, 2006), chap. 4. On public perception of the police, see Emsley, "Policing the Streets," 277–282; Malcolm Anderson, *In Thrall to Political Change: Police and Gendarmerie in France* (Oxford: Oxford University Press, 2011), 23–26; Sarah Horowitz, "Policing and the Problem of Privacy in Restoration-Era France, 1815–30," *French History* 27, no. 1 (2013): 45–68.

21. Harsin, *Policing Prostitution,* xxiii. This process can be understood as an extension of the reduction of prostitutes to "diminished citizenship," as Clyde Plumauzille has termed it, during the French Revolution. Plumauzille, *Prostitution et révolution,* 9.

22. See, for example, "Observations à soumettre au ministre de la police générale de la République," 3 Pairial, An IV (May 22, 1796), DA 221, doc. 2, APP; Report to the Minister of the Interior, February 23, 1828, F7 4338, No. 4, AN; F.F.A. Béraud, *Les filles publiques de Paris et la police qui les régit,* 2 vols. (Paris: Desforges, 1839), 1:4; Letter to Ministre de la Police Générale, n.d. (c. February 13, 1852), DA 221, doc. 99, APP; C. J. Lecour, *La prostitution à Paris et à Londres, 1789–1870* (Paris: P. Asselin, 1870), 17; Charles Virmaître, *Trottoirs et lupanars,* vol. 4, *Paris documentaire (Mœurs)* (Paris: Henri Perrot, 1893), 9; O. Commenge, *Hygiène sociale: La prostitution clandestine à Paris* (Paris: Schleicher Frères, 1897), 480; Petition to Préfet de Police, June 22, 1900, "Boulevard Beaumarchais. Dossier général," JC 40, formerly BM2 20, APP.

23. "Copie de Circulaire," June 14, 1823, "La prostitution en général," DB 407, doc. 1, APP.

disease, in particular syphilis.[24] As Alexandre Parent-Duchâtelet, the most influential nineteenth-century commentator on the subject, argued, prostitution was "similar to a torrent that no one can stop, but that is to a certain extent possible to direct, [that] always tends to rise to the needs and the habits of the population."[25] Inevitable as much as it was necessary, then, this evil could only be attenuated and never fully blocked. Indeed, it had to be made, in some sense, useful, even if such utility had to be constantly disavowed.[26]

The idea of prostitution as both necessary and evil shaped tensions within regulationist approaches to sex work. Regulationist thought reflected Enlightenment faith in the ability of experts to construct systemic responses to social problems. As F.F.A. Béraud, a Restoration-era morals officer, put it in introducing his 1839 book, *Les filles publiques de Paris,* his goal was to "destroy provocation to debauchery by making it, so far as possible, disappear from the public streets . . . [and j]ustify the necessity of a rational antidote against this shameful sickness whose incalculable ravages not only hit impudent men who risk it but also affect the lives of *poor innocent beings*."[27] The "rational antidote" that was regulationism showcased the ability of experts to solve specific social problems, in this case the appearance of venal sex and the spread of venereal disease. However, Béraud also indulged an almost utopian (or dystopian, depending on one's point of view) goal: he wanted to "encourage measures that were both legal and rigorous but that were, above all, radical, with a view to purging the capital of these immoral beings."[28] Caught between a desire, on the one hand, for a "rational antidote" and, on the other hand, for "radical measures" to remove prostitution from the street, Béraud's argument shows how efforts to regulate were always circumscribed within a wish to eliminate as well.[29]

The dialectic between radical and rational measures was reflected in debates over large projects and small-scale interventions with regard to regu-

---

24. Alain Corbin, *Les filles de noce: Misère sexuelle et prostitution au XIXe siècle* (Paris: Flammarion, 1982), 14–24.

25. Alexandre Parent-Duchâtelet, *De la prostitution dans la ville de Paris, considérée sous le rapport de l'hygiène publique, de la morale, et de l'administration* (Paris: J.-B. Baillière, 1836), 1:353. On Parent-Duchâtelet's philosophy, see esp. Charles Bernheimer, *Figures of Ill Repute: Representing Prostitution in Nineteenth-Century France* (Cambridge, Mass: Harvard University Press, 1989), chap. 1.

26. Jann Matlock, *Scenes of Seduction: Prostitution, Hysteria, and Reading Difference in Nineteenth-Century France* (New York: Columbia University Press, 1994), 31.

27. Béraud, *Les filles publiques de Paris,* 1:vi.

28. Ibid.

29. This tension is reflected in Béraud's own relationship to Parent-Duchâtelet's text. Although they share regulationist assumptions, Béraud "reproached" Parent-Duchâtelet for the "scientific" character of the latter's text. See Bernheimer, *Figures of Ill Repute,* 22–23.

lated female prostitution. In late 1828 the prefecture reorganized the morals police and put the dispensary onto a new financial footing, with the Paris Municipal Council funding the institution.[30] In light of these changes, Prefect of Police Louis-Marie Debelleyme created a "Council" for the police des mœurs, renamed the "Commission Spéciale pour la Répression de la Prostitution" in January 1829, and made up of officers of the morals police and doctors attached to the dispensary.[31] The commission met through the end of the Restoration and beginning of the July Monarchy and then again between 1836 and 1851. As these officials responded to complaints, approved new regulations, discussed proposals, and debated budgets, they not only set down the various—and variable—policies that governed female prostitution during the July Monarchy but also produced a politics of space that failed to exceed local intervention into the city's sexual economy. Despite their professed desire to hide away evidence of female prostitution, their unwillingness to countenance truly radical measures reveals their own anxiety at the implications of the regime: that the goal was always as much to ensure the availability of sex work as it was to hide it away.

Decisions made by the commission during its early years highlight administrative efforts to control supply and demand of prostitution through practices of spatial policing. Regulationist policies took on an explicitly class-based sheen as the commission struggled to enable elites to access commercial space that was also used by women who sold sex. Sometimes the authorities simply attempted to clear out areas of the city of prostitutes. For instance, during the meeting of March 11, 1829, the commission turned its attention to the presence of prostitutes around the théâtres des Italiens and de l'Opéra in the present-day ninth arrondissement. The commission, "expressing the desire to see these promenades given back to good society," believed that expelling prostitutes from the area would be well received by local businesses, because doing so would "attract a larger crowd." To that end, the commission decided to ban prostitutes from the area beginning on April 1 of that year.[32] Here, the commission represented the street in zero-sum terms, where the presence of prostitution stood in inverse proportion to the ability of "good so-

---

30. Harsin, *Policing Prostitution,* 14.

31. Debelleyme, March 24, 1828, "Bureau administratif: Commission spéciale," DA 220, doc. 11, APP; Debelleyme, January 12, 1829, "Bureau administratif: Commission spéciale," DA 220, doc. 12, APP; Debelleyme, January 17, 1829, "Bureau administratif: Commission spéciale," DA 220, doc. 13, APP.

32. "Recueil des procès verbaux des séances de la Commission Spéciale pour la Répression de la Prostitution. Registre no. 1," 3e Séance du 11 Mars 1829, DA 221, doc. 5, APP. During the same meeting, the commission decided to ban prostitutes from standing at the doors of maisons de tolérance near the Palais-Royal for "the same reasons."

ciety" to access public space. The construction of approved commercial space necessitated the total elimination of the previously ongoing sexual commerce.

The commission found it difficult to sustain this kind of policy, because it recognized that decisions affecting one area of the city involved consequences for others. For example, during the meeting of July 8, 1829, the commission addressed a number of complaints from business owners and inhabitants of the "rue Lepelletier" [*sic*] near the Royal Academy of Music, not far from the area discussed earlier in the year.[33] Despite its earlier faith in its ability to secure particular neighborhoods from the presence of prostitution, the commission hesitated to intervene in this case. Indeed, the minutes underscore the members' frustration with the volume of the complaints they had received: "The commission painfully understands the difficulty of responding to every complaint of this nature considering that the area where the prostitutes gather during the evening in this neighborhood is very limited in terms of numbers, and one cannot expel them from one side without another becoming encumbered."[34] Implying that the problem in this area was not as bad as elsewhere, the authorities still recommended that prostitutes be banned from the area on days of the opera, pending a report on the subject.[35]

Seeking ways to "dissipate" the "agglomeration" of prostitutes on the streets, as one entry from the commission records put it, the authorities' behavior underscores how late Restoration regulationism shaped street life and policing.[36] Navigating a tension between an ideology that emphasized the importance of a rational and systemic approach and an urban practice premised on street-by-street responses to problems as they emerged, the police constructed a policy intended to clean the streets without any clear standards for achieving the goal. Although regulationism rested on grand assumptions regarding the inevitability of female prostitution and the possibility of state intervention, it remained rather limited in scope when put into practice. While the police sometimes tried to completely remove evidence of prostitution from areas of the city, they ultimately recognized their own limitations. Indeed, it was through the very premises of regulationism that those limitations emerged. For if male desire made female prostitution inevitable, then there was little point in trying to completely remove it. This tension led

---

33. "Recueil des procès verbaux des séances de la Commission Spéciale pour la Répression de la Prostitution. Registre no. 1," 14e Séance du 8 Juillet 1829, DA 221, docs. 15–16, APP. Presumably, the commission was referring to rue le Peletier, in the present-day ninth arrondissement.

34. Ibid.

35. Ibid.

36. "Recueil des procès verbaux des séances de la Commission Spéciale pour la Répression de la Prostitution. Registre no. 1," 16e Séance du 9 Septembre 1829, DA 221, doc. 18, APP.

to street-by-street intervention, encouraged by local conditions around class and commerce, that acknowledged the limits of an expanding police force to remove the sight of prostitution from the street.

Debating Enclosure

Through the course of the late 1820s and 1830s, the prefecture focused its efforts on maintaining a system of tolerated brothels that would enclose female prostitutes while still making them available to themselves, male customers, and doctors. Shifting regulations differed in the particulars, but all revolved around a central goal of ensuring that registered prostitutes only practiced their trade inside registered brothels. These rules shaped police categorization of female prostitutes along two axes: they were either "registered" or "unregistered"—*filles inscrites* (sometimes also called *filles soumises*) or *filles insoumises.* In addition, registered prostitutes could be either *filles en maison* or *filles isolées* (also known as *filles en carte,* for the registration card they carried). The former were prostitutes who lived in a brothel, while the latter were those who lived outside one. The former were "in house," while the latter were "isolated" from it. Thus, prostitutes were partly defined by their position vis-à-vis the tolerated brothel, designated as the only place where sex could be sold. The goal of the early nineteenth-century police was not only to register clandestine prostitutes but also to move them "in house."[37]

The police believed that clandestine street prostitution represented the greatest threat to public morality and health. Since prostitution was inevitable, they argued that it would be better to confine and regulate it within known houses of prostitution. In pursuit of this goal, the prefecture sought out ways of increasing the number of tolerated brothels in Paris. The first article of an 1828 proposed regulation, for example, states simply and clearly that "the number of these maisons is unlimited." This is not to say

---

37. The commission explicitly discussed the difficulty of convincing filles isolées to enter the tolerances in 1830. See "Recueil des procès verbaux des séances de la Commission Spéciale pour la Répression de la Prostitution. Registre no. 1," 27e Séance du 24 Juin 1830, DA 221, docs. 30–32, APP. In 1853 a police report also suggested doing more to make sure that the rules were to the advantage of madams of tolerated brothels rather than filles isolées. "Rapport du 11 Juin 1853," DA 222, doc. 32, 20–21, APP. This theme continued through the Third Republic. A report of a later Commission Spéciale de la Police des Mœurs, compiled by the abolitionist doctor Louis Fiaux, noted that "sadly—for both the doctrine and administrative practices—there have never been sufficient maisons de tolérance to receive all women who live by prostitution or believe that they could only live by it; the police find themselves thereby forced to recognize the *fille isolée*." Conseil Municipal de Paris, "Rapport présenté par M. L. Fiaux, au nom de la Commission Spéciale de la Police des Mœurs," no. 26 (1883), 6–7.

brothels could simply be opened anywhere in the city. Rather, Article Four of the proposal declared, "No house of prostitution may be opened in the neighborhood of royal habitations, churches, religious establishments, or schools."[38] The maison de tolérance would thus enable the police to control the quantitative and the qualitative character of Parisian prostitution. These goals, however, underscore the fact that the police did not really try to "purge" the streets of prostitution. Rather, the police produced new ways of recognizing the availability of venal sex to the populace, or what I refer to as public sexual signs. The brothel could not solve the problem of the visibility of prostitution, because it only redirected, redefined, and reformulated it.

The number of tolerated brothels fluctuated throughout the century, but they did increase from the late 1820s through the 1840s. According to Jill Harsin, who compiled the most complete analysis of statistics drawn from extant published sources, Paris featured around 145 maisons de tolérance in 1825, with about 275 women working within them. At their height, in 1852, Paris possessed 217 tolerated brothels, hosting an unknown number of women. (The 204 tolerances that still existed in 1855 had 1,852 women working in them.) The number of tolerances remained about stable through the first half of the 1850s, when a slow, undeniable decline began. While Paris had 212 brothels in 1850 and still contained 194 in 1860, by 1870 that number was down to 152. At the turn of the century, Paris had only 49 maisons de tolérance left standing.[39]

The causes for this decline are numerous. Shifting police priorities toward the management of street prostitution in the 1840s combined with Haussmannization in the 1850s to reshape the physical spaces of venal sex. It did so in ways that encouraged the use of more informal spaces such as *garnis,* or furnished rooms, cafés, and other public establishments, as well as *maisons de rendezvous,* where rooms were rented on a more short-term basis for prostitutes and their clients.[40] By the end of the century, opposition to

---

38. "Project de règlement no. 5," 1828, "Renseignements généraux: Projets de règlements émanés de l'administration," DA 222, doc. 8, APP. A proposal from the same years drops this declaration, but keeps some of the other language. "Project de règlement no. 6," 1828, "Renseignements généraux: Projets de règlements émanés de l'administration," DA 222, doc. 9, APP.

39. Harsin, *Policing Prostitution,* 309–311. These numbers rise in the very early part of the twentieth century, when the police began also recognizing *maisons de rendezvous.*

40. On the changing shape of the brothel and the maison de rendezvous, see esp. Harsin, *Policing Prostitution,* 307–322. See also Corbin, *Les filles de noce,* 171–189; Lola Gonzalez-Quijano, *Capitale de l'amour: Filles et lieux de plaisir à Paris au XIXe siècle* (Paris: Vendémiaire, 2015), 29–48. For a broader history of the nineteenth-century Parisian brothel, see Laure Adler, *Les maisons closes, 1830–1930* (Paris: Fayard/Pluriel, 2010), esp. chap. 2.

regulated prostitution also encouraged the police to abandon some of their earlier strategies while preserving their essential contours.[41]

Tolerated brothels tended to congregate in particular arrondissements and neighborhoods (Figure 1.1).[42] The placement of maisons de tolérance did not change drastically from the eighteenth century, and the pattern follows that of Parisian population density in the 1830s and 1840s.[43] The center of Paris featured the densest concentration of maisons de tolérance (indicated by the darkest shade on the map), especially in the second arrondissement around the Palais-Royal and the théâtres des Italiens and de l'Opéra, with forty-four tolerances in 1842 and thirty-one in 1854. Other arrondissements with a high number of maisons de tolérance during the same period included the fourth, just east of the Palais-Royal, with between twenty in 1842 and thirteen in 1854; the fifth, just north, with between twenty-three and seventeen brothels in the same years; and the ninth, farther east, with between nineteen and fifteen. Though eventually home to more informal spaces for clandestine prostitution (see Chapter 6), the Left Bank did not host as many maisons de tolérance.

These institutions were unevenly spaced not only throughout the city but also within each arrondissement. While the fifth arrondissement had among the highest number of brothels, almost all of them were in the neighborhood of Bonne Nouvelle: nineteen of twenty-three in 1842 and thirteen out of seventeen in 1854. The Invalides, in the tenth arrondissement in the western part of the Left Bank, had only six out of the ten brothels in the arrondissement in 1842, but by 1854 it had eleven of the sixteen, a growth that can most likely be attributed to the high presence of soldiers around the École Militaire.[44] As Parent-Duchâtelet put it, "There are areas which seem to attract *maisons de débauche,* and others that constantly repulse them."[45]

The spread of maisons de tolérance in Paris did not much change with their numerical decline (Figure 1.2). The new arrondissements that followed the incorporation of the suburbs did little to hide the essential consistency in the organization of tolerated brothels in the center of the city. The quartier

---

41. Harsin, *Policing Prostitution,* 335. On the abolitionist movement in France, see Corbin, *Les filles de noce,* 315–344; Bernheimer, *Figures of Ill Repute,* 211–212; Jean-Marc Berlière, *La police des mœurs sous la IIIe République* (Paris: Seuil, 1992), chap. 4; Karen Offen, "Madame Ghénia Avril de Sainte-Croix, the Josephine Butler of France," *Women's History Review* 17, no. 2 (2008): 239–255.

42. Note that the included map and description refer to pre-1860 arrondissements.

43. Plumauzille, *Prostitution et révolution,* 75; Ann-Louise Shapiro, *Housing the Poor of Paris, 1850–1902* (Madison: University of Wisconsin Press, 1985), 9.

44. Alexandre Parent-Duchâtelet, *De la prostitution dans la ville de Paris considérée sous le rapport de l'hygiène publique, de la morale et de l'administration,* 3rd ed., vol. 1 (Paris: J.-B. Baillière, 1857), 324–325.

45. Ibid., 322.

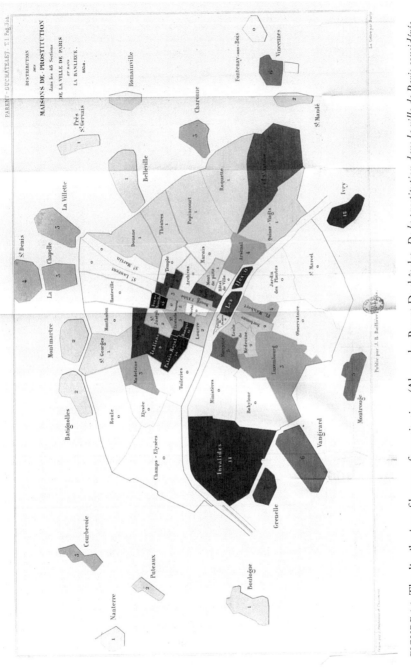

FIGURE 1.1. The distribution of houses of prostitution. (Alexandre Parent-Duchâtelet, *De la prostitution dans la ville de Paris considérée sous le rapport de l'hygiène publique, de la morale et de l'administration*, 3rd ed., 2 vols. [Paris: J.-B. Baillière, 1857], 1:324. Courtesy Bibliothèque Nationale de France.)

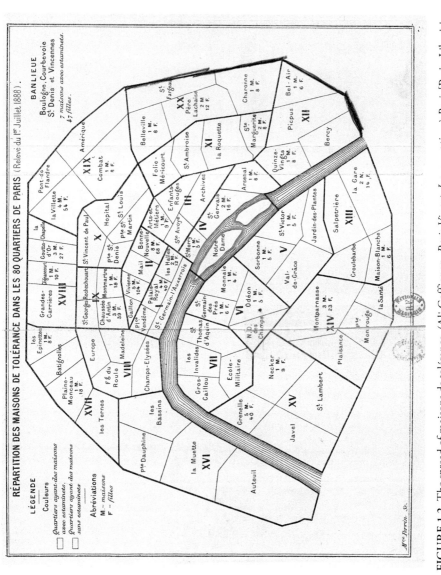

FIGURE 1.2. The spread of maisons de tolérance. (Ali Coffignon, *Paris-Vivant: La corruption à Paris* [Paris: Librairie Illustrée, 1888], 36. Courtesy Bibliothèque Nationale de France.)

of Bonne Nouvelle, for instance, now in the second arrondissement, still had among the highest number of maisons de tolérance, with eight houses and 68 women working in them out of thirteen houses and 187 women in the whole arrondissement. The area closest to the Palais-Royal, however, did see a relative decline, most likely due to the concerted efforts of the police to clear out the area that began in the 1840s. The Left Bank still did not possess a high number of tolerated brothels, but their decline elsewhere in the city made the area more important in relative terms.[46] What this later map ultimately shows, therefore, is that while tolerated brothels remained in the same general areas of the city, they were simply not as central to the business of venal sex as they had been during the July Monarchy.

The most complete attempt to enclose female prostitutes in the maisons de tolérance took place between April 14, 1830, and the July Revolution of that year, when a regulation enunciated by Prefect of Police Claude Mangin was briefly in force: "It is absolutely forbidden to prostitutes to present themselves on the public streets in order to excite, directly or indirectly, debauchery. It is equally forbidden for them to appear for any reason in the arcades, in public gardens, or on the boulevards." The ordinance restricted all acts of prostitution to the tolerated brothels; those filles isolées who did not live in the brothel would have to go to one "after the lighting of the streetlamps." Although the ordinance revolved around hiding the body of the prostitute, it still permitted houses of prostitution to "indicate themselves by a lamp and, early on, by an older woman who will stand by the door."[47] The comprehensiveness of the order speaks to a desire for systemic regulation in ways that constantly ran up against the more local interventions of the preceding years.

However, despite appearances, the regulation did not actually attempt to completely enclose female prostitutes. Limitations on where prostitutes could appear complemented a constant, regular circulation of filles isolées. These women, joining their compatriots in the tolerances, had to march "directly" to the lighted brothel, "dressed simply and with decency, abstaining from all standing still, from all promenades, and, from all provocation," after the streetlights were lit each night. Although the ordinance downplayed the visual presence of the prostitute by forcing her into simple, "decent" dress, it nonetheless pushed her into public space by regimenting her movement to and from the tolerance. As the brothel drew in the neighborhood's prostitutes at the beginning of the evening and expelled them precisely at eleven o'clock, it participated in remaking Parisian space into a kind of heterosexual system wherein these nodes

---

46. Ali Coffignon, *Paris-Vivant: La corruption à Paris* (Paris: Librairie Illustrée, 1888), 70.
47. Mangin, April 14, 1830, "Répression: Voie publique: Décisions," DA 223, doc. 12, APP.

of sexual commerce constantly provoked without "provocation."[48] Despite its reputation, therefore, the ordinance was never actually an attempt to "remove all evidence of prostitution from the sight of the public."[49] Transforming female prostitutes from "public" to cloistered women required an enduring commitment to the centrality of the brothel to urban space.

Despite eventual disagreement between Mangin and his fellow administrators regarding the age of registration, the ordinance received plaudits from the commission.[50] When the commission met to assess the immediate effects of his ordinance on June 24, 1830, they declared, "The public scandal of prostitution has almost completely disappeared. One sees only a small number of prostitutes circulating about the streets; and those who show themselves are dressed so decently, they maintain an affect so reserved, they take so many precautions not to be remarked on, that only experienced eyes can recognize them." Even if the ordinance had not entirely pushed sex work indoors, it did achieve the goal of disciplining the prostitute. Aware of the regulations that constrained them, these women remade their behavior, taking care to avoid the attention of the police and potential clients—or so the police reported. However, the commission admitted that Mangin's ordinance had done little to encourage filles isolées to become filles en maison—the number of the latter increased by only 45 between April 30, 1830, and late June of that year, despite a rather large increase in the number of tolerated brothels from 187 to 200 during the same period, which means the average number of women living in the tolerances remained stable at about 5.6.[51]

Mangin's rules stand as the apogee of administrative efforts to push female prostitutes into tolerated brothels. Despite their short life span, they became touchstones among the populace, associated with the men who promulgated them, the regulationist system, and the Restoration as a whole. For example, unidentified Parisians laid out their response to Mangin's order in a series of pamphlets that appeared just before the July Revolution.[52] As Jann

---

48. Ibid.

49. Harsin, *Policing Prostitution*, 43.

50. Ibid., 29.

51. "Recueil des procès verbaux des séances de la Commission Spéciale pour la Répression de la Prostitution. Registre no. 1," 27e Séance du 24 Juin 1830, DA 221, docs. 30–32, APP. These numbers differ slightly from those available in the published sources, which claim 1,052 women living in 198 maisons de tolérance in 1830 and 1,071 women living in 205 maisons de tolérance in 1831, for an average of about 5.3 women per house. See Harsin, *Policing Prostitution*, 309.

52. I was able to locate twenty of the pamphlets in the catalog of the Bibliothèque Nationale de la France. They are as follows: "Projet d'un nouveau règlement concernant les filles publiques et les maisons de prostitution, tendant à en diminuer le nombre, sans employer la rigueur, et sans attenter à la liberté des prostituées. Soumis à M. le Préfet de Police. Par un Ami de la Charte,

Matlock has shown, although the pamphlets often replicate regulationist assumptions of a "politics of visibility," they also use constructions of space to make new claims on the city, which made the prostitute into a symbol to be

Dans l'intérêt du Commerce et des Mœurs" (Paris: Libraires du Palais-Royal, 1830); Virginie, "Deuxième pétition adressée à M. Le Préfet de Police, par les filles publiques de Paris, la première, a cause de sa nullité, étant restée sans réponse, suivie de lettres de condoléance de leurs consœurs des départemens" (Paris: Marchands de Nouveautés, 1830); "À MM. les Députés. Projet de pétition sur la liberté individuelle, par un spartiate, de ceux que vulgairement on nomme voleurs: et a l'appui de la pétition des filles publiques" (Paris: Marchands de Nouveautés, 1830); Engin, "Réponse de M. Engin, aux pétitions des filles publiques suivie de deux scènes historiques de révolte occasionnées par la nouvelle ordonnance de police (Paris: Marchands de Nouveautés, 1830); "Le vrai motif de la captivité des femmes soumises, et leurs plus grands ennemis dévoilés" (Paris: Marchands de Nouveautés,1830); "Aux Ministres!!! Nouvelle pétition des filles publiques de Paris, tendant à obtenir de LL. EE. la révocation de l'ordonnance attentatoire à leurs liberté, rendue contre elles" (Paris: Libraires du Palais-Royal, 1830); Laure, "Prière romantique de Laure, dite la Séduisante, à tous les amateurs des prêtresses de Vénus et aux augustes défenseurs de Thémis, au sujet de l'ordonnance qui défend aux charmantes déesses de Paphos de sortir de leurs temples, publiée par un amoureux en délire" (Paris: Marchands de Nouveautés, 1830); "La Paulinade, grande conspiration de la fameuse Pauline et des 20.000 filles publiques de Paris, contre M. Mangin et ses agens. Poème romantique, en trois chants dans le genre adapté par l'auteur d'Hernani" (Paris: Marchands de Nouveautés, 1830); "Les filles en cage ou Déguerpissons! Par un abonné au cachet des maisons de plaisir de la capitale" (Paris: Peytieux, 1830); "Plainte et révélations nouvellement adressées par les filles de joie de Paris à la congrégation, contre l'ordonnance de M. Mangin, qui leur défend de circuler dans les rues pour offrir leurs charmes aux passans (Paris: Garnier, 1830); César, "Pétition d'un souteneur à M. le préfet de police de Paris, à l'occasion de l'ordonnance qu'il vient de rendre contre les filles publiques, appuyée d'une lettre d'un fruitier de la rue Froidmanteau" (Paris: Principaux Libraires au Palais-Royal, 1830); "Complainte authentique, originale et seule véritable, sur la grande catastrophe des filles de Paris" (Paris: Marchands de Nouveautés, 1830); "Réponse de M. le Préfet à toutes les pétitions et réclamations des filles publiques de Paris" (Paris: 1830); Rosine, "Observations soumises par une fille de joie à M. le préfet de police, Sur les dangers que les hommes et les honnêtes femmes ont à craindre des effets de son ordonnance qui défend aux filles prostituées de sortir de chez elles; le tort qu'elle fait au commerce, et sur les moyens de réparer tant de maux sans nuire aux bonnes mœurs" (Paris: Marchands de Nouveautés, 1830); M.J.M, "Épitre à M. Mangin au sujet de l'ordonnance attentatoire à la liberté des femmes" (Paris: 1830); Pauline, "Pétition des filles publiques de Paris à M. le préfet de police, au sujet de l'ordonnance qu'il vient de rendre contre elles" (Paris: 1830); "Doléances des filles de joie de Paris, à l'occasion de l'ordonnance qui leur défend de se montrer en public, arrangées en complainte par l'une d'elles, enrichies de notes et adressées aux nymphes" (Paris: Libraires du Palais-Royal, 1830); "Grande, veritable et lamentable complainte romantique de ces demoiselles, écrite sous la dictée d'une ci-devant nymphe du No 113, accompagnée de notes et commentaires" (Paris: Gaultier-Laguionie, 1830); Théodore, "50,000 voleurs de plus à Paris, ou réclamations des anciens marlous de la capitale contre l'ordonnance de M. le préfet de police, concernant les filles publiques" (Paris: Marchands de Nouveautés, 1830); "Le Tocsin de ces demoiselles, ou Mémoire à consultée adressé à tous les barreaux de France, et dénonciation aux cours royales, au sujet d'un arrêté de M. Mangin, contre les filles publiques, suivi de plusieurs lettres édifiantes et curieuses" (Paris: Marchands de Nouveautés, 1830). Note that publisher information is generally lacking; distributors are listed as available, following the catalog of the Bibliothèque Nationale.

deployed against the government of Charles X.[53] One pamphlet, for instance, authored by "a friend of the Charter"—referencing the limited constitution of the regime—proposed a different regulation that was "less severe than the ordinance of M. le Préfet." The first article declared:

> Allow all prostitutes to freely move about wherever and without fear that they will be arrested, not including cases of infractions against the regulation. Place, on all areas where many prostitutes promenade, an inspector specially charged to observe, stop those who make obscene or gross remarks, or who insult anyone, whether with words or gestures. He will also prevent anyone from mistreating them.[54]

This "friend of the Charter" thus accepts many of the premises of regulation. Article One deploys the idea of public decency, arguing that prostitutes were capable of working in public without indulging in the "obscene" acts that would otherwise threaten it. In order to ensure that prostitutes remain well-behaved, the pamphlet still encourages a direct police role in managing sex work, inscribing these women under the eye of the inspector. Subsequent articles also accepted the need for medical inspections, for registration, and for continued use of the maisons de tolérance. And yet, in its emphasis on the need for prostitutes to remain outside—and, indeed protected by the police as they went about their business—it also constructs a different relationship between sex, the city, and its residents. The proposal called for prostitutes to carry an ostentatious numbered medal, a card with her name and address, as well as her medical card. By "showing these three objects to any man who wanted to spend a moment with her," potential clients "would be able to assure themselves that the girl they had chosen was healthy and easily recognizable, should she take anything from him."[55] Just as for the police, a well-ordered city necessitated properly managed houses of prostitution, the presence of prostitutes in public could also become an indication of well-functioning city space.

Other pamphlets were written in the voice of prostitutes themselves. In one, the pseudonymous author, Rosine, explains that "most men with depraved tastes do not like going to known brothels." With Mangin's ordinance, Rosine could only ask, "What will these men do now when their lustful plea-

---

53. Matlock, *Scenes of Seduction*, 76–77. Matlock notes that the *Bibliographie de France* "lists twenty-one pamphlets and one print relating to the Mangin ordinances on prostitution." Ibid., 327.

54. "Projet d'un nouveau règlement concernant les filles publiques et les maisons de prostitution," 2.

55. Ibid., 3.

sures torment them?" She responds, "They will insult the first woman that they meet alone on the streets or in little frequented areas."[56] Indeed, the pamphlet is explicit on this point, linking the ability of prostitutes to move about the city with the protection of "honest women." It concludes by arguing, "It is therefore necessary, for the peace of mind of honest women, and for the good of commerce, that we move about freely."[57] The pamphlet thus links a politics of space to regulationist understandings of male desire. As an uncontrollable "passion," male desire required outlets. If it could not target a known prostitute, it would instead be directed at an honest woman. In order to prevent this from happening, prostitutes had to be allowed to move about the city attracting men. The liberty of the prostitute would thereby ensure the social stability that Mangin had intended to guarantee by locking them up. Thus, the pamphlets reveal how regulationists had successfully defined the range of the debate over liberty, class, and gender during the early part of the century. Written in the name of liberty, these arguments still took up the concern with urban social control that was so prominent in the regulationist discourse they supposedly opposed.

It is no coincidence that the pamphlets circulated primarily around the Palais-Royal, one of the first spaces in Paris where evidence remains of residents and business owners also intervening in debates over regulation.[58] Since the eighteenth century, prostitution in the Palais-Royal fed off of its reputation as a commercial space where women and men were expected to interact with one another. Prostitution played a role in making the Palais-Royal into a popular space of commerce, both sexual and nonsexual.[59] By the final years of the Restoration and especially during the July Monarchy, however, the police began to intervene fairly forcefully into the life of the area. They sought to clear it of clandestine prostitution and entice prostitutes into the brothels. The attempt to eliminate clandestine prostitution from the Palais-Royal represents the spatial strategies at the heart of the regulationist project while also showcasing the difficulties the police faced in putting them into practice.

On July 23, 1824, the merchants of the Palais-Royal sent a petition to the Ministry of the Interior asking that the authorities do more to expel the prostitutes from the area. Associating the problem of prostitution with a variety of social ills and political dangers, the petition's authors declared that by forcing the prostitutes out, they would be able to create a

---

56. Rosine, "Observations soumises par une fille de joie," 3–4.

57. Ibid, 7.

58. The archives only occasionally reveal the voices of these men (and occasionally women) during the early part of the century, but they became a cacophony during the Third Republic. On these letters, see Chapter 5 herein.

59. Plumauzille, *Prostitution et révolution,* 94–114.

magnificent bazaar where all the riches of the world would pile up, the most successful commercial space of the capital due to the affluence of foreigners, which will only increase when wives and mothers can present themselves without worrying about being insulted, without worrying about subjecting the eyes of their children to the image of prostitution.[60]

The petition constructs a dual binary that contrasts selling sex with selling goods and prostitutes with "wives and mothers." And yet the image of the "magnificent bazaar" cannot help but evoke the orientalist image of sensual delights in the wares the merchants themselves purvey, wares their female customers and their children would be gazing on as well. The problem, perhaps, was less that sex or images of sex were being sold and more that these businessmen failed to profit from it. Prostitutes comprised, in this sense, competition. By placing sexual (and, in this case, somewhat racialized) imagery under their own power, they would both profit from it. The request for police intervention, then, was as much a demand for the protection of their own economic power as it was one for the elimination of prostitution.

In response to the petition, the police explained to the minister of the interior why it was not possible to simply expel the prostitutes from the area. For the most part, the report follows a standard regulationist line: "Prostitution is a fact that is not in the power of the authorities to destroy," and trying to do so would lead the prostitutes to simply invade other spaces.[61] Here, however, the police added an essential caveat to its considerations. One reason that the police were reticent to attempt to rid the Palais-Royal of prostitution actually lay in its existing reputation: "There is no one who does not know in advance what sort of scandalous scenes he may be shocked by if curiosity leads one to this place."[62] In other words, one could take advantage of the existence of what was, in essence, a red-light district avant la lettre. One could hardly be surprised by the sight of a prostitute should one's "curiosity" draw one to a well-known space of sex. Regulationist thought could take the merchants' concerns into account only to a certain extent. The existence of a space already associated with venal sex proved advantageous to a police force that was unable and unwilling to try to eliminate it from the city.

The contrast between the 1824 petition, asking for prostitutes to be ex-

---

60. Copie de la Pétition adressée à S. Ex. M. le Ministre de l'Intérieur le 23 Juillet 1824 par M. M. les marchands du Palais Royal, July 23, 1824, "Répression: Lieux interdits," DA 222, doc. 3, APP.

61. Letter to Minister of the Interior, August 2, 1824, "Répression: Lieux interdits," DA 222, docs. 6–7, 2-4, APP.

62. Ibid, 7.

pelled, and the 1830 pamphlets, asking for prostitutes to be welcomed, in the same space speaks to conflicting interpretations of how public sex was understood at the time as well as a shift in the approach taken by the authorities over the 1820s. Later complaints, including one request from a representative of the Duc d'Orléans himself, renewed the request for police to clear the area of female prostitutes.[63] These efforts were part of a growing effort to remake the class basis of the area. The director of the *Cosmorama* (an entertainment featuring large-scale images of real-world sights), for instance, wrote in the name of "persons of distinction, even ecclesiastics of the highest rank," who have made known their discomfort.[64] These requests were received with more sympathy by the police, who began making piecemeal efforts to keep prostitutes away from certain areas of the Palais.[65] By the end of the 1820s, the Palais-Royal became caught up in the broader shifts in police strategy undertaken first by Prefect Debelleyme then by Prefect Mangin.[66] Indeed, a specific interdiction on the ability of prostitutes to use the Palais-Royal survived Mangin's fall.[67]

Two views of the relationship between space, sex, and commerce thus remained in play simultaneously. On the one hand, prostitution and commerce complemented each other; on the other hand, the two conflicted and needed to be kept distinct. For instance, in his book, F.F.A. Béraud presented an imaginary interlocutor who blamed efforts to rid prostitutes from the Palais-Royal and other busy places for hurting commerce in those areas by decreasing the number of people going there.[68] However, Béraud rejects this argument and claims that "even if it were true[,] . . . it would not be sufficient reason to allow them [prostitutes] back in because of the spectacle that repulses public morality, a spectacle more immoral in the enclosure of a *palais,* than on a boulevard or a street."[69] Béraud thus shifts the grounds on which the claim to manage space was made. While in the 1820s, the concentration of prostitution at the Palais-Royal was an advantage insofar as it kept it away

---

63. Badouin to Préfet de Police, December 16, 1828, "Répression: Lieux interdits," DA 222, doc. 10, APP.

64. Genin to Préfet de Police, July 10, 1827, "Répression: Lieux interdits," DA 222, doc. 8, APP.

65. Préfet de Police to Commissaire de Police du quartier du Palais-Royal, December 22, 1828, "Répression: Lieux interdits," DA 222, doc. 11, APP.

66. It was Debelleyme who first laid down a fairly strict policy on the use of the streets by women who sold sex. See his circular of April 27, 1829, DA 226, doc. 12, APP. See also Harsin, *Policing Prostitution,* 42.

67. Girod, A. September 7, 1830, "Répression: Voie publique: Arrêté du 7 Septembre 1830: Abrogation implicite de l'arrêté du 14 Avril précédant," DA 223, doc. 28, APP.

68. Béraud, *Les filles publiques de Paris,* 1:202–204.

69. Ibid., 204.

from other areas, now it was a disadvantage, because concentration was, by definition, dangerous. Conceding that sex could attract people and that this may indeed benefit the shops of the area, Béraud still refused to admit that this was sufficient reason to allow prostitutes the freedom to pursue their business. By the 1830s, the police tended to agree with those who advocated the latter opinion, which encouraged police attempts to more forcefully ensure that spaces of commerce remained free of venal sex.

Promoting Tolerated Prostitution

Although both Parisians and the authorities long remembered Mangin's efforts in largely positive terms, later regulations never really tried to replicate them.[70] The immediate replacement, announced on September 7, 1830, declared that "prostitutes are forbidden from appearing on the streets in a manner that makes themselves known before the lighting of the lamps and from staying there after eleven o'clock in the evening."[71] Here, the prohibition on entering public space was undercut by the rest of the article. While it exhibits the same desire to ban prostitutes from appearing on the streets, it also acknowledges the impossibility of doing so. Women who sold sex may be on the streets so long as they did not "make themselves known." Indeed, the final line of Article One simply states "Their conduct must be decent," while the second article bans them from "provoquer à la débauche" (provoking debauchery).[72] The ordinance proceeds through a series of restrictions on their movement in public space by banning them from moving about in groups, from using the Palais-Royal and other gardens, and from areas around taverns and the like. Contrasted with Mangin's ordinance, which essentially stated that prostitutes could not appear in public at all, the sheer detail of its replacement speaks to a shift away from broad attempts to manage the problem back to more precise interventions into the life of the street.

At the same time, administrators continued to emphasize the importance of the tolerance as a space of venal sex and a solution to the problem of street prostitution. The idea of increasing the number of brothels to house and employ sex workers, however, ran up against administrators' fears of disorder and discouraged the authorities from taking active measures to promote

---

70. Later references to Mangin's efforts include Prévoite, March 25, 1838, F7 9305, AN; Lamarche to Préfecture de Police, January 17, 1846, DA 221, doc. 70, APP; G. Delessert, "Circulaire no 12: Manière de procéder à la répression des désordes [sic] causés par les filles publiques," February 10, 1841, "Renseignements généraux: Projects de règlements émanés de l'administration," DA 222, doc. 12, APP; Béraud, Les filles publiques de Paris, 1:183.

71. Girod, September 7, 1830.

72. Ibid.

the expansion of tolerated houses. The commission took up the question of increasing the number of tolerated brothels when it reconvened in 1836.[73] At their meeting of October 4 that year, the police reported a decline of tolerated brothels from 220 to 186 but also complained about the "incessant" increase in the number of prostitutes as well as the growth of clandestine brothels.[74] In response, at their next meeting, an unnamed member of the commission suggested offering all lodgers known to be housing prostitutes a choice: from a specific date—to be determined—they could either remain garnis, and thus submit to all the regulations that governed such establishments, or become maisons de tolérance. In doing so, this commissioner hoped, the authorities would encourage lodgers to choose the latter course, which would, in turn, push other clandestine houses of prostitution to do the same.[75]

However, another unnamed member of the commission objected to this optimistic suggestion. This member noted that it would be hard to determine how long a period to allow the lodgers to decide which course they wanted to take. In the meantime, he feared that the lodgers, under the misconception that the new rules foreshadowed a crackdown, "would refuse their houses to the prostitutes, a great number of whom would find themselves without shelter." In addition, he feared, those who did request to become tolerances would probably be precisely those who the authorities would most likely want to shut down in the first place, and there was no way to guarantee that sufficient numbers would request to become brothels to house the women, which would only disrupt "the state of sanitation and that of public order." Ultimately, the commission agreed that they should enforce the existing regulations in order to encourage landlords either to stop hosting clandestine prostitution or to request to become tolerances until there were enough to "constrain prostitutes to enclose themselves within them." This process should take place "successively and over the totality of all neighborhoods infested by these clandestine houses, beginning with those that featured the most 'maisons clandestines.'"[76] The project of moving through the whole city with a progressive crackdown against clandestine brothels contrasts with the fundamentally conservative nature of the proposal that essentially maintained the status quo and showcases the authorities' hesitance to reformulate their approach to urban sexual policing after Mangin's brief tenure.

---

73. The four-year hiatus is left unexplained in their reports.

74. "Recueil des procès verbaux des séances de la Commission Spéciale pour la Répression de la Prostitution. Registre no. 2," 46e Séance du 4 Octobre 1836, DA 221, doc. 2, APP.

75. "Recueil des procès verbaux des séances de la Commission Spéciale pour la Répression de la Prostitution. Registre no. 2," 47e Séance du 5 Décembre 1836, DA 221, docs. 3–4, APP.

76. Ibid.

Despite calling for sex work to occur only in tolerated brothels and lamenting the decline in the number of such institutions, the commission remained largely unwilling to actually take steps to increase their number even when presented with the opportunity to do so. In July 1837 the commission discussed requests from six landlords to convert their houses into tolerances. Four of these requests came from locations on the rue Pierre-Lescot and the rue Fromenteau in the first arrondissement; the other two were located on the rue de la Contrescarpe St. Antoine, in the eighth arrondissement (now the boulevard de la Bastille in the twelfth arrondissement). Neither group was granted permission to become maisons de tolérance. The police argued that the first was located too close to an area near the Palais-Royal where they had been encouraging other clandestine houses of prostitution to close down. Granting permission to those that remained would reward their bad behavior, place the administration in an awkward position, and encourage those that had closed to try again. The other two, the police explained, were located in an area of the city that "is deserted and obscure during the night and is quite far from the center of surveillance, that incidentally the two houses under consideration are well known for habitually receiving miscreants and thieving prostitutes, and that should some awful event occur, one would not fail to blame the lack of foresight by the administration which allowed two places of debauchery in so isolated a space."[77]

While the commission was unanimous in rejecting the application of the first four brothels, one commissioner did speak up in support of turning the final two into tolerances. This commissioner argued that allowing these garnis to become tolerances would enable the police to keep a closer eye on them. Increased surveillance remained, after all, the purpose of these regulations. The commission ignored this argument, however, and instead followed the police's wishes by suggesting that the two lodgers be prosecuted in order to prevent this *"coupable industrie"* from returning.[78] The commission and the police thus rejected the request of the garnis near the center of the city *and* those in more isolated areas. In doing so, they frustrated our ability to unravel the precise conditions under which they would have been willing to increase the number of tolerances, which was, after all, the ostensible goal. Presented with arguments in line with their regulationist ideology, the authorities nonetheless preferred to deploy their considerable power in an attempt to eliminate rather than create new spaces of prostitution.

---

77. "Recueil des procès verbaux des séances de la Commission Spéciale pour la Répression de la Prostitution. Registre no. 2," 48e Séance du 6 Juillet 1837, DA 221, doc. 4, APP.

78. "Recueil des procès verbaux des séances de la Commission Spéciale pour la Répression de la Prostitution. Registre no. 2," 48e Séance du 6 Juillet 1837, DA 221, docs. 4–5, APP.

And yet the police still seemed surprised when Parisians themselves asked them to eliminate brothels from their neighborhoods. In 1834 the prefecture received a letter complaining about a brothel on the rue du Chantre in the first arrondissement. The letter claimed that while the brothel had been in the neighborhood for quite a while, the problems it represented were getting worse. The writer, a man named Jerôme, blamed this state of affairs on broader social changes: "Each day sees morality and social habits more in keeping with the refinements and tastes of the comfortable, which results in disadvantages that had previously been unperceived and unimportant but today become an insurmountable obstacle to the habitation of peaceful and honest people." According to the writer, recent urban works had isolated the street from the "general circulation," which had contributed to making prostitution more apparent within the neighborhood.[79] Jerôme's complaint thus combines changes in urban space and in social mores to create a claim for police intervention in order to preserve the value of the rents of the neighborhood. His attack on the neighborhood prostitutes stands as a classed attempt to make room for his own investment in a changing neighborhood.

In response, the police launched a brief investigation. The resulting report, sent to the minister of the interior, noted that this was actually the second complaint from Jerôme. It not only affirmed that the two brothels in the neighborhood had been there for some time but also claimed that Jerôme's complaints were the first the police had received. In response to Jerôme's first complaint, the officer investigated the situation and made sure the regulations were enforced more carefully. The officer believed that these efforts "were followed with perseverance" and would be well received by Jerôme. Instead, the report continues, "I can only express my surprise at the insistence with which he [Jerôme] demands the closure of a brothel which, if I am to believe the reports that have been delivered to me, has always been kept with order." That said, the prefect concludes by explaining to the minister, "If public prostitution is an evil without a solution in large cities, one of those sad necessities we must suffer, at the very least, your excellence [the minister of the interior] can be persuaded that I am bringing all my efforts to enclose it in the narrowest limits."[80] If Jerôme wanted to emphasize the "evil" of prostitution, the police highlighted its "necessity." The police, fearful of social disorder represented by those proprietors who hid clandestine prostitution, evinced surprise that city residents would feel the same about regulated brothels, even as the authorities themselves hesitated to increase their number. The well-ordered brothel was to represent the successful management of

---

79. Jerôme to Police, January 24, 1834, F7 9305, AN.
80. Préfet de Police to Ministre de l'Intérieur, July 7, 1834, F7 9305, AN.

public sex, but it remained in a rather ambiguous position insofar as it always wrote sex onto the street.

The police expressed exasperation at continued requests to clean the city streets. Faced with an increasing number of complaints from Parisians who lived in neighborhoods where prostitutes gathered near maisons de tolérance, the head of the morals police addressed "the efforts he had taken to give to satisfaction to these complainants" at an 1844 meeting of the commission. However, these efforts had failed to satisfy Parisians, who "would like, for the most part, for us to keep prostitution away from their residences, without worrying about how that would affect other inhabitants."[81] The torrent could not be stopped, in other words; it could only be redirected. The commission considered the possibility of trying to spread out the maisons de tolérance evenly throughout the city as a way of achieving a sort of balance, but the police deemed this idea "impractical[,] . . . because prostitution naturally adapts itself to those areas where it happens by virtue of the general movement of the population."[82] Afraid that any effort in that direction would have the effect of decreasing the number of brothels, the commission resigned itself to asking the police to respond to these complaints within established limits. Regulationism as such seemed to have constrained the ability of the authorities to act. Fearful of actually increasing the number of spaces for women to sell sex, they remained convinced that prostitution was inevitable in the city. Having constructed this system of sexual regulation in the first place, the police and its allies seemed incapable of controlling the very sexual economy that they had created.

Producing Sexual Space

As these discussions reveal, decisions regarding how to manage the appearance of prostitution were far more complex than binary oppositions between the visible and the invisible, the street and the brothel, the revealed and the hidden. The police strove to control *how* not *whether* venal sex appeared to the populace. This process involved more than granting permission to tolerances; it also entailed the production of a system of signification that would allow people to recognize public sex in order to either enter such spaces or—preferably—avoid them. More than enclosure, the circulation of sexual knowledge would solve the fundamental contradiction at the heart of the regulationist project. By enabling Parisians and visitors to recognize a maison de tolérance,

---

81. "Recueil des procès verbaux des séances de la Commission Spéciale pour la Répression de la Prostitution. Registre no. 2," 60e Séance du 7 Mai 1844, DA 221, doc 18, APP.
82. Ibid.

the police acknowledged the inevitability of prostitution while providing the necessary tools for all city residents to participate in managing it.

The process of enclosing the body of the prostitute actually revealed it in new ways. While the prostitutional body could not be trusted to provoke and incite sexual desire in passing men because of the threat to other women, the tolerated brothel apparently could. Put differently, the tolerated brothel was both a physical space and a symbolic imprint on which the authorities reoriented the signs of sex to their own ends. In order to do so, the police struggled to locate an appropriate marker of tolerated prostitution. First they permitted retired prostitutes and other older women—known as *marcheuses*—to beckon men indoors. Then they replaced them with a large address number to indicate the existence of tolerance. The body of the prostitute thus became fully subsumed under the numerical sign of well-regulated urban space, even as such indicators continued to advertise the availability of venal sex to all who saw them.

While it remains the case that brothels tried to hide sexual activity from those who passed them by, they still had to find ways to invite men inside. The ground floor of maisons de tolérance, for instance, were required to have windows "of ground glass, and no windows may be opened more than a few inches."[83] These requirements speak as much to the desire to hide sexual acts as they do to preventing women from soliciting sex from the windows. Nevertheless, the police sanctioned several exterior reminders of the uses of the brothel. In 1817 the police recognized the use of marcheuses, "women who invite [men], in a rather imperceptible manner, to enter a maison de tolérance where the women, kept on a particular footing, do not go on the street."[84] The marcheuse underscores how regulators tried to have it both ways. On the one hand, she was often a former prostitute who was explicitly permitted to hawk sex; on the other hand, the police argued that her age and manner prevented the kinds of problems that emerged with prostitutes who solicited on the streets.

Here, then, the use of the body to signal sex becomes folded into the broader administrative apparatus of the tolerance itself, so long as it remained "imperceptible." The police thus enabled the activity of a particular kind of "public woman" just as they depended on madams to run the brothels. In this respect, the marcheuse stands as the inversion of the *portière* of the first half of the century. The working-class portière managed apartment buildings and, through her daily activities, was able to observe the interior lives of those

---

83. Bernheimer, *Figures of Ill Repute,* 20.

84. "Observations sur les femmes publiques d'un certain âge, connues sous le nom de marcheuses," June 17, 1817, DA 226, doc. 8, APP.

who inhabited them. In addition, by virtue of her station at the building's entrance, she regulated just who did and did not also have access. She therefore came to represent a female obstacle to male observation of the Parisian interior and a barrier to men's sexual access to women.[85] However, rather than a barrier, the marcheuse actually became the entry point to heterosexual sex. She represents effective control over the working-class female body, rendering her useful to the proper functioning of the urban environment and those who inhabited it.[86]

The police contrasted the public presence of prostitutes with that of marcheuses. At some point during the Restoration, the prefecture began to allow brothels to send out two prostitutes to solicit at the doors of certain tolerances. This practice, Prefect of Police Debelleyme later claimed in agreement with the commission, tended to attract crowds of young men. In response, beginning on May 1, 1829, the prefecture forbade the practice and instructed the madams to replace them with "a domestic of advanced age whose presence will not cause the same harm."[87] Although the police believed that this decision may have the effect of increasing the number of filles isolées on the streets—their reasoning is left unexplained—they argued that a "just severity repeated as often as the circumstances merited" would succeed in eliminating these "exterior manifestations" from the "eyes of the public."[88]

Mangin's 1830 ordinance codified this practice by allowing maisons de tolérance to light their doors with a lantern and to place an "old woman" at the door.[89] When the commission met to assess the new rule, they lauded this decision, arguing that "the domestics placed at the doors of the maisons de tolérance in general solicit the passers-by, but this kind of provocation . . . is much less shocking than that which had been done by the prostitutes themselves and in much greater numbers."[90] The commission thus distinguished between modes of solicitation even as they claimed to want to eliminate all solicitation. One could not have a regulationist system without a means of signaling its existence. The signs of its success were made evident by the signs of sexual commerce themselves.

The use of the marcheuse provided the means for the police to disavow the fact that they had put their own stamp on a different kind of sexual

---

85. Marcus, *Apartment Stories*, 42–50.

86. Thanks to one of my anonymous readers for pointing out the connection between the marcheuse and the portière.

87. "Circulaire du 27 Avril 1829," DA 226, doc. 12, APP.

88. Ibid.

89. Mangin, April 14, 1830, "Répression: Voie publique: Décisions," DA 223, doc. 12, APP.

90. "Recueil des procès verbaux des séances de la Commission Spéciale pour la Répression de la Prostitution. Registre no. 1," 27e Séance du 24 Juillet 1830, DA 221, doc. 30, APP.

presence on the street. While they claimed to be hiding prostitution from the public at large, they had actually rendered it differently visible, available to those who recognized the marcheuse for who she was and responded to her call. The signs of prostitution were in the process of being transformed, taken away from the individual prostitute and granted to the madam, but only with the explicit permission of the police. Situated in the neighborhoods of the city, standing in the doorways, enticing young men, the literal signs of prostitution no longer signified disorder but rather safe containment. The irony of producing public signs of sex in order to safely enclose sex serves only to highlight the instability of the system as it was being enunciated.

Eventually the police risked allowing more women to move about the city in order to locate clients for the brothels, but they had difficulty deciding how many and in what manner they should be allowed to do so. An 1842 circular declared, "Madams who, until now, had the ability to let two prostitutes leave in the evening, may from now on have a domestic at their door and a single prostitute outside if they have six pensioners or more and only a domestic at their door if they have only five or less." The women allowed to leave to solicit had to follow a "route that was large enough so that her presence was not remarked on."[91] However, the police still received complaints about sexual solicitation. An 1843 letter to the police, for example, foreshadowed later police efforts to signal the maison de tolérance and suggested the use of "two lamps of a uniform color outside the door" to replace the women who solicited on the street.[92] An 1844 report tried to differentiate between the kinds of circulation the prefecture could and should allow. The report made no demand that prostitutes "should remain arbitrarily enclosed within their domiciles" but complained about those who left the tolerance to solicit rather than to leave in order to take care of their "errands and for their health." Any "intelligent officer" should be able to tell the difference between the two kinds of movement, the report argued. In particular, prostitutes were taking advantage of the "latitude" of the police to gather with the filles isolées of the neighborhood. In addition, the report asked for the domestics who were placed at the doors of the brothels to be forbidden from soliciting "by gesture or by word," because they were "generally the object of complaints by the proprietors and lodgers." The author suggested that "a simple show or sign would in part satisfy these recriminations that their presence and conduct give rise to."[93] The authorities thus struggled to reckon with their repeated acknowledgment of the need to increase the number of

---

91. Circulaire no. 14, September 20, 1842, DA 226, doc. 23, APP.

92. Letter to Préfet de Police, February 15, 1843, DA 221, doc. 65, APP.

93. Rapport trimestriel, April 15, 1844, DA 226, doc. 40, APP.

brothels, to display the brothels, and to allow the brothels to serve the sexual needs of the populace with their simultaneous desire to decrease the number of prostitutes who showed themselves and claim that the brothels somehow remained separate from the normal operation of the city.

The inability of the police to fully reconcile this tension partly explains the gradual decline of the maisons de tolérance, even as they continued to emphasize the need to monitor and identify female prostitutes. Police attitudes changed little in the wake of the 1848 Revolution that ushered in the Second Republic. In April 1848 the police noted how the February Revolution of that year had temporarily "interrupted" the regulationist system, which caused "prostitutes to forget to observe their regulatory obligations."[94] However, in the prior month, the now "citizen" prefect of police and the dispensary decided to "resume their ordinary functions" and, among other items, "proceed as in the past to examine requests for tolerances in order to diminish the number of prostitutes circulating to the benefit of the tolerances."[95] The politics of sexual regulation changed little in the transition from monarchy to republic.

However, the police did face newfound challenges as republican discourse circulated about the city. About a month before the outbreak of the June Days—when the Second Republic brutally suppressed the workers of Paris who were demanding the new government fulfill its social commitments—a group of madams wrote to the police to ask for a change in the laws that had "hit them under the fallen government." Claiming that these "poor souls" had been "tyrannized," they asked for "a bit more liberty," including the right to allow more of their employees to leave the brothel, promising that they would "avoid indulging in any insults toward passers-by." As a guarantee, they assured the prefect that they would "place an old woman next to them, in order to avoid any scandal."[96] The madams thus took up many of the terms of regulation even as they laid claim to greater freedom under the Second Republic.

Such hopes were not to be fulfilled. With the rise of the Second Empire, the police decided to reassess their practices and drew up an extensive report on past efforts to regulate prostitution in light of best practices for the future. In the report, the police recommended getting rid of the marcheuses: "The domestics called marcheuses, former prostitutes whose debauchery and drunkenness has degraded and [made conditions] a thousand times more shocking

---

94. "Répression de la prostitution," April 27, 1848, "Répression. Voie publique. Circulaire du 27 Avril 1848. Circulation des filles publiques sur la voie publique et répression," DA 223, doc. 119, APP.

95. "Recueil des procès verbaux des séances de la Commission Spéciale pour la Répression de la Prostitution. Registre no. 2," 61e Séance, March 21, 1848, DA 221, doc. 19, APP.

96. Letter to Préfet de Police, May 16, 1848, DA 226, doc. 163, APP.

FIGURE 1.3. The distinctive sign of the nineteenth-century brothel: the gros numéro. (Eugène Atget, *Maison close: 106, avenue de Suffren* [c. 1910–1912]. Courtesy Bibliothèque Nationale de France.)

than the prostitutes, would be eliminated."[97] There is no explanation for this shift in tolerance for the appearance of the marcheuse beyond the report's use of Mangin's efforts to clear the streets as a guide.[98] It is also possible that the police realized that the use of an actual woman was simply too great a reminder of the sexual purposes of the maisons de tolérance or that it gave too much freedom to the woman so employed. In any case, the report suggests replacing the marcheuse with what would become known as the *gros numéro*: the number of the house would be painted in a large size (fifty centimeters was recommended in 1853 and increased to sixty centimeters at some point during the Second Empire) on or above the door of the brothel (Figure 1.3). The report explained, "This number will be able to appear singular to the passers-by, but it has nothing shocking nor scandalous about it."[99] The gros numéro remained the distinctive sign of the brothel through the rest of the century,

97. "Rapport du 11 Juin 1853," DA 222, doc. 32, 19, APP.
98. Ibid., 18.
99. Ibid., 19.

"sufficiently known to the public to prevent any unwelcome surprise," according to Second Empire morals officer Félix Carlier.[100] The physical body of the prostitute could only exceed the limitations placed on her—whether by police regulations, age, or some other attempt to imprint the signs of regulationism on the prostitute. The number, in some ways the ultimate sign of effective administration, replaced her physical body entirely—or so they hoped.

All of these various attempts by the police to simultaneously ensure the visibility of prostitution and hide it away avoided explicitly situating either the maison de tolérance or the business of prostitution in light of the neighborhoods where they were actually built. Regulationism was, in this sense, a gigantic project of disavowal. On the one hand, regulationists acknowledged prostitution as evidence of "filth," a vice that "infected" the city; on the other hand, they provided the very means for that filth to become more fully integrated into urban space. Police practice assumed the presence of prostitution in the city and in many ways reinforced it. It therefore follows that the police themselves integrated prostitution into the city of Paris and the lives of Parisians. And yet, at the same time, they police willfully denied that this was what they were doing. They recognized prostitution as antagonistic to the growth of business, to the use of the city by "honest" men and women, and to the continued safety, security, and health of the population more broadly. While prostitution was constructed as an immoral "other" to the populace, it was simultaneously integrated into the lives of those who inhabited and used city space.

Conclusion

During a late 1837 meeting of the commission, a letter was read aloud and described in the minutes. Written by a resident of the rue St. Anne in the first arrondissement, the letter complains about the prostitutes who were using the rues St. Anne, Thérèse, and Villedo to solicit sex. So many of them were doing so, according to the writer, that "it was no longer possible to pass by without being assailed, followed, and touched in the most obscene manner." The writer demanded not only that prostitutes be banned from using these streets but also that "a yellow lamp be placed at the windows of the maisons publiques in order to make them known to those in need and to foreigners."[101] The writer thus asked the police to render prostitution simultaneously less and more noticeable. The lamp may have indeed served as a moralizing warning,

---

100. Carlier reports the size as sixty centimeters. See Carlier, *Les deux prostitutions,* 130.

101. "Recueil des procès verbaux des séances de la Commission Spéciale pour la Répression de la Prostitution. Registre no. 2," 50e Séance du 1 Décembre 1837, DA 221, doc. 6, APP. The writer is left unnamed, but the commission refers to him as "he."

but it did so only in that it illuminated a house of prostitution in the first place. In an era where street lighting was far from complete, one can imagine how this strategy would illuminate one house at the expense of its neighbors, creating a shining light of sexual depravity in the neighborhood.[102]

The spatial contours of regulationism never exceeded the tension embedded within the "necessary evil" nomenclature that demanded prostitutes' simultaneous presence and absence in nineteenth-century Paris. On the one hand, regulationists consistently decried the moral degradation that prostitution brought in its wake. They emphasized the disorders that attended the public presence of prostitutes and worried about the effects their presence had on both young men and women who encountered them. On the other hand, regulationists also refused the possibility of eliminating prostitution, because they saw it as the inevitable outcome of urban growth. Even their most extreme attempt to purify the public streets of evidence of venal sex—Mangin's 1830 ordinance—did not attempt to eliminate prostitution entirely from the city. Torn between repugnance and acceptance of prostitution, regulationists strove to place it under their own imprimatur in order to render its nuisances the least problematic while ensuring its continued role in serving the sexual needs of the male populace. In order to do so, they sought out the spaces of prostitution, attempted to capture them in an administrative apparatus, and rendered them knowable to both the police and those who sought them out. Doing so revolved around the maison de tolérance as the only proper location for practicing prostitution, but ultimately their efforts spread out, rather than localized, evidence of venal sex on the streets of Paris.

In attending to the ways in which the maison de tolérance signified sex in the public spaces of Paris, I am indebted to Sharon Marcus's emphasis on how the categories of "public" and "private" did not always align with spatial orientations of exterior and interior.[103] While it is true that the police strove to discipline the body of the prostitute by reducing her ability to display herself and by forcing her inside, they ultimately consistently referred to that ultimate signifier of the private in public—sexual desire—as a sign of their own administrative success. I want to emphasize how this project disrupted the construction of prostitutes as a "people apart."[104] Instead, the attempt to manage prostitution effectively made it more, not less, central to nineteenth-century Parisian life. Rather than either actively destroy or create new spaces

---

102. Perhaps realizing that this would be the case, the commission recommended lighting the entirety of the streets. The meeting notes concluded by reiterating the commission's relatively new conviction that "the absolute ban on prostitutes on the public streets . . . is impossible, as experience has demonstrated." Ibid.

103. Marcus, *Apartment Stories,* 7–8.

104. Parent-Duchâtelet, *De la prostitution dans la ville de Paris,* 1st ed., 4.

for venal sex, the authorities preferred to ensure that Parisians knew how to recognize those that already existed. The creation of a system of signs to indicate the presence of venal sex, alongside an unwillingness to drastically intervene in the sexual economy of the city, highlights how the knowledge of urban sexual possibility became a central feature of the city. As put into practice, regulationism demanded, in other words, that people "watch" for sex in their daily lives.

Both prostitutes and the police provided the means for knowing what kind of establishment and what kind of person one encountered as people moved about the city. The struggle to determine how this sexual knowledge would be defined and spread in part shaped the struggle between the two groups. Knowledge of public sex became even more important as the nineteenth century wore on. First, expert moralists, scientists, and sociologists produced a greater and greater number of works dedicated to enumerating the increasingly complex signs of sex in the city. This kind of knowledge expanded beyond the ability to tell which maison was or was not a brothel; expanded beyond concern with forms of female sexual deviancy; and required urban walkers to pay close attention to signs written onto the bodies of everyone they encountered, to listen to the sounds of the city, and even to guard against—or invite—an indiscreet touch. Second, Haussmann was more willing to disrupt established patterns of social life than July Monarchy administrators. Haussmannization, in the end, had the effect of making sex seem to be everywhere. No longer restricted to the brothels or to specific areas of the city, the possibility of a sexual encounter came to be seen as omnipresent. Finally, new sexual spaces made it clear that heterosexual sex was not the only kind offered on the streets of Paris. The apparent ability of other kinds of spaces besides the brothels to incite and entice men put into question the very foundations of regulationism as a "necessary evil."

2

PUBLIC HYGIENE, PUBLIC SEX, AND PUBLIC URINALS

Alexandre Parent-Duchâtelet did not begin his career as an explorer of brothels and prostitutes. Rather, he understood these subjects in light of his role as a public hygienist interested in all the "filth" of the city. The sewers of the city held a particular interest for him, and when he turned his attention away from the underground and toward the prostitutes of Paris, he refused to distinguish between the two.[1] Introducing *De la prostitution dans la ville de Paris* (1836), Parent-Duchâtelet noted people's surprise that he would choose female prostitution as the subject of a major work, especially in light of his constant visits into the depths of Paris's underground: "If I could, without scandalizing anyone, enter the sewer [*cloaques*] . . . and live, to some extent, in the middle of all that human communities withdraw from as the most abject and most disgusting, why would I blush at a sewer of another kind (a sewer, more squalid, I admit, than any other), in the well-founded hope of doing some good, by examining it under all the guises that it offers?"[2] Just as a modern city needed to drain away its physical waste, it also required

---

1. Charles Bernheimer, *Figures of Ill Repute: Representing Prostitution in Nineteenth-Century France* (Cambridge, Mass: Harvard University Press, 1989), 15. On Parent-Duchâtelet's other work, see Donald Reid, *Paris Sewers and Sewermen: Realities and Representations* (Cambridge, Mass: Harvard University Press, 1991), esp. 74–77, 95–106.

2. Alexandre Parent-Duchâtelet, *De la prostitution dans la ville de Paris, considérée sous le rapport de l'hygiène publique, de la morale et de l'administration* (Paris: J.-B. Baillière, 1836), 1:7.

a "seminal drain," as it was sometimes called, to manage any excess male sexual need.[3]

The successful management of the city's waste stood for the successful management of the entire urban environment, including the social milieu that both inhabited and made it in the first place.[4] To Victor Hugo, for instance, the sewer stood as the repository of history itself, repressing the conflicts, crises, and problems that had defined the city of Paris.[5] According to Hugo, the sewer always contained the possibility of failed management, disorder, and overflow as well: "Sometimes, the sewer of Paris took itself to overflow, as if that unappreciated Nile were suddenly seized with wrath. . . . At intervals, this stomach of civilization digested badly, the cloaca flowed back into the city's throat, and Paris had the aftertaste of its slime. . . . The city was indignant that its mire should have such audacity and did not countenance the return of the ordure. Drive it away better."[6] Hugo viscerally situates the failure of the sewer as a broader call to management not just of physical waste but also of the metaphorical body of "civilization" itself. This rumination reflects as well the implicit fears of an emerging expert cadre, represented in Hugo's book by the Napoleonic sewer explorer Pierre Emmanuel Bruneseau and in our story by Parent-Duchâtelet, who worked not to contain the "excesses" of the city but to channel them instead.[7]

In any event, a large-scale renovation of the sewers was duly made during Haussmann's Second Empire renovations. Between 1851 and 1870, Paris witnessed the building of two hundred miles of sewers; by the end of the Second Empire it had four times as many miles as it had in 1851.[8] This transformation

3. Louis Fiaux, *La police des mœurs devant la Commission Extraparlementaire du Régime des Mœurs* (Paris: Félix Alcan, 1907), 1:212. See also A. Granveau, *La prostitution dans Paris* (Paris: 1868), 138–139; *Commission Extraparlementaire du Régime des Mœurs: Procès-verbaux des séances* (Melun, France: Imprimerie Administrative, 1909), 259.

4. Reid, *Paris Sewers and Sewermen,* 4.

5. Rosalina de la Carrera, "History's Unconscious in Victor Hugo's *Les Misérables,*" *MLN* 96, no. 4 (1981): 839–855.

6. Victor Hugo, *Les misérables* (Paris: Gallimard, 1951), 1288–1289. Translation is from Victor Hugo, *Les misérables,* trans. Charles E. Wilbour (New York: Modern Library, 1992), 1092.

7. On the relationship between Hugo and Parent-Duchâtelet, see Briana Lewis, "The Sewer and the Prostitute in *Les Misérables:* From Regulation to Redemption," *Nineteenth-Century French Studies* 44, nos. 3–4 (2016): 266–278.

8. David H. Pinkney, *Napoleon III and the Rebuilding of Paris* (Princeton, N.J.: Princeton University Press, 1958), 131–132. On the transformation of the Paris sewers during the nineteenth century, see also Barrie M. Ratcliffe, "Cities and Environmental Decline: Elites and the Sewage Problem in Paris from the Mid-Eighteenth to the Mid-Nineteenth Century," *Planning Perspectives* 5 (1990): 189–222; David P. Jordan, *Transforming Paris: The Life and Labors of Baron Haussmann* (New York: Free Press, 1995), 267–277; David S. Barnes, *The Great Stink of Paris and the Nineteenth-Century Struggle against Filth and Germs* (Baltimore: Johns Hopkins University Press, 2006), esp. 52–58.

was both quantitative and qualitative. The confusion of the past was reworked into a newly rational system that paralleled the myths of Haussmannization more broadly as a sudden break between the old medieval Paris and the new modern city.[9] Despite his absence from the city during his Second Empire exile, Hugo captured the new underground: "At present the sewer is neat, cold, straight, correct. It almost realizes what is understood in England by the word 'respectable.'"[10] Indeed, the construction of a "respectable" sewer highlights the socio-moral aspects of a form of urbanism explicitly designed to produce and perpetuate forms of social discipline, aligned with the apparent values and needs of a nascent middle class.[11] And yet Hugo emphasizes that this transformation remains—probably inevitably—incomplete: "Do not trust in it [the sewer] too much, however. Miasmas still inhabit it. It is rather hypocritical than irreproachable."[12] The attempt to channel the excesses of Paris would be only partially successful. The city may have appeared well ordered, but underneath it still contained its ruinous potential.

This chapter brings together sex and sewers in order to show how efforts to manage the city tended to be diverted by those who used it. At precisely the same time that the police were trying to encourage a greater number of "seminal drains," public hygienists were demanding that the administration build or encourage the construction of urinary drains in the form of public urinals. These two institutions complemented one another as they combined to mold and discipline the people of Paris by conditioning ways of seeing. The maison de tolérance strove to control not only women who sold sex but also how men could buy it; the public urinal demanded not only that men hide urination but also that others refrain from looking inside. This enforcement of modes of looking and encounter was premised on a dual strategy: both institutions were to be plentiful and noticeable but only to those who sought them out and only insofar as they hid what went on inside of them. Together, the brothel and the urinal struggled to produce a particular social and sexual organization of Paris premised on men's ability to access public space and the women they encountered there.

The exact connection between the brothel and the urinal was only ever implicit, but as facilities meant to enable men's access to public space they complemented one another. The maison de tolérance incited heterosexual desire, and urinals enabled men to move about the city and thus toward (or away from) brothels. In this respect, it is no coincidence that the *Annales*

9. On this myth, see David Harvey, *Paris, Capital of Modernity* (New York: Routledge, 2006), 1–18.

10. Hugo, *Les misérables* (1951), 1294. Translation from Hugo, *Les misérables* (1992), 1097.

11. D. Harvey, *Paris, Capital of Modernity,* 149–150.

12. Hugo, *Les misérables* (1951), 1295. Translation from Hugo, *Les misérables* (1992), 1097.

d'hygiène publique et de médecine légale immediately followed an 1871 article by the public hygienist Alphonse Chevallier, on the need to increase the number of public urinals in Paris, with a study of clandestine prostitution by Félix Carlier, the head of the morals brigade during the Second Empire.[13] The *Annales,* the most important nineteenth-century journal of medical-juridical discourse, understood that both issues fell under its purview to "sometimes aid the legislator in the preparation of laws, often enlighten the magistrate regarding their application, and always ensure, alongside the administration, the maintenance of public health," as the journal's 1829 prospectus put it.[14] Both the maison de tolérance and the public urinal thus shaped a relationship between health, law, and order that developed between the July Monarchy and early Third Republic, premised on the need to enable men to move about the city, complete bodily functions, and do so without compromising themselves in front of women.[15]

The construction of public urinals for men shaped gender and sexual relations in the public spaces of nineteenth-century Paris. The urinal directed, propelled, and otherwise pushed men toward their proper objects by enabling them to inhabit public space while adhering to certain standards of bodily propriety by physically emphasizing their existence in the first place.[16] The infrastructure of the city, thus read, produces compulsory forms of bodily propriety and sexuality by helping ensure men's access to women. However, the attempt to channel male desire toward the maison de tolérance by, in part, physically enabling men to move about the city was ultimately frustrated by visions of a different kind of desire: that between men themselves.[17]

13. M. A. Chevallier, "Note sur la nécessité de multiplier et d'améliorer les urinoirs publics," *Annales d'hygiène publique et de médecine légale* 2, no. 36 (1871): 285–291; Félix Carlier, "Étude statistique sur la prostitution clandestine à Paris de 1855 à 1870," *Annales d'hygiène publique et de médecine légale* 2, no. 36 (1871): 292–308.

14. "Prospectus," *Annales d'hygiène publique et de médecine légale* 1, no. 1 (1829): v.

15. On the relationship between public hygiene, morality, and social order more broadly, see, for instance, Andrew R. Aisenberg, *Contagion: Disease, Government, and the "Social Question" in Nineteenth-Century France* (Stanford, Calif.: Stanford University Press, 1999), and Joshua Cole, *The Power of Large Numbers: Population, Politics, and Gender in Nineteenth-Century France* (Ithaca, N.Y.: Cornell University Press, 2000).

16. My interpretation here is inspired by Sara Ahmed, who argues that spatial relationships enforce "orientations" that together construct sexuality itself. People's relationships to one another and to other objects are actively directed: "The concept of 'orientations' allows us to expose how life gets directed in some ways rather than others, through the very requirement that we follow what is already given us." Sara Ahmed, *Queer Phenomenology: Orientations, Objects, Others* (Durham, N.C.: Duke University Press, 2006), 21.

17. As Christopher Prendergast has argued, "Prostitution . . . was commonly figured via the analogy of the sewer. In addition, we might perhaps have expected, via the whole imaginary of

The appropriation of public urinals by men who sought sex with other men put into question the underlying premise of regulationism by revealing other possible avenues for the expression of male desire that challenged the construction of compulsory heterosexuality in the first place.[18] The authorities' struggle to manage the urinal—in particular, the inability of the police to tell the difference between those using the urinal as intended and those seeking out sex with other men—ultimately highlights the incommensurability between visions of a managed form of male desire and how it was actually enacted on the streets of Paris. Regulationism struggled not simply because of a decline in the number of maisons de tolérance, shifting forms of male heterosexual desire, and shifting police tactics, but also because the theory was premised on a false understanding of male desire in the first place. That men could so easily be led astray by the temptations of the urinal only underscored the mistaken assumption that male desire was necessarily oriented toward the opposite sex. The urinal revealed, instead, the thin line dividing forms of desire in the nineteenth century and ultimately undercut the very distinctions that seemed to structure the public culture of the city.

The Public Urinal and the Making of Modern Paris

The appearance of public urinals on the streets of Paris marked an instantiation of a philosophy of urban hygiene that united moral with behavioral and urban concerns. The first concerted effort to build public urinals occurred under Prefect of the Seine Rambuteau during the July Monarchy, which led to his name being attached to the first type of facility to appear, the *colonne Rambuteau*.[19] The construction of public urinals only increased over the course of the century. In 1840 Paris featured around 500 facilities, but by 1893 the boulevards, parks, and train stations possessed more than 3,500.[20] This increase occurred as a cohort of public hygienists increasingly demanded greater administrative attention to men's bodily behavior for the sake of the moral and physical health of the populace.

---

the cloacal, some allusion, if only unspoken, to the heavily tabooed area of the anal-erotic and so to the theme of homosexuality." Christopher Prendergast, *Paris and the Nineteenth Century* (Oxford, U.K.: Blackwell, 1992), 100.

18. This chapter thus follows Matt Houlbrook's call to examine the ways that public urinals were used, not just how they were policed. See Matt Houlbrook, "The Private World of Public Urinals: London, 1918–57," *London Journal* 25, no. 1 (2000): 52.

19. On the term *colonne Rambuteau*, see Lucien Rigaud, *Dictionnaire d'argot moderne* (Paris: Paul Ollendorff, 1881), 321.

20. Régis Revenin, *Homosexualité et prostitution masculines à Paris: 1870–1918* (Paris: L'Harmattan, 2005), 36.

As such, these facilities reflect a newfound concern with public health that associated progress with urban cleanliness. In his *Dictionnaire d'hygiène et de salubrité* (1852–1854), for instance, Ambroise Tardieu, the medical pathologist now most famous for his treatment of male pederasty (see Chapter 3), associated public hygiene with civilization itself. Introducing the book, he declared that his goal was "only to provide a quick look at the principles of public hygiene, at its development and current condition within the most advanced people in civilization."[21] The connection between hygiene and civilizational progress generally also implicated public urinals specifically. As J. Barbey d'Aurevilly once sarcastically exclaimed, "Factories and latrines, here is what the civilization of the nineteenth century arrogantly plants on its rivers!"[22] On the one hand, there existed the manufacture of goods that evoked industrialization; on the other hand, were facilities designed to safeguard public health while perpetuating emerging norms of bodily hygiene and display. Public urinals, put simply, contributed to the management of the city by safeguarding health and safety while also encouraging hygienic social practices among the citizenry.

Urinals comprised part of the broader debate over what to do with Paris's waste.[23] Despite the real increase in the length of the sewers, Haussmann did not require landowners to actually connect to the expanded system—an idea that would have been vociferously opposed by both property holders and cesspit cleaners—because they were primarily intended to drain away water, not human waste.[24] By the mid-1870s and 1880s, a full-blown debate

---

21. Ambroise Tardieu, *Dictionnaire d'hygiène publique et de salubrité, ou répertoire de toutes les questions relatives à la santé publique, considérées dans leurs rapports avec les subsistances, les épidémies, les professions, les établissements et institutions d'hygiène et de salubrité,* 2nd ed. (Paris: J.-B. Baillière, 1862), 1:v. On the public health movement of nineteenth-century France, see Ann F. La Berge, *Mission and Method: The Early Nineteenth-Century French Public Health Movement* (Cambridge: Cambridge University Press, 1992); Sean M. Quinlan, *The Great Nation in Decline: Sex, Modernity, and Health Crises in Revolutionary France, c. 1750–1850* (Aldershot, U.K.: Ashgate, 2007).

22. J. Barbey d'Aurevilly, *Memoranda* (Paris: Rouveyre et G. Blond, 1883), 22–23.

23. Parisian elites had become progressively more concerned over the problem of human waste beginning in the late eighteenth century. See Ratcliffe, "Cities and Environmental Decline," 192–195. On the importance of water and waste disposal to Haussmann's Paris more broadly, see esp. Peter S. Soppelsa, "The Fragility of Modernity: Infrastructure and Everyday Life in Paris, 1870–1914" (Ph.D. diss., University of Michigan, 2009), chap. 5, https://deepblue.lib.umich.edu/handle/2027.42/62374, accessed November 14, 2017; Matthew Gandy, *The Fabric of Space: Water, Modernity, and the Urban Imagination* (Cambridge, Mass: MIT Press, 2014), chap. 1

24. According to Barrie M. Ratcliffe, only 22 percent of dwellings were connected in the early 1850s; it was only with the promulgation of tout-à-l'égout in the 1880s and its adoption in 1894 that the entire city was finally to be connected to the sewer system. Ratcliffe attributes the slow pace of change to "the slow evolution of technology," the relative inefficacy of the *Conseil de salubrité,* divisions within the hygienist movement that weakened its ability to galvanize the

erupted over a *tout-à-l'égout* (everything into the sewer) system that would unite forms of drainage and eventually connect all buildings in the city to the sewer system.[25] The precise solution to the problem of human waste in Paris remained very much in doubt through the course of the nineteenth century. Urinals and latrines, whether in private homes or in public spaces, often simply drained into the street or required transport to cesspools.

While some public hygienists focused on the need to ensure the cleanliness of latrines and urinals inside private dwellings, others emphasized the importance of encouraging Parisians to use those placed in public.[26] In order to accomplish this feat, expert commentators did not hesitate to draw on the power of the police. In 1850 the police banned public urination in an ordinance that also admonished Parisians to "sacrifice the bad habits that they may have contracted."[27] The portrayal of public urination as a "habit" understates the significance of what was being asked. By deploying state power to enforce a certain kind of bodily prohibition, administrators brought to bear considerable efforts designed to refashion Parisians' relation to their own bodies and the spaces they inhabited. While the ordinance explicitly rests its legitimacy on "frequent and well-founded complaints," it also encouraged those complaints by reducing a once-common practice—public urination—to a "bad habit."[28] The ordinance, in other words, participated in a reconfiguration of male Parisians' relationship to public space by drawing a new division between appropriate and inappropriate behavior. The public urinal became both a reminder of and a solution to this problem.

Some public hygienists emphasized the need for more facilities rather than police intervention. Twenty years after the ban on public urination, Chevallier argued that the lack of facilities was making "walls lacking openings, boards that surround construction, buildings being demolished, pavement of bridges, angles of certain streets, public monuments, and up to the

---

public, and the "vested interest" of property owners and the city. Ratcliffe, "Cities and Environmental Decline," 195, 200–204. On Haussmann's view of sewers, see Soppelsa, "Fragility of Modernity," 376; Gandy, *Fabric of Space,* 38–43.

25. On the debates surrounding tout-à-l'égout during the 1880s, see esp. Gérard Jacquemet, "Urbanisme parisien: La bataille du tout-à-l'égout à la fin du XIXe siècle," *Revue d'histoire moderne et contemporaine* 26, no. 4 (1979): 505–548; Aisenberg, *Contagion,* 105–112; Barnes, *Great Stink of Paris,* 52–58.

26. The public hygienist Jean-Baptiste Fonssagrives, for instance, claimed that any "serious municipality" would use its powers under the law on insalubrious housing to conduct a house-by-house inspection of latrines. J.-B. Fonssagrives, *Hygiène et assainissement des villes* (Paris: J.-B. Baillière, 1874), 163. On the Law on Insalubrious Dwellings, see Aisenberg, *Contagion,* chap. 2.

27. "Salubrité publique—ordinance," *Annales d'hygiène publique et médecine légale* 1, no. 44 (1850): 470. On this ordinance, see also Barnes, *Great Stink of Paris,* 79–80.

28. "Salubrité publique," 470.

slightest crevices . . . public urinals and disgusting cloacae."[29] The entire city threatened to turn into a urinal if administrators failed to build their own. Indeed, Chevallier's focus on the fluctuating materiality of the city—his list of at-risk spaces, such as barriers blocking access to urban works and demolished buildings, included several spaces related to construction and reconstruction—reveals a certain anxiety at the possibility of losing control as government administrators and urbanists transformed the city. As Haussmannization destroyed vast swaths of the city, administrators fretted over their ability to ensure that such destruction remained carefully controlled. The public urinal stood as one small way for them to do so, by reminding men of how to behave in public.

Others argued that the police needed to enforce the use of public urinals. Public hygienist Jean-Baptiste Fonssagrives, for instance, argued that "the cleanliness of the city" was not the responsibility of individuals but rather "is imposed and executed by the authorities, and the most recalcitrant profit as much as the most submissive. It's the great power of public hygiene to be authoritative and to force people to not resist the good it wants to do for them."[30] Adrien Proust, Marcel Proust's father, agreed, cited Fonssagrives, and declared that "a severe police [force] is absolutely essential[,] . . . because, without it, all the precaution that can suggest hygiene will remain absolutely superfluous."[31] Fonssagrives's and Proust's emphasis on enforcement highlights an underlying anxiety. The simple appearance of public urinals was not sufficient to change behavior, because public urination was not universally acknowledged as a "bad habit." Rather, because Paris's male population saw urinals as "superfluous," their use had to be actively enforced. Therefore, men's relation to public space itself had to be reshaped and reconstructed.

Circulation and the City

Public hygiene helped facilitate proper circulation—in all senses of the word—in nineteenth-century Paris.[32] As David Harvey notes, the hygienic sciences of the nineteenth century were inscribed on the city because Haussmann "cast the city as a living body whose vital functions must be cleansed" through "the circulation of air, water, sewage."[33] Circulation indeed defined

---

29. M. A. Chevallier, "Note sur la nécessité de multiplier et d'améliorer les urinoirs publics," 286.

30. Fonssagrives, *Hygiène et assainissement des villes,* 143.

31. A. Proust, *Traité d'hygiène,* 2nd ed. (Paris: G. Masson, 1881), 640.

32. Nicholas Papayanis, *Horse-Drawn Cabs and Omnibuses in Paris: The Idea of Circulation and the Business of Public Transit* (Baton Rouge: Louisiana State University Press, 1996), 1.

33. D. Harvey, *Paris, Capital of Modernity,* 260.

the urban culture of the nineteenth century, and public urinals had a clear role to play by enabling not only a quantitative increase of men about the street but also a qualitative change in how men interacted in public. Public facilities represented and enforced new modes of male bodily propriety in public by teaching men to hide their bodily functions from other passers-by. The creation of this form of bodily shame necessitated a kind of class discipline wherein growing middle-class expectations were produced through city space. The urinal, therefore, participated in the attempt to constrain the ways that both women and men could use public space in order to maintain the fiction of a "bourgeois" city.

Until the very end of the nineteenth century, the provision of public urinals was predicated on different assumptions about the public needs of men and women. Fonssagrives, for instance, responded to those who opposed new public urinals by claiming, "It is in vain to bring up, as proof of the possibility of going without them, the example of the other sex; there is no parity in this matter between the withdrawn and sedentary life of the gynaeceum and the exigencies of exterior life . . . which drive men in great cities."[34] Fonssagrives used the urinal to inscribe gender difference onto the physical form of the urban environment. Rather than the contrasting signs for "Ladies" and "Gentlemen" in a single restroom, as in Jacques Lacan's famous depiction, it is the absence of women's facilities that produced gendered space in nineteenth-century Paris and enforced a different kind of discipline on women's bodies.[35] This argument unites the physical environment, hygienic discourse, and the material body to perpetuate the fiction that women were excluded from public space.[36] This idea could be sustained only until the end

34. Fonssagrives, *Hygiène et assainissement,* 163–164.

35. Jacques Lacan, *Écrits: A Selection,* trans. Alan Sheridan (New York: W. W. Norton, 1977), 151–152. On the history of gender-segregated toilets in Europe more broadly, see Sheila L. Cavanagh, *Queering Bathrooms: Gender, Sexuality, and the Hygienic Imagination* (Toronto: University of Toronto Press, 2010), 32–33. On this issue in another context, see Andrew Brown-May and Peg Fraser, "Gender, Respectability, and Public Convenience in Melbourne, Australia, 1859–1902," in *Ladies and Gents: Public Toilets and Gender,* ed. Olga Gershenson and Barbara Penner (Philadelphia: Temple University Press, 2009), 75–89.

36. On women's public presence in nineteenth-century Paris, see Janet Wolff, "The Invisible *Flâneuse*: Women and the Literature of Modernity," *Theory, Culture, and Society* 2, no. 3 (1985): 37–46; Griselda Pollock, *Vision and Difference: Femininity, Feminism, and Histories of Art* (London: Routledge, 1988), esp. chap 3; Elizabeth Wilson, *The Sphinx in the City: Urban Life, the Control of Disorder, and Women* (Berkeley: University of California Press, 1992), esp. chap 4; Aruna d'Souza and Tom McDonough, eds. *The Invisible* Flâneuse*? Gender, Public Space, and Visual Culture in Nineteenth-Century Paris* (Manchester, U.K.: Manchester University Press, 2006); Catherine Nesci, *Le flâneur et les flâneuses: Les femmes et la ville à l'époque romantique* (Grenoble, France: Ellug, 2007); Ruth E. Iskin, *Modern Women and Parisian Consumer Culture in Impressionist Painting* (Cambridge: Cambridge University Press, 2007); Temma Balducci,

of the century, when women's facilities did appear in the city just as women's shopping became so key to its productive capacity.[37]

Just as the absence of women's facilities enforced a particular view of women's bodies, so too did the presence of public urinals help construct a male body that depended on well-managed internal and external management. If the nineteenth-century city figuratively "revolved" around the men who inhabited it, then, according to Fonssagrives, that movement was necessarily masculine. As men moved to and fro throughout the city, their very bodies, "agitated," required urinary relief in ways that women's simply did not. In light of this apparently essential difference, toleration for the sight of public urinals had to increase in inverse proportion to that of male public urination. Those who opposed public urinals, he argued, did so out of "prudishness" rather than "practicality."[38] Circulation about the city thus also entailed circulation within the body. Just as men required the ability to physically move about the city, so too did their internal systems require the free circulation enabled by the public urinal.

The body and the city thus paralleled one another as the constant movement on the streets and below ground enabled and provided for bodily circulation. For example, in 1856 Alphonse Chevallier's son, A. Chevallier *fils,* related the dangers of "holding it in" through the case of one of his father's friends, a member of the Conseil de salubrité, a Dr. Juge. According to Chevallier, "Because of the small number of urinals [in Paris], men find themselves placed between a hard necessity either to put themselves in contravention of the law or to contract an illness that can sometimes have the most grave consequences." The dangers this imposed on men was illustrated by Juge, who, after finding it "impossible" to urinate during a long journey, "took to his bed, called for a surgeon, and was sick more than three months due to this accident."[39] About fifteen years later, Chevallier *père* referenced this story but downgraded Juge's

---

Gender, Space, and the Gaze in Post-Haussmann Visual Culture: Beyond the Flâneur (London: Routledge, 2017). For other contexts, see also Lynda Nead, *Victorian Babylon: People, Streets, and Images in Nineteenth-Century London* (New Haven, Conn.: Yale University Press, 2000); Sarah Deutsch, *Women and the City: Gender, Space, and Power in Boston, 1870–1940* (New York: Oxford University Press, 2000).

37. On women's shopping in the nineteenth century, see Judith R. Walkowitz, *City of Dreadful Delight: Narratives of Sexual Danger in Late-Victorian London* (Chicago: University of Chicago Press, 1992), 46–50; Erika Diane Rappaport, *Shopping for Pleasure: Women in the Making of London's West End* (Princeton, N.J.: Princeton University Press, 2000); Lisa Tiersten, *Marianne in the Market: Envisioning Consumer Society in Fin-de-Siècle France* (Berkeley: University of California Press, 2001).

38. Fonssagrives, *Hygiène et assainissement,* 163.

39. A. Chevallier, "Notice historique sur la conservation, la désinfection et l'utilisation des urines," *Journal de chimie médicale, de pharmacie et de toxicologie et revue des nouvelles scientifiques nationales et étrangères* 2 (1856): 382.

condition to death, "which caused the most painful impression."[40] Whether he lived or died, Juge's circumstances reflect the body/city dualism being constructed. For it was as Juge moved about the city and the country that he found it impossible to allow his own body to properly circulate. Therefore, as the body was conditioned to the moral prerogatives of private urination in public, so too it was reshaped to physically require the urinal for relief. The processing of normal bodily functions here serves as a metaphor for the larger desire for smooth circulation in Paris itself.[41] The health of the street and society ensured the health of the physical body.

Modern urban life was thus secured in part by public urinals, which enabled men to move about their city without discomfort, neither having to stop their promenades early nor break the law by disobeying new strictures regarding bodily hygiene and urban sanitation. Placement and design were intended to fulfill all of these goals at the same time. First, urinals needed to be placed in ways that ensured constant and consistent access to them. Indeed, a proper urinal emplacement, according to the elder Chevallier, would be able to serve enough people so as to "not expose the public to too long a wait," thus ensuring constant circulation of men in and out of them.[42] Fonssagrives, citing Chevallier, called for advertising the number of urinals at "each street entrance" on a plaque.[43] Doing so would allow the public, on their promenades, to know whether they would be able to quickly stop to relieve themselves without being forced to take a detour.

The architects who designed public urinals participated in efforts to build them in ways that would facilitate smooth movement. One urinal in the Champs-Élysées, for instance, smoothly blended into the path, creating an optional U-turn while the promenade's greenery served as an effective screen (Figure 2.1). By simply turning into the urinal, one could stop, answer nature's call, and then continue on one's stroll in the same direction. The need to urinate, then, did not interrupt the promenade; instead, it created a small turn in the path, a detour rather than break. Unlike, say, brothels, urinals were not destinations in and of themselves; rather, they enabled men to move somewhere else. Their eventual appropriation by men seeking sex with other

---

40. M. A. Chevallier, "Note sur la nécessité de multiplier et d'améliorer les urinoirs publics," 290.

41. As Alain Corbin has argued, "The phantasm of loss[,] . . . the desire to ensure the smooth running of the social physiology of excretion, the concern to keep a record of men and goods and to ensure their circulation, were all part of the same process." Alain Corbin, *The Foul and the Fragrant: Odor and the French Social Imagination* (Cambridge, Mass: Harvard University Press, 1986), 116.

42. M. A. Chevallier, "Note sur la nécessité de multiplier et d'améliorer les urinoirs publics," 285.

43. Fonssagrives, *Hygiène et assainissement des villes,* 165.

FIGURE 2.1. Urinal with eight boxes, made of cast iron and slate, in the Champs-Élysées public garden, Paris (eighth arrondissement), circa 1870. (Photograph by Charles Marville. Paris, Musée Carnavalet. © Charles Marville/Musée Carnavalet/Roger Viollet.)

men thus put into question the very principles that linked the body, hygiene, and the city to processes of social discipline.

Urinals were also explicitly designed to hide the men who used them from the prying eyes of the public, evidenced by their increasing complexity as the century wore on. The oldest type of urinal was a simple column that left the user exposed to the street (Figure 2.2). By the end of the century, these older columns began to be replaced by *urinoirs lumineux,* lighted urinals that, in one design at least, featured a large column in the center of two or three fully hidden pissoirs (Figures 2.3 and 2.4).

The most basic type of public urinal, *urinoirs d'angle,* consisted of two walls that pointed out from a building toward one another and created a vague triangular space in which one or two receptacles were placed. The frequent lack of water to flush out these urinals completely—urine was supposed to drain underneath the pavement—caused an unpleasant odor and degraded the enamel. Moreover, passers-by could easily view those using the facilities. The third type of public urinal, the *urinoirs de face,* featured multiple stalls with a surrounding wall that isolated people from the street; a

FIGURE 2.2. Urinal, cast iron and brickwork, rue du Faubourg Saint-Martin, Paris (tenth arrondissement), circa 1870. (Photograph by Charles Marville. Paris, Musée Carnavalet. © Charles Marville/Musée Carnavalet/ Roger Viollet.)

FIGURE 2.3. Urinal with two boxes and doors, cast iron (old model), 44 rue de Rennes, Paris (sixth arrondissement), circa 1870. (Photograph by Charles Marville. Paris, Musée Carnavalet. © Charles Marville/Musée Carnavalet/ Roger Viollet.)

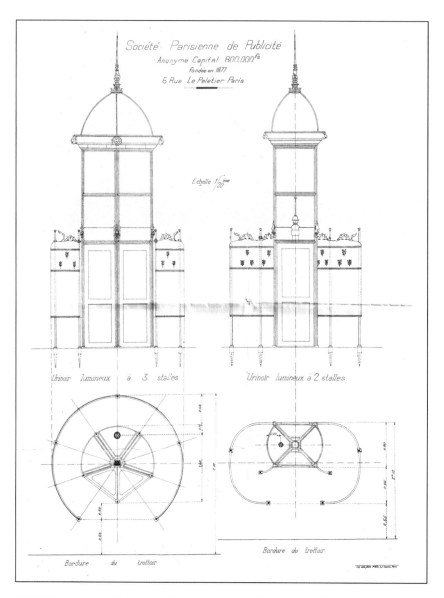

FIGURE 2.4. Plan for lighted public urinals, Société Parisienne de Publicité, 1897. (Archives de Paris, VO3 419.)

trough underneath each pissoir collected the urine and prevented it from reaching the street surface (Figure 2.5). Finally, the *urinoirs publics en kiosque* came in a variety of forms in high traffic areas, notably the Palais-Royal (Figure 2.6). These fully enclosed pavilions featured multiple isolated stalls and total isolation from the street.[44]

---

44. Ibid., 165–167.

FIGURE 2.5. Urinal with six slate boxes, rue Rambuteau, at the corner of the rue Baltard, Paris (first arrondissement), 1876. (Photograph by Charles Marville. Paris, Musée Carnavalet. © Charles Marville/Musée Carnavalet/Roger Viollet.)

FIGURE 2.6. Cabinet water closet by Dorion, avenue des Champs-Élysées, Paris (eighth arrondissement), circa 1870. (Photograph by Charles Marville. Paris, Musée Carnavalet. © Charles Marville/Musée Carnavalet/Roger Viollet.)

No urinal design totally effaced a prior one, but one does sense a gradual trend toward enclosure as the century approached its conclusion. The provision of urinals therefore revolved around hiding the body as much as it did around urination. For instance, in 1874, in response to a complaint by the prefect of police, an engineer with the Service Municipal des Travaux Publics drew up a report on two urinals on the Pont de l'Archeveché that were posing "difficulties . . . from the point of view of decency." The report suggested "completely getting rid of the urinals placed at insufficient angles for hiding the persons who stop there and replacing these with masonry, in order to divert the public." Urinals located just off the bridge, on the quay, should have "screens in sheet metal at each side [which] . . . will completely hide the people who stop there."[45] The actual note from the prefect of police does not appear in the archives, but his interest speaks to the importance of the issues at play. The dual goal of diversion and invisibility encapsulates the spatial logic of the public urinal. They not only provided space for excretion but actively hid bodily functions and moved people along their way as well.

In this vein, builders also designed the facilities to contribute to the aesthetics of the city or, at the very least, to not detract from them. Both Chevallier and Fonssagrives emphasized the importance of designing urinals in relation to their environments, with Fonssagrives stressing the "elegant . . . [and] very agreeable architecture" of the some of the column-style urinals and the "very agreeable ornamental effect" of the "screens supporting a candelabra" in the kiosk-style facilities.[46] This emphasis on aesthetics became a requirement for those seeking permission to build certain public urinals; the list of obligations for a concession to build four *chalets de nécessité* for both men and women in the bois de Boulogne during the 1890s stipulated that "they should strongly present a decorative appearance, in harmony with their placement."[47] The goal was not simply to heighten the aesthetic effects of certain specific kinds of modern infrastructure but to use such ornamentation to disavow the reasons why urinals were necessary in the first place.

For some administrators, no decoration could ever succeed at accomplishing this goal. For example, Louis Masson, Inspecteur de l'Assainissement de Paris, wrote in 1892, "Thanks to the progress of sanitary science, we have, in certain cities, come to render urinals acceptable from the point of view of smell, but their presence on public thoroughfares is no less shocking, and

45. Rapport de l'Ingénieur ordinaire, "Archevêché (Pont de l'): Amélioration des urinoirs," May 29, 1874, V.O3 419, Archives de Paris.

46. Fonssagrives, *Hygiène et assainissement des villes,* 167; M. A. Chevallier, "Note sur la nécessité de multiplier et d'améliorer les urinoirs publics," 285.

47. Société des Chalets de Nécessité, "Adjudication du droit d'exploitation de quatre chalets de nécessité à installer dans le bois de Boulogne," December 23, 1893, Pérotin/10653 39, 3, AP.

all the elegance provided to the construction of edifices which shelter them, cannot completely conceal their purpose."[48] In Masson's opinion, no matter how successful scientific advancements were at eliminating the smell, no matter how aesthetically pleasing one tried to make public urinals, they would always remind passers-by of their filthy purpose, a state of affairs destined to "only give incomplete satisfaction to the public."[49] Comparing Parisian public urinals to those found in London, Masson concluded that building them underground, completely out of sight, where, one supposes, such filth belonged, was the best solution. Banishing formerly public bodily functions to a realm not recognized as belonging to the social order at all would protect the populace from the threats represented by bodily waste. The threat the filth contained by the urinals posed would finally be eliminated.

Had French authorities followed Masson's recommendation, however, they would have eliminated one of the urinals' primary advantages: advertising. Throughout the nineteenth century, a number of ventures used urinals for street publicity. In the 1840s, Drouart and Company built some of the first of the *colonne* type of urinals for use in advertising.[50] By the 1860s, the company was advertising its exclusive three-hundred-franc service of ten bill postings on the urinals of Paris: six along "the entire length of the boulevards," one on the boulevard Sebastopol, and three on the quays, both the left and the right bank.[51] In addition, in response to the municipal council in 1897, the Société Parisienne de Publicité offered to replace its column urinals—which were "no longer in harmony with new installations and no longer responsive to hygienic needs and modern propriety"—with new illuminated urinals in exchange for an extension of their concession.[52] This advertising company clearly saw great potential in public urinals. New consumption patterns nicely complemented public hygiene facilities. In fact, advertising could help disguise the water closet itself, turning it almost into any other kiosk that could be seen on the streets of Paris. Advertising served as an ornamental measure itself and, in moving consumer desires, also distracted passers-by from the activities taking place inside the facilities.

The urinal, therefore, not only "diverted" passers-by. It also complemented the emergence of a society of consumption predicated on a particular deployment of desire. As urinals became more complex and more gender inclusive

---

48. Louis Masson, *"Les Conveniences" à Londres* (Paris: Ch. Schlaeber, 1892), V.O3 425, 3, AP.

49. Ibid.

50. Conseil Municipal de Paris, *Année 1872 Procès-Verbaux* (Paris: Imprimerie Municipale, 1873), 167–168.

51. "Advertisement for Drouart and Co.," n.d., F21 1046, AN.

52. Ch. Durand to Menant, September 10, 1897, V.O3 419, AP.

between the 1840s and 1890s, they increasingly participated in the growth of consumer society. The public urinal did more than deflect passers-by from the sight, sound, and smell of male bodily functions; through advertising it also attempted to divert pleasure. By encouraging the purchase of goods and participation in consumer culture, the urinal elicited pleasure that was rooted not in abject bodily functions but rather in the department store, the café, or the dance hall. As an administrative tool meant to contribute to the circulation of male bodies, the urinal can be placed within the broader project of satisfying male desire in ways that complemented an emerging urban system predicated on the movement of bodies through public space. The urinal enabled men to access other spaces of pleasure. That the public urinal emerged to facilitate men's access to public space at precisely the same moment when the police were finding new ways of cordoning off working-class women highlights the relationship at work. Urinals and brothels participated in a shared goal: the production of forms of male bodily practice that revolved around the exercise of particular kinds of desires. Intended as a space of hygiene rather than desire, the urinal nevertheless helped men find locations to fulfill those other needs.

Diverting Hygiene, Disrupting Desire

Certain spaces, such as parks, cafés, and brothels, enabled Parisians to safely indulge their desires while other spaces, such as public urinals, facilitated those entertainments but were not sites of desire themselves. This complementarity is nicely illustrated by the use of public urinals to advertise treatment for venereal disease, as reported by *La Lanterne* in 1888.[53] If the regulationist system represented by the brothels largely revolved around preventing the spread of venereal disease, then urinals also had a place in this economy of male desire. Both enabled men to avoid the consequences of their sexual desires. And yet, by reminding its users of the threat of venereal disease, the urinal also reminded them of sexual desire. In this way, the urinal itself became a space of desire. The circulatory functions of the penis—in both urinary and sexual terms—were united in the space of the public urinal.

Such a union, however, never remained constrained within the heterosexual assumptions of regulationism. Instead, public urinals became the most important rendezvous for men seeking sex with other men in nineteenth-century Paris. Over one-third of William Peniston's sample of 328 pederasts from the 1870s were arrested at urinals, primarily those "near the Bourse in the First Arrondissement and along the Champs Elysées in the Eighth

---

53. Ali Coffignon, *Paris-Vivant: La corruption à Paris* (Paris: Librairie Illustrée, 1888), 275–280.

Arrondissement."[54] Other urinals widely used during the period include those at train stations, parks, and gardens; along the Seine; and near Les Halles.[55] In all, men used urinals in almost half of Paris's twenty arrondissements to seek sexual encounters with other men; taking into account the incomplete nature of the evidence, more were undoubtedly used as well. By the 1860s at the latest, Paris found itself dotted with queer spaces in the guise of the public urinal.

Men who used public urinals for same-sex sexual encounters developed techniques to transform them into their own spaces. We can witness this process through a series of police records from the 1860s, when the police turned their attention to the facilities near the markets of Les Halles. A report of March 4, 1861, describes two sets of these urinals. Each one contained a small waiting room that "could contain five to six persons" and three stalls, which were separated by "thick boards." According to the police, around eight o'clock every night men began using the urinals to locate sex with other men:

> They enter into a stall as soon as one is free; if all the stalls are oc-cupied, they enter into the vestibule and pass a quarter of an hour by examining the physiognomy of the people who enter and leave, un-button themselves five or six times during this length of time in order to pretend to urinate and then leave these urinals to recommence the same little game in those opposite; however, as soon as they notice that they are being followed by an individual that they suppose to be one of them, before reentering the other latrines, they stop again at a urinal in the open. . . . [He] unbuttons himself again and if the individual who followed him does the same, they immediately enter into conversation, walk together with their new friends and eventu-ally leave together, and do not reappear for the rest of the evening.[56]

The nightly ritual of cruising here appears in the police report in an almost anthropological vein.[57] The urinals stood at the center of a complex dance as the men moved in and out, around and between the facilities, looking to meet other men to take elsewhere. The importance of solicitation itself

---

54. William A. Peniston, *Pederasts and Others: Urban Culture and Sexual Identity in Nine-teenth-Century Paris* (New York: Harrington Park Press, 2004), 140.

55. Revenin, *Homosexualité et prostitution masculines à Paris,* 36–40.

56. Rapport: Attentat aux mœurs, March 4, 1861, DA 230, doc. 295, APP.

57. These descriptions are similar to those from other times and places. See, for example, Laud Humphreys, *Tearoom Trade: Impersonal Sex in Public Places* (New York: Aldine, 1970), esp. chap 4; Houlbrook, "Private World of Public Urinals," 54.

is highlighted in Chapter 4, but for now it is worth emphasizing how the physical space of the urinal shaped the particular ways men met one another. The provision of a waiting area enabled multiple men to cruise at once, while the stalls justified the exposure of the genitals. At the same time, the relative openness of the facilities to observation enabled men to recognize one another and meant that the actual sexual act often took place elsewhere. The urinal drew men in, brought them together, and allowed them to consummate whatever kind of encounter they wished. Not all encounters necessarily led to sex. In fact, according to the report, some men spent their entire evenings around these facilities, making them into a social, as well as sexual, space.

At the same time, the men who used the urinals to locate sexual partners molded the physical space to their own needs. Underscoring the intimacy of police observation, the report noted that the stalls of the urinals often had holes punched through the dividers. According to the police, these holes served three purposes. First, someone in one stall could easily look into the next, because the holes were at eye height when the stall's occupant was seated. Second, by putting three fingers through one of the holes, a person could signal interest in his neighbor, who would then be able to reciprocate. Third, "these holes serve to satisfy the passions of these dangerous beings. They are placed in such a fashion that the pederasts can indulge in acts against nature even as each one stays in the stall that he occupies."[58] The urinal was thus modified to provide for the specific needs of the men who appropriated it. Even as the urinal's essential function of providing a semiprivate space in public was maintained, even exacerbated by the particular strategies of recognition employed by the men who went there, the urinal itself was turned to new purposes.

From a kind of voyeurism, to a tool for signaling sexual interest, to facilitator of the sexual act itself, these "glory holes," as we would call them today, show how urinals were constructed through a dialogue between those who used them and those who built and policed them. About a year after the aforementioned report, the police superintendent wrote another that focused exclusively on the issue of the holes between the urinal stalls. He noted that he had ordered them filled with plaster "but, several days afterward, the plaster had been removed and I had to recommence the work, which was then rendered once again necessary due to the persistence of the individuals who frequent these toilets with the intention of committing their ignoble acts there."[59] In order to prevent this constant back-and-forth, the superintendent asked that the prefect of the Seine give the order to put up plates of

---

58. Rapport: Attentat aux mœurs, March 4, 1861, DA 230, doc. 295, APP.
59. Rapport: Au sujet de trous pratiqués dans les cloisons des latrines des halles, March 24, 1862, DA 230, doc. 302, APP.

sheet metal that would prevent their vandalism in the future, thus forcing the administration to come face-to-face with the material consequences of sexual desire.[60]

Attempts to prevent the appropriation of public urinals with material changes to the urban landscape were not limited to filling in some holes or replacing a few walls with sheet metal. Lighting became a preferred solution. In the summer of 1865, the police discussed the possibility of lighting the urinals along the Seine and some of the arches formed by the river's bridges, which were also used by men who sought sex with other men.[61] In May of that year, they recommended lighting the urinals of the Solférino Bridge, as well as those that lined the Seine from the neighborhoods of Grenelle in the western section of the city to Bercy in the eastern section, and closing them each night at seven o'clock in order to prevent their being used "evening and night as the rendezvous of pederasts." A note overlaid on the report implies that closing the urinals at night would not be desirable, as doing so would lead to "problems that we have wanted to avoid from the point of view of cleanliness," but that lighting the urinals and the arches of the bridges was "important."[62] Attempting to balance two competing interests—hygiene and propriety—the administration was forced to admit the power of men who sought sex with other men to reshape urban space. Indeed, so powerful was this appropriation that they ended up literally highlighting—illuminating— its existence in order to bring it into the open for better policing.[63]

Responses to the appropriation of public urinals were not limited to the state. During the winter of 1889 and 1890, André Cassard, a builder specializing in flooring and woodworking, corresponded with the prefecture of the Seine in an attempt to negotiate a contract to build new public urinals along the Seine. Cassard claimed that although the approximately forty urinals along the banks of the Seine were kept in "as great a state of cleanliness as possible," they remained not "open to everyone" due to a general "repugnance of which the cause is not unknown by the Service de l'assainissement." Cassard then linked this repugnance to "the dregs of the population who meet there and . . . the shameful acts which are committed there."[64] Presumably, Cassard meant to imply men who sought sex with other men. These "dregs of society" had turned public facilities into their own semiprivate space. In other

60. Ibid.

61. "Eclairage des ponts sous les arches de ponts," June 1, 1865, DA 230, doc. 344, APP; "Eclairage des premières arches de tous les ponts," June 21, 1865, DA 230, doc. 345, APP.

62. Rapport, May 19, 1865, DA 230, doc. 343, APP.

63. Many thanks to one of the anonymous reviewers for helping me clarify this point.

64. André Cassard to Préfet de la Seine, September 24, 1889, 2, V.O3 425, AP.

words, illicit sexual activity had so contaminated these facilities of public hygiene that respectable citizens could no longer use them.

Attempting to justify his contract, Cassard did not recommend increased surveillance by the police as did some of his hygienist and law enforcement contemporaries. Instead, in order to justify his plans, Cassard emphasized placement and design. In particular, he suggested destroying the urinals on the banks of the river and building new facilities on the quays, in alignment with the parapets.[65] Presumably, though Cassard remains vague, raising the urinals to street level would bring them more fully into the public purview, preventing their takeover by the "dregs" of society. In other words, Cassard proposed a material reaction to antisocial behaviors, one that, in the end, would probably only provide greater publicity to the urinals and their varied uses. The beginning of a cycle can be discerned in this reaction. The municipal government authorized a series of public urinals that were then claimed by sexual dissidents who, through their actions, rendered the facilities so symbolic of their presence as to prevent others from using them. In response, a builder proposed not to attack the people who created the problem but to build new urinals that would prevent the social practices that caused the problem in the first place.

The attempts to "fix" this problem through changes to the physical structure of the city reflects a faith in the ability of space to reshape how people behaved. However, it also highlights how such efforts formed part of a more complicated, dialogic process. Beginning in the July Monarchy and accelerating in the Second Empire and Third Republic, the administration of Paris built enclosed spaces in public specifically designated for genital functions. Men who sought sex with other men quickly understood the opportunity the edifices provided: here they could encounter other men, shielded from prying eyes, and justify their presence through their bodily needs. In response to this appropriation, the state and private interests reshaped the urinal to prevent this kind of use. And the cycle began again.

"A Kind of Erotic Madness"

The attempt to make urinals recognizable and plentiful, capable of hiding men in order to ensure their access to public space, opened these facilities to appropriation for same-sex sexual activity. Urinals became destinations themselves, fulfilling a more varied set of desires than those imagined by the authorities and public hygienists. The use of public urinals for men seeking sex with other men thus put into question the entire apparatus set up to

---

65. Ibid.

manage the male body. Efforts were made to explain the appropriation of public urinals by men who sought sex with other men, but they did so in ways that ultimately confounded any attempt to situate the facilities within a heterosexual economy of desire. Rather than helping men move about, the urinal enticed them to stay inside. Carlier described those who came to the urinals as having a "kind of erotic madness, which brought [men] each night to the same place" that police attempts to manage only publicized.[66] By providing a space for this madness, ensuring that passers-by witnessed it, the urinal put into question the assumption of heterosexuality in the nineteenth-century city.

By drawing in different kinds of men, confounding the difference between men who sought sex with other men and those who did not, and enticing men who did not even realize they desired other men, the urinal disrupted the regulationist assumption of inevitable male desire directed toward women. It could also incite same-sex desire. Carlier, for his part, argued that the odor of the facilities functioned as a kind of aphrodisiac for some pederasts.[67] In doing so, he implied that the urinal itself provided the very enticement that drew in men for sex. Figured as madness, this attraction stood for a loss of control, the very justification for men's access to public space in the first place. The use of public urinals by men seeking sex with other men diverted their purpose and forced commentators to wrestle with their inability to impose clear meaning on the city.

The madness Carlier referred to had an almost banal source: "curiosity." As knowledge of men's use of public urinals spread, the desire to know could be used as an excuse for one's presence in a urinal, even as the sexual implications remained clear. In 1876 a member of the municipal council, the Comte de Germiny, was arrested for soliciting sex from a working-class man named Edmond-Pierre Chouard. Explaining his presence in the urinal, Germiny claimed that after seeing some men hanging out near the facility, he went to investigate: "I wanted to assure myself of what was happening there," because "I had heard of the troubles they were causing."[68] Germiny thus explains his presence as a kind of slumming. He had heard rumors of what was going on at public urinals and decided he needed to see it firsthand. The common sexual underpinnings of the slumming narrative, however, undercut his claim to pure investigative observation.[69] At the same time, his arrest caused

---

66. Félix Carlier, *Études de pathologie sociale: Les deux prostitutions (1860–1870)* (Paris: E. Dentu, 1887), 302.

67. Ibid., 305.

68. Quoted in Peniston, *Pederasts and Others,* 154.

69. Seth Koven, *Slumming: Sexual and Social Politics in Victorian London* (Princeton, N.J.: Princeton University Press, 2004), 8.

a widely publicized scandal, which in turn could only have increased other men's knowledge of the sexual possibilities of public urinals.[70]

In a similar case, Henri Joseph Duval, the forty-seven-year-old mayor of the commune of Chanteloup, in what was then the Seine et Oise department (just northwest of Paris), was arrested in a public urinal near the Palais de la Bourse. According to the police report from the night of his arrest, Duval "went from stall to stall and, without urinating, revealed his erect genitals to every man who arrived in order to urinate, while masturbating with his right hand and craning to see into the compartments to the right and left of his own in order to see the penises of the men next to him, which he did ten times in a row in the space of thirty minutes."[71] Duval, the police claimed, then proceeded to enter a different urinal before "finally, not finding any men who would respond to his shameful provocations, returned for the twelfth time, without even rebuttoning his pants," to the original urinal, where he proceeded to masturbate again, with two police officers watching from the next stall, at which point he was arrested. The sheer detail of the description—the police twice noted which hand he used to masturbate—underlines the situation that Duval had found himself in.

And yet Duval still tried to excuse his behavior through innocent curiosity. Interrogated that evening, he explained that he "had a weakness for staying in diverse urinals, in the situation where I was found; I was pushed there, not out of a shameful passion, but rather out of an almost invincible curiosity to see if what I had heard about the urinals was true."[72] As one of the rare moments where the voice of the marginal appears in the archives, it is tempting to read Duval's statement as an excuse, a lie, or even false consciousness. However, taken on its own terms, his emphasis on his desire to see and understand underscores the power of a discourse that made the urinal into a draw against which men had to resist. Indeed, according to one of the arresting officers—the somewhat notorious *inspecteur des mœurs* Achille Rabasse—Duval claimed at the time of his arrest that he "had yielded to the yearning [*désir*] of an unhealthy curiosity."[73] The multivalence of the word *désir* here

---

70. On this case, see William A. Peniston, "A Public Offense against Decency: The Trial of the Count de Germiny and the 'Moral Order' of the Third Republic," in *Disorder in the Court: Trials and Sexual Conflict at the Turn of the Century,* ed. George Robb and Nancy Erber (New York: New York University Press, 1999), 12–32.

71. Déposé, May 23, 1876, "Duval (Henri, Joseph); outrage à la pudeur, 15.6.1876," D2U6 37, AP.

72. Procès-verbal, May 23, 1876, Dossier "Duval (Henri, Joseph); outrage à la pudeur, 15.6.1876," D2U6 37, AP.

73. "Notes tenues par le Greffier soussigné, en exécution des Articles 155 et 189 du Code d'Instruction criminelle pour M. Le Procureur de la République, contre Duval, Henri Joseph,

points to how curiosity proved a double-edge sword for both the accused and the accuser. While on the one hand it could be innocent, a desire to know, it was always also premised on a somewhat uncontrollable will to pleasure, a desire to experience. That it seemed a useful claim, one that Duval repeated at his arrest and while under interrogation, underscores how curiosity implicated all men: anyone with knowledge of the urinals or who simply passed them by could also find themselves struck with a desire to know that became an experience of pleasure.

This kind of curiosity disrupted attempts to root same-sex desire in particular male bodies, a goal of the police and the medical establishment, who sought ways of distinguishing between those appropriating the urinals for sex and innocent men. In *La corruption à Paris,* the moral commentator Ali Coffignon presented his readers with the supposed explanation of one person who had been drawn to the urinals. "It is not my fault," the anonymous man explains. "I look entirely like a man, but I am not one, being in a complete state of incapacity from the sexual point of view." If anything "caused" the anonymous man's same-sex desire, it was the urinal itself. It was his sterility that gave rise to a "curiosity that took me to know how other men were made in this regard." This curiosity, once it took hold, "became an obsession, and little by little, due to this furious desire that I had to be like other men, that I arrived at giving into pederasty."[74] Coffignon's account is riven with ellipses and thus evades any definitive accounting of the man's true desires; indeed, he concludes the story by "leaving it to doctors to seek out what is real in this explanation." Its ambiguity, however, evokes a strange accounting of same-sexual desire. Rather than attraction *to* other men, it was a desire *to be like* other men that led him to the urinal in the first place. The urinal provided a homosocial space in which this "furious desire" turned from an opportunity to gaze on other men in order to become like them into an opportunity to be penetrated by them. The urinal thus enabled a dangerous slippage between homosociality and homosexuality.[75]

I emphasize this point in order to highlight how the urinal became essen-

---

47 ans, Propriétaire et Maire de la Commune de Chanteloup," June 15, 1876, Dossier "Duval (Henri, Joseph); outrage à la pudeur, 15.6.1876," D2U6 37, AP.

74. Coffignon, *La corruption à Paris,* 331.

75. In this sense, Coffignon underscores conflicting notions of male friendship and male same-sex sexual activity as the nineteenth-century drew to a close. On the relationship between male sociability and homosexuality in nineteenth-century France, see, for example, Brian Joseph Martin, *Napoleonic Friendship: Military Fraternity, Intimacy, and Sexuality in Nineteenth-Century France* (Durham: University of New Hampshire Press, 2011). For a broader theorization of "homosocial desire," see esp. Eve Kosofsky Sedgwick, *Between Men: English Literature and Male Homosocial Desire* (New York: Columbia University Press, 1985).

tially diversionary, disordering the attempt by the police to manage the sexual life of the city. The brothel, remember, was meant to facilitate male sexual need. Even as it declined through the second half of the nineteenth century, it remained a key site of sexual initiation.[76] The curiosity of young men that so concerned regulationists was supposed to be heterosexually directed. The signs of sex placed within the city—the marcheuse, the gros numéro—and the attempt to wrest control of these signs from women's bodies only gained administrative force insofar as that primary assumption held. The urinal threw that assumption into question, because it provided another site of sexual experience, but one between men. In Coffignon's example, the narrator's attempt to cure his sterility led him to enjoy passive sex with other men and, as he explains, "I have incidentally remarked that a great number of passive subjects are, like me, incapable of a virile act."[77] In other words, the attempt to cure sterility led not to heterosexual sexual excitement but rather to the discovery of other kinds of sexual pleasures. He thus productively confused identification with desire. In doing so, he not only highlighted the continuing understanding of homosexuality as a vice that threatened all men but also revealed a failure to promote heterosexuality.[78]

The power of the urinal undermined the logic of regulationism that shaped police supervision of public sex. In order to ensure the proper functioning of the urban economy, sexual and otherwise, the police strove to ensure that public urinals were used as intended. This quest, however, demanded they be able to separate men who were using the facilities to urinate and those who were seeking out sex. Most men arrested in public urinals were accused under the law against "public offenses against decency," a vague statute that defined

---

76. Lola Gonzalez-Quijano, "Entre désir sexuel et sentiments: L'apprentissage amoureux des étudiants du quartier latin du second XIXe siècle," in *Les jeunes et la sexualité: Initiations, interdits, identities (XIXe–XXIe siècle),* ed. Véronique Blanchard, Régis Revenin, and Jean-Jacques Yvorel (Paris: Éditions Autrement, 2010), 181. On the construction of masculinity in public space more broadly, see Anne-Marie Sohn, *"Sois un homme!" La construction de la masculinité au XIXe siècle* (Paris: Seuil, 2009), esp. chap. 2.

77. Coffignon, *La corruption à Paris,* 131.

78. As sexologists and other experts began to understand inversion and homosexuality as in-born, the connection with impotence lost favor. In his rather unique *Uranisme et unisexualité* (1896), for instance, Marc-André Raffalovich argued that impotence cannot cause inversion, because castration did not necessarily kill heterosexual desire. However, he still argued that impotence among "uranists" often led them to agree to other kinds of sexual acts and were often "passive, effeminate, or exhausted virile men." Marc-André Raffalovich, *Uranisme et unisexualité: Étude sur différentes manifestations de l'instinct sexuel* (Lyon: A. Storck, 1896), 8–9. Translation is from Nancy Erber and William A. Peniston, trans., *Marc-André Raffalovich's "Uranism and Unisexuality: A Study of Different Manifestations of the Sexual Instinct,"* ed. Philip Healy and Frederick S. Roden (New York: Palgrave Macmillan, 2016), 44.

the meaning of neither "public" nor "decency."[79] The nature of the law thus provided an opening to those who wished to assert a role in the enforcement of law, notably the medical establishment (see Chapter 3). In 1878 one such doctor, Maurice Laugier, published an article in the *Annales d'hygiène publique et médecine légale* that addressed precisely this problem. Laugier recognized the potential difficulties in regulating offenses against public decency in spaces built to enable activities that could, given the right context, also appear indecent. Laugier defined the offense as "including gestures, touches, exhibition of sexual organs in not only a public space but also a place accessible to public view, [performed] with either an obscene intention or simple negligence on the part of the accused."[80] Laugier rested his definition of the statute on the publicness of a particular act. A public offense against decency did not only have to occur in public places, but could also take place in areas accessible to the public. This potential publicness overshadows the intent of the act, as "simple negligence" could also lead to breaking the law. Left vague, however, remained the key term "decent." The indecent act thus had to be defined on a case-by-case basis.

Laugier did not address cases of drunkenness or other forms of mental incapacity, and instead emphasized situations involving those arrested for actions that may have appeared obscene at first glance but could actually be justified given specific circumstances. In particular, he emphasized the possibility that a man may have a medical condition that necessitated frequent use of public urinals.[81] For instance, one of Laugier's six examples featured a man who attracted police attention due to his "very prolonged stay in a urinal and the maneuvers that he was exercising on his penis." The accused requested an examination, claiming that he suffered from a "disease of the urinary tract."[82] The examination undertaken, Laugier determined that the man did indeed suffer from difficulty urinating, a problem ameliorated by his masturbation-like activity and his lengthy stays in the public urinals. The cause of the accused man's gestures, in other words, justified his otherwise "offensive" act, distinguishing him from the pederasts who also frequented the urinals. Laugier thus asserted his ability to tell the difference between the decent and the indecent in the public urinals and, by implication, those drawn to them for the right or wrong reasons. In doing

---

79. On this law, see esp. Marcel Iacub, *Through the Keyhole: A History of Sex, Space, and Public Modesty in Modern France,* trans. Vinay Swamy (Manchester, U.K.: Manchester University Press, 2016).

80. Maurice Laugier, "Du rôle de l'expertise médico-légale dans certains cas d'outrage public à la pudeur," *Annales d'hygiène publique et médecine légale* 2, no. 50 (1878): 165.

81. Ibid., 166–167.

82. Ibid., 170.

so, he redrew the problem of the public urinals: they may divert some men but not all of them.

Laugier saw doctors as a corrective to a police force relying, by necessity, on shaky evidence. He advised men to take care to avoid the attention of the police while using the public urinals but remained confident that a proper medical exam, requested by a conscientious magistrate, could save "the honor of an entire family" in the event of police error.[83] Laugier's evidence, however, was not so clear cut, because pederasty supposedly caused the very medical problems that could justify one's presence in the urinal in the first place. For instance, another doctor, Alfred Becquerel, in his brief recapitulation of the ideas of the most important commentator on the subject, Ambroise Tardieu (see Chapter 3), claimed that both active and passive pederasty could have an adverse effect on urinary and fecal movement. The active pederast possessed a "singular deformation of the penis," which among those with a "voluminous penis" could be seen in a "urinary meatus . . . [that exited] to the side," while the passive pederast suffered from "incontinence of fecal matter."[84] To take one specific example, Becquerel includes hemorrhoids in his list of positive signs of passive pederasty, while Laugier's fourth example features a man whose large hemorrhoid served as a legitimate medical reason for not only his excessive stay in a public urinal but also the movements he was making with regard to his anus.[85] Perhaps it was awareness of this contradiction that made Tardieu himself, writing in 1857, wary of attributing too much explanatory power to hemorrhoids.[86] Nevertheless, while Laugier claimed urinary disease could exonerate a person accused of pederasty at a urinal, Becquerel argued that pederasty potentially caused urinary conditions. Certainly, if one could ask the doctors themselves to explain the apparent contradiction, they would defer to their expertise as doctors and their consequent ability to tell the difference between exculpatory and inculpatory evidence. In any case, the written record implies that the signs of pederasty could exculpate a pederast.

The ambiguous position of those who entered the urinal was demonstrated by the blackmail narrative that surrounded it. Medical and legal commentators identified the susceptibility of men who sought sex with other men to blackmail as a danger to social peace.[87] Threatening to reveal that an

---

83. Ibid., 173.

84. Alfred Becquerel, *Traité élémentaire d'hygiène privée et publique,* 6th ed. (Paris: P. Asselin, 1877), 845.

85. Ibid.; Laugier, "Du rôle de l'expertise médico-légale," 170–171.

86. Ambroise Tardieu, *Étude médico-légale sur les attentats aux mœurs,* 3rd. ed. (Paris: J.-B. Baillière, 1859), 147–148.

87. On sexual blackmail in the nineteenth-century in a broader context, see Angus McLaren, *Sexual Blackmail: A Modern History* (Cambridge, Mass: Harvard University Press, 2002).

individual was a pederast, whether true or not, relied on the indeterminacy of sexual deviance. It thus played on a dual anxiety: the difficulty in avoiding being taken for a pederast and the difficulty in identifying those who actually were. Blackmail became an almost omnipresent danger, enabling commentators to indulge their storytelling while emphasizing that the dangers posed by the spaces of male same-sex sexual desire were very real indeed. For instance, in his memoir, the police inspector Gustave Macé provided an explicit account of blackmail in the Parisian public urinals. Working in a pair, one blackmailer entered a public urinal at Les Halles and propositioned someone. Upon exiting the urinal with the victim in tow, the accomplice approached and addressed the first blackmailer and said, "I know him [the victim]. . . . I am an inspecteur des mœurs, we have observed him for a long time, and we will conduct him to the police station."[88] The false agent then interrogated the victim about his familial situation, implying his potential disgrace if the incident became known, while the bait encouraged the victim to pay off the fake officer.[89] Unlike the commentators who described them, blackmailers recognized that the truth of the individual's actual sexual desires mattered little inside a space already associated with the stigma of filth and same-sex desire. Whether the victim had such desire mattered little in the blackmail narrative, because the very fact of being in the urinal was sufficient evidence of possible deviance. Within the urinal, the distinction between innocent and guilty, the curious and the deviant, broke down.

The police themselves had no choice but to reckon with this possibility. When Count Germiny was arrested in December 1876, he tried to fight off the undercover agents of the vice squad until a uniformed officer arrived at the scene. He excused his conduct by claiming that "he feared that he had been set up by criminals."[90] In the context of the blackmail narrative, his fear was quite justified; inside the urinal, the symbol of authority, the police, was put into question. Indeed, Yves Guyot, member of the municipal council of Paris and critic of the morals police, explicitly pointed out the problem: "Some men, knowing that an individual should never resist a police agent for fear of capture and of condemnation for outrages against agents, pretend to be employees of the prefecture. . . . Sometimes they address themselves to men that they accuse of pederasty, because they entered a urinal. It is necessary to distrust the urinals; they are ambushes of the honorable Rabasse's band."[91] Blackmailers, according to Guyot, needed no further evidence than

---

88. Gustave Macé, *La police parisienne: Mes Lundis en prison* (Paris: G. Charpentier, 1889), 158.

89. Ibid., 158–159.

90. Peniston, "Public Offense against Decency," 20.

91. Yves Guyot, *La police* (Paris: G. Charpentier, 1884), 273.

the act of entering the public urinal in order to find a target; "because they entered a urinal," individuals could believably be "accuse[d] of pederasty." The intermingling of men, the arbitrary means by which the police arrested people, and the inability of examiners to unravel their own contradictions rendered the space susceptible to the specific tactics used by blackmailers. In other words, the arbitrary actions of the police, supposedly founded on the "science" of hygiene and forensics, rendered their authority susceptible to believable usurpation by blackmailers in the first place. The police themselves became suspect; no one could be sure who was and was not a proper representative of authority. While Guyot begins his passage by warning against those who could so easily disguise themselves as police officers, he ends by warning against the police themselves.

Conclusion

In *La corruption à Paris,* Coffignon reproduced the article that appeared in *La Lanterne* in July 1888 complaining about the appearance of placards advertising treatment for venereal disease in the public urinals of Paris. British urinal postings, the newspaper explained, instruct their users to "Please adjust your dress before leaving. In Paris, it's entirely different, the public facilities seem to indicate that the entire population is gnawed on by the most abominable maladies." In Paris the advertisements promised a "cure without mercury of all venereal disease. Doctor X. . . . Easy treatment follows, even while traveling."[92] According to the paper, the urinals of London performed the duty they were intended to accomplish: preserve the purity of the public street. The urinals of Paris did the opposite: they reminded the city of its seemingly eternal impurity.[93] The article's argument rests on the particular nature of these ads, most of which, the newspaper argues, were posted by charlatans. But it also points to how the urinals' use for this kind of publicity gave rise to the very problems it claimed to solve: "Is it dignified that a city that respects itself permits such vile postings? The Parisian, from his youth, is in this way familiarized with the sad results of debauchery; being still a child, his curiosity is awoken by these unwholesome inscriptions."[94] These reminders were thus read not as an effective warning as to the consequences of soliciting sex from a prostitute but as an incitement to do so in the first

---

92. Coffignon, *La corruption à Paris,* 275–276.

93. Coffignon's book was published during a veritable "venereal panic" in France. See Corbin, *Les filles de noce,* 386–405; Harsin, *Policing Prostitution,* chap. 7; Judith Surkis, *Sexing the Citizen: Morality and Masculinity in France, 1870–1920* (Ithaca, N.Y.: Cornell University Press, 2006), chap. 7.

94. Coffignon, *La corruption à Paris,* 276.

place. The urinal had thus been appropriated by fraudulent doctors who, in claiming to cure venereal disease, were creating the conditions that would only spread it faster.

The reminder of venereal disease in the public urinal can be seen as a double failure. First, the advertisement awakens the urinal user to that other use of his penis, undercutting the propriety the facilities were meant to ensure. Second, in doing so, the man's "curiosity" was awakened, and he was thus directed not to the café, for instance, but to the prostitute. Implicit, however, was another possibility: having excited him, the young man perhaps would be drawn to explore those enticements right then and there. Indeed, one could read the ad against the *Lanterne*: drawn to the public urinal out of curiosity, the men who read the advertisement were instructed in how to disavow same-sex sexual activity. The painful urination that came with some forms of venereal disease parallels the kinds of urinary infections that served to disavow same-sex sexual activity in the urinals and thus could remind those using the urinals of what to say if caught by the police. Regulationism's failure here is of another kind and rests on its inability to actually distinguish between the kinds of desires that animated the sexual economy of Paris in the first place.

Although built to facilitate the social discipline of male bodies as they moved through the modern city, the urinal ultimately confounded the ability of administrators to manage and determine the meaning of transforming spaces.[95] Indeed, it represents a broader failure in the regulationist project. While the police may have created their own signs of sex, they were ultimately more successful in establishing the importance of recognition in general than in the particular meanings they ascribed to the various institutions and practices of nineteenth-century hygiene and sexual management. The concern over the multiple meaning of advertisements about venereal disease highlights the recognition that sometimes the cure created the disease. In other words, the attempt to manage the sexual life of the city did more to make sex central to how Parisians understood and encountered the city than it did to fully determine how sexual encounters would be felt, experienced, and represented in everyday life.

Before the emergence of modern homosexual identities, the public urinal enabled men of diverse desires to interact with one another, use one another as cover when caught, and find pleasure together. The urinals thus illustrate

---

95. The example of the public urinal thus supports Michel de Certeau's cautionary critique of urban discourses that claim to understand the totality of the city, as well as his admonition to scholars, by way of a critique of Foucault, to be wary of attributing too much power to disciplinary practices and panoptic discourses. Michel de Certeau, *The Practice of Everyday Life*, trans. Steven Rendall (Berkeley: University of California Press, 1984), 45–49.

how the project of modernity, never fully grasped even by those constructing it, will always provide some opportunities for social activity outside the purview of the normal, the acceptable, and the productive. I refuse to unravel the various contradictions in the uses and discourses of public urinals in Paris during the second half of the nineteenth-century.[96] Rather, I allow them to remain confused spaces in which new and unexpected possibilities for pleasure emerged in the modern city. However, as the next chapter shows, this confusion brought forth a reaction among those tasked with managing the city that entailed a shift in the discourse of sexual regulation. Increasing evidence that the transforming spaces of Paris were being used for supposedly illicit, deviant, or otherwise asocial pleasures forced the police, administrators, and other expert commentators to direct their regulationist impulses toward other figures besides the female prostitute. As attempts to render the city knowable and amenable to policing, these efforts to understand multiple kinds of public sexual activity were a response to the confusion symbolized by the public urinal. However, as we shall see, such efforts to manage the sexual life of Paris may have shaped how individuals understood the sexual possibilities of the city, but they failed to determine how people responded to them.

---

96. Here I am inspired by Lee Edelman's conclusion to his examination of post–World War II public restrooms. Lee Edelman, *Homographesis: Essays in Gay Literary and Cultural Theory* (New York: Routledge, 1994), 169–170.

PART II

3

ON PROSTITUTES AND PEDERASTS

In 1837 the famous criminal-turned-detective François Vidocq published his dictionary of criminal argot, where he described the prison *tante,* or fairy: a "man who has the taste of women, the woman of the male prison."[1] Vidocq did not understand pederasty as necessarily innate; rather, it was "nothing more than a vice of those associations of men who live outside society."[2] Most men resisted this vice, but in prison they often "succumbed," and even formed "marriages" between "audacious thieves" and "young pederasts."[3] "Is there any spectacle that more disgusts all of humanity, than to see men renounce the privileges of their sex," Vidocq asks, "in order to take up the tone and manners of those sad creatures [*ces malheureuses créatures*] who sell themselves to the first comer, to see them lap at the hand that hits them, to smile at the person who hurls insults at them?"[4]

Vidocq's description not only inverts the gender of pederasts in both psychic and bodily terms—pederasts have "women's taste" and are "the women

---

1. E. F. Vidocq, *Les voleurs: Physiologie de leurs mœurs et de leur langage,* 2 vols. (Paris, 1837), 2:160. Vidocq would be fictionalized in Honoré de Balzac's *Comédie humaine* as the recurring character Vautrin, whose prison relationship with Théodore Calvi is described in *Splendeurs et misères de courtisanes.* Honoré de Balzac, *La Comédie humaine,* vol. 6, *Études de mœurs: Scènes de la vie parisienne,* ed. Pierre-Georges Castex, (Paris: Gallimard, 1977). On this relationship, see Laure Murat, "La tante, le policier et l'écrivain: Pour une protosexologie de commissariats et de romans," *Revue d'histoire des sciences humaines* 2, no. 17 (2007): 54–57.

2. Vidocq, *Les voleurs,* 2:161.

3. Ibid., 2:161–163.

4. Ibid., 2:164.

of the prison"—but also defines same-sex relations through a fundamental inequality. The "marriages," he describes, for example, were usually consummated between an older, more experienced prisoner—the audacious thief—and a younger one and were characterized by dependency and physical and mental abuse. Indeed, such relations formed a kind of prostitution: they could only remind the former thief of "those sad creatures," gendered female, who "sold themselves." These relationships provided enough emotional sustenance that the pair "would no longer seek to escape," but they remained founded primarily on a form of inequality that could be understood only in light of their fundamental venality.[5]

The notion of the pederast as essentially a kind of prostitute quickly escaped the prison and percolated through nineteenth-century expert and popular discourse. As policing increasingly focused on maintaining order on the streets, forensic scientists, public hygienists, and moral commentators likewise turned their attention to a broader range of behavior, including sexual behavior, in public during the 1850s.[6] This chapter argues that if the female prostitute represented a unique combination of both moral and physical danger to the city, then prostitution itself proved an apt discourse with which to attack men who sought sex with other men as well.[7] As Jeffrey Weeks once argued regarding nineteenth-century London, "[In] terms of social obloquy, all homosexual males as a class were equated with female prostitutes."[8] The construction of the tante as a third sex relied on a discourse of prostitution that associated male same-sex sexual activity with an essential venality.[9] It was not just "femininity," therefore, that modified the gender of the pederast into a "third sex" but a particular kind of femininity that was, in

---

5. Ibid., 2:163.

6. On police attention to the street, see esp. Quentin Deluermoz, *Policiers dans la ville: La construction d'un ordre public à Paris (1854–1914)* (Paris: Publications de la Sorbonne, 2012), 45–47. On Second Empire policing more broadly, see Howard C. Payne, *The Police State of Louis Napoleon Bonaparte, 1851–1860* (Seattle: University of Washington Press, 1966); Quentin Deluermoz, "Police Forces and Political Crises: Revolutions, Policing Alternatives, and Institutional Resilience in Paris, 1848–1871," *Urban History* 43, no. 2 (2016): 232–248.

7. Andrew R. Aisenberg, *Contagion: Disease, Government, and the "Social Question" in Nineteenth-Century France* (Stanford, Calif.: Stanford University Press, 1999), 59–60.

8. Jeffrey Weeks, "Inverts, Perverts, and Mary-Annes: Male Prostitution and the Regulation of Homosexuality in England in the Nineteenth and Early Twentieth Centuries," in *Hidden from History: Reclaiming the Gay and Lesbian Past,* ed. Martin Bauml Duberman, Martha Vicinus, and George Chauncey (New York: New American Library, 1989), 200.

9. Laure Murat, *La loi du genre: Une histoire du "troisième sexe"* (Paris: Fayard, 2006), 31–39. Elsewhere, Murat also notes the incongruity in the use of a French-language "feminine word to designate a character whose biological sex is masculine" as a way of signaling the discordance of the pederast within a binary gender system. Murat, "La tante, le policier, et l'écrivain," 55.

essence, already corrupted.[10] Female prostitution anchored how moral commentators understood the appearance of male same-sex desire on the streets of Paris during the Second Empire and early Third Republic. If the turn to prostitution was a turn to vice, then the curiosity that led to pederasty was the same. If, as I have argued, male same-sex sexual activity posed a particular problem to regulationism insofar as it put into question assumptions about the direction of male desire, then it was regulationism that had to be reconciled to male same-sex sexual activity. By producing another kind of female prostitute, the authorities justified their own attention to male same-sex sexual activity on the streets of mid-nineteenth-century Paris.

The morals police were tasked with regulating both female prostitution and male pederasty, but their primary focus remained squarely on female prostitution.[11] Indeed, the wealth of material on female prostitution contained in the police archives threatens to totally overshadow that documenting male same-sex sexual activity. The very stationery symbolized their priorities: a turn-of-the-century document ordering a raid on a wine merchant and hotel that was "signaled as serving as the refuge of pederasts" has the word "pederasts" replacing the crossed-out, printed words *filles de débauche* in the header.[12] Too often, however, the imbalance of the archives has implicitly justified exclusive attention to female prostitution by historians, even those supposedly interested in the morals police more broadly.[13] Historians who have examined male same-sex sexual activity have shown that the police conflated male same-sex sexual activity and male prostitution but have generally treated female prostitution only as a useful point of comparison.[14] The systems that caught up both female prostitutes and men who sought sex with other men, however, were fundamentally intertwined in ways reflected by the very structure of the archives.[15] The sheer attention paid to female prostitution by the nineteenth-century police should not be seen as an obstacle to comprehending male same-sex sexual activity. Rather, the former shaped how the police and other authorities approached the latter.

This is not to say that the police treated each group the same way. While

---

10. Murat, *La loi du genre,* 52–53.

11. Jean-Claude Féray, *"Pédés:" Le premier registre infamant de la préfecture de police de Paris au XIXe siècle suivi d'un dictionnaire des noms propres et noms communs les plus significatifs du register et d'annexes* (Paris: Quintes-feuilles, 2012), 15.

12. Untitled, September 11, 1901, "Rue des Tournelles, 32," JC 44, formerly BM2 28, APP.

13. Jean-Marc Berlière, *La police des mœurs sous la IIIe république* (Paris: Seuil, 1992).

14. Régis Revenin, *Homosexualité et prostitution masculines à Paris, 1870–1918* (Paris: L'Harmattan, 2005), 114–122; William A. Peniston, *Pederasts and Others: Urban Culture and Sexual Identity in Nineteenth-Century Paris* (New York: Harrington Park Press, 2004), 28–30.

15. Andrew Israel Ross, "Sex in the Archives: Homosexuality, Prostitution, and the Archives de la Préfecture de Police," *French Historical Studies* 40, no. 2 (2017): 267–290.

the absence of pederasty from the penal code offered some protection to men who sought sex with other men, the absence of prostitution placed women who sold sex under the authority of the police themselves. As William Peniston has described, while a woman who sold sex became a prostitute at the expense of her many other social roles, men so accused remained "clerks, servants, artisans, or laborers" as well. While female prostitutes were differentiated from their clients, male prostitutes were not. While female prostitutes had little legal recourse once arrested, men accused of same-sex sexual activity maintained at least some protection.[16] Women accused of prostitution, once inscribed, were always and only prostitutes, to the police at least.[17] This contrast speaks to men's privilege and to the difficulty the police faced in actually defining the pederast. In this sense, the apparent coherence of the category of the prostitute—underscored by police confidence in identifying her—contrasts problematically with the apparent incoherence of the pederast.

The differences in how the police treated female prostitutes and male pederasts highlight the complicated interplay between social behavior and identity. Men who misbehaved in public retained a measure of agency vis-à-vis the police, as they received the protection of the law and relied on their roles as fathers, husbands, and workers to justify their public presence. At the same time, however, that very possibility disrupted any attempt to ground their actions exclusively in light of their sexual behavior. The man caught in flagrante delicto did not simply become a pederast in the way women caught selling sex were labeled. These distinctions reflect in some ways the double standard that protected the male client of the female prostitute, which ensured and perpetuated male privilege in public and their access to working-class women.[18] This is not to reinscribe gender as a static category and sexuality as a fluid one as if the prostitute symbolizes the former and the pederast

---

16. Peniston, *Pederasts and Others,* 29–30.

17. This despite the fact that women who turned to prostitution often did so out of economic need and that prostitution was often therefore a temporary expedience. On the economic situation of female prostitutes in nineteenth-century France as well as the effects of their inscription onto the rolls, see Jill Harsin, *Policing Prostitution in Nineteenth-Century Paris* (Princeton, N.J.: Princeton University Press, 1985), chap. 6. On this theme in other geographic contexts, see, for example, Christine Stansell, *City of Women: Sex and Class in New York, 1789–1860* (Urbana: University of Illinois Press, 1987), chap. 9; Keely Stauter-Halsted, *The Devil's Chain: Prostitution and Social Control in Partitioned Poland* (Ithaca, N.Y.: Cornell University Press, 2015), chap. 2.

18. For a definition of the sexual double standard, see Judith Walkowitz, *Prostitution and Victorian Society: Women, Class, and the State* (Cambridge: Cambridge University Press, 1980), 3. On some of the particularities of the "double standard" in France at the end of the nineteenth century, see Michèle Plott, "The Rules of the Game: Respectability, Sexuality, and the *Femme Mondaine* in Late-Nineteenth-Century Paris," *French Historical Studies* 25, no. 3 (2002): 531–556.

the latter.[19] Rather, it is to highlight how gender—along with class—shaped the process through which sexual behavior became codified, represented, and eventually attached to sexual identities as well. Indeed, the figure of the female prostitute enabled a discourse that gradually reduced the ability of men who sought sex with other men to be anything but a pederast. Put differently, the female prostitute enabled the eventual emergence of the homosexual.

Key actors in this process were medical professionals, participating in a Europe-wide trend toward the integration of forensic science with policing.[20] During the 1850s, forensic pathologists in France, such as Ambroise Tardieu, participated in the production of early images of the "invert" that would appear in sexological discourse by the end of the century, but they did so in ways that still emphasized the importance of the "sexual act itself, specifically anal penetration."[21] This unique combination—an emphasis on

19. Biddy Martin, "Extraordinary Homosexuals and the Fear of Being Ordinary," *differences* 6, nos. 2–3 (1994): 101.

20. On the relationship between the medical profession and policing in nineteenth-century France, see Robert A. Nye, *Crime, Madness, and Politics in Modern France: The Medical Concept of National Decline* (Princeton, N.J.: Princeton University Press, 1984), esp. chap. 2; Ruth Harris, *Murders and Madness: Medicine, Law, and Society in the Fin de Siècle* (Oxford, U.K.: Clarendon Press, 1989). On forensic medicine in other contexts, see Ian A. Burney, *Bodies of Evidence: Medicine and the Politics of the English Inquest, 1830–1926* (Baltimore: Johns Hopkins University Press, 2000); Katherine D. Watson, *Forensic Medicine in Western Society* (London: Routledge, 2011), esp. chap. 3.

21. Scott Spector, *Violent Sensations: Sex, Crime, and Utopia in Vienna and Berlin, 1860–1914* (Chicago: University of Chicago Press, 2016), 81. Vernon Rosario in particular has emphasized the link between forensic approaches to same-sex sexual behavior and "inversion" in the French context. See Vernon A. Rosario, "Pointy Penises, Fashion Crimes, and Hysterical Mollies: The Pederasts' Inversions," in *Homosexuality in Modern France,* ed. Jeffrey Merrick and Bryant T. Ragan Jr. (New York: Oxford University Press, 1996), 146–176. "Inversion" entered the French lexicon and French sexology with the publication of Jean-Martin Charcot and Valentin Magnan's article "Inversion du sens genital." See Jean-Martin Charcot and Valentin Magnan, "Inversion du sens génital et autres perversions sexuelles," *Archives de neurologie* 3 (1882): 53–60, and 4 (1882): 296–322. On the development of these ideas in different national contexts, see Robert A. Nye, "The History of Sexuality in Context: National Sexological Traditions," *Science in Context* 4, no. 2 (1991): 387–406. On "inversion" in some other contexts, see George Chauncey, "From Sexual Inversion to Homosexuality: Medicine and the Changing Conceptualization of Female Deviance," *Salmagundi,* nos. 58–59 (1982–1983): 114–146; Gert Hekma, "'A Female Soul in a Male Body': Sexual Inversion as Gender Inversion in Nineteenth-Century Sexology," in *Third Sex, Third Gender: Beyond Sexual Dimorphism in Culture and History,* ed. Gilbert Herdt (New York: Zone Books, 1994), 213–239; Heike Bauer, "Theorizing Female Inversion: Sexology, Discipline, and Gender at the Fin de Siècle," *Journal of the History of Sexuality* 18, no. 1 (2009): 84–102; Chiara Beccalossi, *Female Sexual Inversion: Same-Sex Desires in Italian and British Sexology, c. 1870–1920* (New York: Palgrave Macmillan, 2012). On the broader development of psychological interest in sexuality, see esp. Harry Oosterhuis, *Stepchildren of Nature: Krafft-Ebing, Psychiatry, and the Making of Sexual Identity* (Chicago: University of Chicago Press, 2000); Arnold I. Davidson, *The Emergence of Sexuality: Historical Epistemology and the Formation of Concepts* (Cambridge, Mass: Harvard University Press, 2001).

specific behaviors combined with the conviction of the pederast's essential difference—intersected with an ongoing discourse around the female prostitute, ultimately uniting the two as the male pederast was remade into a venal subject him- (or her-) self.[22] As this medical discourse was subsequently taken up and expanded on by the police and moral commentators, the male pederast became associated with the female prostitute, which had the potential to justify applying a regulationist logic—if not regulationism itself—to the problem of male same-sex sexual activity in public space.

The Problem of Regulation and the Public Offense against Decency

The legal context for the policing of "public indecency" emerged out of shifting conceptualizations of male same-sex sexual activity during the eighteenth century, when the police began to reconceive sodomy and male-male sexual activity as social problems rather than sin. The cross-class mixing and secrecy that were already associated with male same-sex sexual activity concerned the police as they increasingly defined their role as the guardians of social order.[23] As threats to that order, pederasts—as they became increasingly known—received the attention of regular "pederasty patrols."[24] The transition of male same-sex sexual activity from a religious to a state concern occurred in tandem with the gradual extension of police power over society more broadly. This change involved categorizing same-sex sexual activity in new ways. No longer just one kind of sin among others, pederasty began to represent a distinct kind of person who acquired—somehow—this particular taste.[25]

---

22. In this respect my argument builds on Laure Murat's examination of the "third sex" in nineteenth-century French police, medical, and literary discourse. Murat investigates how French discourse—in dialog with the ways marginal individuals interacted with one another and with the authorities—created shifting conceptualizations of gender outside the male-female binary and "designated a marginal and stigmatized sexuality" at the same time. Murat, *La loi du genre,* 13–14, 21.

23. Michel Rey, "Police et sodomie à Paris au XVIIIe siècle: Du péché au désordre," *Revue d'histoire moderne et contemporaine* 29, no. 1 (1982): 123–124. On the policing of male same-sex sexual activity in the eighteenth century, see also Michael Sibalis, "The Regulation of Male Homosexuality in Revolutionary and Napoleonic France, 1789–1815," in *Homosexuality in Modern France,* ed. Jeffrey Merrick and Bryant T. Ragan Jr. (New York: Oxford University Press, 1996), 80–101; Jeffrey Merrick, "Commissioner Foucault, Inspector Noël, and the 'Pederasts' of Paris, 1780–3," *Journal of Social History* 32, no. 2 (1998): 287–307.

24. Merrick, "Commissioner Foucault," 288–289.

25. Ibid., 301–303. See also Thierry Pastorello, "L'abolition du crime de sodomie en 1791: Un long processus social, répressif et pénal," *Cahiers d'histoire: Revue d'histoire critique* 112–113 (2010): 197–208.

In general, Enlightenment thinkers did not oppose the regulation of sodomy by the police but questioned the punishment as part of their broader critique of absolute authority.[26] Some, however, did call for a "more liberal" approach that distinguished between private and public acts and argued that "the private act of sodomy, no matter how depraved it seemed, should be tolerated, perhaps even decriminalized, by the state."[27] This position was most forcefully and explicitly put by the Marquis de Condorcet, who argued, "Sodomy without violence cannot be placed under criminal law. It violates no man's rights."[28] Even *philosophes* of this bent, however, continued to argue that pederasty committed in public should be either policed or subject to "public opprobrium."[29] These arguments may have influenced the French Revolutionaries—though, as Michael Sibalis notes, they did not actually explain their reasoning—when they left any mention of sodomy out of the new law code of 1791, an omission that was then perpetuated by Napoleon's Penal Code of 1810.[30]

Just as it left out prostitution, then, French law left the police without explicit means of regulating men who sought sex with other men. Instead, the penal code laid out a series of articles on various sexual offenses (*attentats aux mœurs*), which included prohibitions on pornography and other "immoral" publications, rape and sexual assault, the incitement to debauchery, adultery, bigamy, and, most important for our purposes, "offenses against public decency."[31] However, the police did not take the absence of male same-sex sexual activity from the law codes as a sign of greater social tolerance toward men who sought sex with other men.[32] Rather, by using the legal structure to harass and arrest men who sought sex with other men, the police actually became more repressive after the Revolutionary era, and especially during the middle of the century, than they had been before.[33]

That said, sodomy or pederasty was never as high a priority of the nineteenth-century Paris police as female prostitution. In an 1843 regulation, for

26. Rey, "Police et sodomie," 124.

27. Bryant T. Ragan Jr., "The Enlightenment Confronts Homosexuality," in *Homosexuality in Modern France,* ed. Jeffrey Merrick and Bryant T. Ragan Jr. (New York: Oxford University Press, 1996), 22.

28. Jean-Antoine-Nicolas de Caritat, marquis de Condorcet, *Œuvres complètes,* 21 vols. (Brunswick, Germany: Vieweg, 1804), 7:374. On this quotation, see Rey, "Police et sodomie," 124; Ragan, "Enlightenment Confronts Homosexuality," 22.

29. Ragan, "Enlightenment Confronts Homosexuality," 22–23.

30. Sibalis, "Regulation of Male Homosexuality," 82.

31. *Code pénal, suivi d'une table alphabétique et raisonnée des matières* (Paris: P. Didot l'Aîné et Firmin Didot, 1810), 81–83. See also Sibalis, "Regulation of Male Homosexuality," 82–84; Peniston, *Pederasts and Others,* 16–19.

32. Laure Murat, *La loi du genre,* 28–30.

33. Sibalis, "Regulation of Male Homosexuality," 96.

instance, the police set down the responsibilities of the morals brigade regarding "Public Offenses against Decency, Sodomy," only after a long list of clauses regarding female prostitution. The article stated, in total: "The surveillance of inspectors of the morals police extends to all crimes of public offenses against decency and principally to acts of sodomy, but they should expressly abstain from all acts that could have the character of provocation and try above all to catch the person in the act. / The act of attempted or completed sodomy in a public space constitutes the infraction of a public offense against decency."[34] When, in 1878, the police updated this regulation, they left this clause unchanged, which reflects a broader stability in police approaches to the issue in the nineteenth century.[35] All morals officers were to turn their attention to offenses against decency, which, in this case, specifically referred to male same-sex sexual activity.[36] Instructed to not act as agents provocateurs, they still had to be close enough to see the actual act, defined here as "attempted or completed sodomy."[37]

Interpreting the "public offense against decency" in a relatively restricted manner, the police created a new problem for the authorities. How often, one wonders, did the police actually witness "attempted," let alone "completed," sodomy? For example, a police report from 1843 claimed that "pederasts come together every day at the Galerie d'Orléans at the Palais-Royal, and it is at this gallery that they very openly provoke debauchery, [but] we have no idea where they take the people that they provoke."[38] The mystery was solved by the arrest about a month later of two men who described in some detail

---

34. "Prostitution: Instructions réglementaire du 16 Novembre 1843," "Prostitution: Traite des Blanches: Vagabondage spécial, Prostitution des mineurs: Jurisprudence," DB 408, APP. See also Jean-Claude Féray, "Pédés," 15-16.

35. Préfecture de Police, "Service des Mœurs: Règlement," October 15, 1878, DA 851, 9, APP.

36. Article 330 was, of course, used to police other kinds of sexual behavior as well. It was particularly important to artists and theater owners, especially toward the end of the century and into the twentieth. Marcela Iacub, *Through the Keyhole: A History of Sex, Space, and Public Modesty in Modern France,* trans. Vinay Swamy (Manchester, U.K.: Manchester University Press, 2016), 71.

37. It is interesting to note the similarities between this interpretation of the law and the problems faced by German police and jurists in the pre-Nazi period. The infamous Paragraph 175, which forbade male homosexual acts in Germany, often required evidence of anal penetration for prosecution. On this aspect of Paragraph 175, see Geoffrey J. Giles, "Legislating Homophobia in the Third Reich: The Radicalization of Prosecution against Homosexuality by the Legal Profession," *German History* 23, no. 3 (2005): 339–354; Robert Beachy, *Gay Berlin: Birthplace of a Modern Identity* (New York: Vintage, 2014), chap. 2; Laurie Marhoefer, *Sex and the Weimar Republic: German Homosexual Emancipation and the Rise of the Nazis* (Toronto: University of Toronto Press, 2015), 73–74.

38. Rapport, December 28, 1843, "Palais-Royal. Dossier général," JC 33, formerly BM2 32, APP.

the local establishments that served the men who came to the Palais-Royal.[39] And yet the reticence of the police to intervene, even when these men were "very openly" soliciting, points to how, even as the police referred to the existence of indecent pederasts, they continued to define the indecent around specific acts of pederasty.

The absence of pederasty from the law codes thus posed a conundrum for the police. While they were sure that certain same-sex sexual behaviors indicated a deviant and dangerous personality, they had little legal recourse unless they witnessed an actual act. This tension between knowledge of the person and that of behavior shaped police approaches to public same-sex sexual activity in nineteenth-century Paris. The lack of a clear definition of the "indecent" provided an opening for men to seek sex with other men without contravening the law, an opening not offered to women who sold sex. This tension frustrated the police, who nevertheless sought to manage the existence of public same-sex sexual solicitation. One 1853 report made this point explicit, listing known pederasts but complaining that since their "immoral acts take place in their interiors, only chance could lead to their arrest."[40] Men who sought sex with other men thus managed to appropriate the spaces of Paris, remain known to the citizens and to the police, and still evade arrest by ensuring they never behaved too indecently nor too publicly. Solicitation may have been public, but it was often not indecent enough to justify an arrest. As the criminologist Alexandre Lacassagne put it later, in 1878, "It is publicity that the law punishes. By public offense, it means acts and actions contrary to good morals, but not obscene propositions or injury by words."[41] Even as the police defined these men as pederasts on the basis of their observable behavior, they remained reticent to intervene without actually witnessing an act of pederasty.

This tension between the moral imperatives of street policing and the letter of the law became more acute as the century wore on. After receiving a number of anonymous letters drawing the police's attention to areas where pederasts were meeting in 1869, the police drew up a short report that noted: "Surveillance has frequently been undertaken in the areas indicated, and one does see there individuals stationing themselves at the access point of the urinals, stopping there five or six times and pretending to urinate, but they do not engage in any touching, and their entire ring consists simply of soliciting among themselves."[42] The officer acknowledged the problem, identified

---

39. Rapport, January 28, 1844, "Palais-Royal. Dossier général," JC 33, formerly BM2 32, APP.

40. Rapport, August 9, 1853, DA 230, doc. 247, APP.

41. Alexandre Lacassagne, *Précis de médecine judiciaire* (Paris: G. Masson, 1878), 452.

42. Rapport: Réponses à des lettres signalant des rendez-vous de pédérastes, March 23, 1869, DA 230, doc. 356, APP.

his ability to step in, but also noted the difficulty he faced in gathering the firsthand evidence he believed he needed for an arrest. In fact, he concluded his report by arguing, "It is impossible with the current state of legislation to intervene in such conditions."[43] One sees a similar lament in a surveillance report from 1872: "It is true that pederasts sometimes promenade under the galleries and in the garden of the Palais-Royal," it claimed, "but up until now we have yet to notice enough evidence of a nature to justify their arrest."[44] They had identified pederasts but would not arrest them without seeing pederasty.

This is not to say that the police followed a completely hands-off approach to men who sought sex with other men in public. Certainly the very fact of surveillance undercuts any possible claim that men who sought sex with other men in nineteenth-century Paris escaped censure or the weight of police oppression. In fact, the police sought a variety of ways around these limitations. Anti-vagrancy statutes, for instance, were sometimes used to confine pederasts. In 1820 the *commissaire de police* of the Tuileries neighborhood wrote to the prefecture lamenting that because they were not willing to allow "these infamous sodomites" the time to "let themselves be caught in the act, I have no choice but to arrest them on strong suspicion" and hold them for a night for not having their papers.[45] Ten years later the same strategy was used when eighteen men were arrested at the Palais-Royal for "not having any papers and were known for engaging in the infamous taste of pederasty, from which they make their living."[46] Félix Carlier, head of the morals brigade during the Second Empire, claimed that the authorities used a law of July 9, 1852, allowing the police to "expel for two years from the department of the Seine any individual found without refuge or means of existence," against pederasts.[47] The charge of vagrancy, as with many other petty crimes used to excuse police harassment of the working class and newcomers to the city of

---

43. Ibid.

44. Rapport: Surveillances au Palais Royal, July 1, 1872, "Palais-Royal. Dossier général," JC 33, formerly BM2 32, APP.

45. De Marug, August 5, 1820, DA 230, doc. 3, APP. John Merriman has described the use of vagrancy laws and the right of the police to ask anyone for their papers in the context of the early nineteenth century in John Merriman, *Police Stories: Building the French State, 1815–1851* (Oxford: Oxford University Press, 2006), 118–120. The use of vagrancy to police sexual behavior was also common in London. See Michal Shapira, "Indecently Exposed: The Male Body and Vagrancy in Metropolitan London before the Fin de Siècle," *Gender and History* 30, no. 1 (2018): 52–69.

46. Rapport: Arrestation sur la voie publique de plusieurs pédérastes, September 19, 1832, DA 230, doc. 19, APP.

47. Félix Carlier, *Études de pathologie sociale: Les deux prostitutions (1860–1870)* (Paris: E. Dentu, 1887), 472. I was drawn to this passage in Carlier's book by Sylvie Chaperon, *Les origines de la sexologie (1850–1900)* (Paris: Payot et Rivages, 2012), 66.

Paris, thus also served as a useful tool for managing public evidence of same-sex sexual activity. The crossing of gender privilege (the assumption that men had the right to the city) with class privilege (some men had more rights to the city than others) shaped the interaction between the police and men who sought sex with other men. In this respect, the policing of male same-sex sexual activity rested on a process of class discipline that complemented the policing of female prostitution.

The use of vagrancy to harass men who sought sex with other men could only ever be haphazard in nature; the strategy's very reliance on the class status of its victims underscores its relative limitations. By the Second Empire, the police started to put together more systematic processes for monitoring, managing, and arresting men who sought sex with other men. For example, Louis Canler, the head of the Sûreté during the Second Republic, began to maintain a list of known pederasts, a practice that was continued through the Second Empire.[48] These records, unfortunately for the historian but perhaps fortunately for the accused, were not consistent in laying out the reasons for any individual arrest, if there even was one. The goal was to compile compromising information rather than to necessarily facilitate arrest.[49] As such, these registers illustrate the relative lack of protection social class provided to some men who sought sex with other men. Indeed, it demonstrates the reverse: that evidence of same-sex sexual desire could puncture the prerogatives of class.

During the early Third Republic, the police kept another register of "Pederasts and Others," which more carefully noted the crime and punishments for each relevant entry, of which "public offense against decency" was the most common.[50] The register does record some cases where someone was taken in for the crime in flagrante delicto, as in the cases of Ernest Porin and Jérome Dziersbicki, who were arrested together near the Bourse on May 15, 1873.[51] In other cases the police had to find other reasons for an arrest. For instance, on September 18, 1874, the police detained a man named Ernest Féron for "*outrage à la morale publique et aux bonnes mœurs* [offense against good morals], for having had shameful relations with a person named Rousseau for six months." Féron, then, was not arrested for any specific act, nor for having committed an act against public "decency," but rather under part of the legal code more often used against pornography and illicit publications. Perhaps this decision explains why he was let go after his interrogation, de-

48. Féray, "*Pédés,*" 13–15. These are the registers BB4 and BB5 in the APP.
49. Claude Féray's point that the register may have first emerged as a means of monitoring political foes may explain the lack of rigor in its record keeping. Féray, "*Pédés,*" 16–19.
50. William Peniston analyzed this register in his *Pederasts and Others.*
51. "Pédérastes et divers," BB6, 4, APP.

spite having given "a most complete confession."[52] The police, therefore, well understood the limits the penal code placed on them. Some agents may have wanted to arrest "pederasts," but they were often forced to be on the lookout for acts of pederasty. The case of Féron's lover Rousseau stands as a useful example. The police turned their attention to Rousseau two days after Féron's arrest and took him in along with a man named Charles Weber. Both Rousseau and Weber were charged with offenses against public decency (Rousseau was additionally charged with corrupting a minor, as Weber was nineteen years old), because Weber's "door had been left open onto the street."[53] The records are too fragmentary to trace the full contours of this love triangle—though the police do note that the three of them shared an address—nor do they confirm my own suspicion that Féron gave the other two up during his "complete" interrogation or by leaving that door open (or both). They do note, however, that both Rousseau and Weber were sentenced to jail time (Rousseau received two years, Weber six months) and a two-hundred-franc fine. That open door enabled the police to see or imagine themselves seeing the two men in the act and then to prosecute and sentence them. Indeed, the very fact that the police made sure to note in the register that the door was open indicates its significance to justifying the arrest in the first place.

The difficulties the police faced underscore the irony at the heart of their project. While they enunciated written instructions and called commissions to design a system that regulated female prostitution, those captured by it ultimately had no legal protection. While no consistent framework governed how the police approached men who sought sex with other men, pederasts still possessed certain protections under the law. This contradiction can be well illustrated by a pair of arrests. When Louise Odessa Lapie was arrested for "Prostitution on the boulevards as an unregistered prostitute [and for] soliciting men," she was punished "administratively," meaning she was handled internally by the police, without referral to the judicial system.[54] When her sometime companion—seemingly both in bed and out of bed—Georges Alexandre Gondouin was arrested for public offenses against decency a year later "for a series of offenses in a urinal of the Champs-Élysées," he was sentenced to a year of prison and a two-hundred-franc fine.[55] Thus, women who sold sex had a kind of semi-official status endowed by the police, but their relationship with the authorities was essentially "arbitrary." In contrast, while men who sought sex with other men had no clear and identifiable re-

---

52. Ibid., 63.

53. Ibid. The charge of corruption of a minor was applied when the "victim" was under the age of twenty-one. See Revenin, *Homosexualité et prostitution masculine,* 171.

54. "Péderastes et diverses," BB6, 27, APP.

55. Ibid., 62.

lationship with the authorities, they found themselves prosecuted under an actual law.

One possible response to the police's difficulty was to redefine pederasty as a kind of prostitution. In doing so, they would be able to puncture men's relative protection, which existed only because of the incoherence of the law itself. To the police, the apparent clarity of the category of the prostitute—underscored by police confidence in identifying them—contrasted with the apparent incoherence of men who sought sex with other men. The need to witness an act was as much a requirement of the penal code as it was an indication of the police's relative lack of confidence in knowing who was and was not a pederast. Our own difficulty today in determining the precise circumstances under which a man would be arrested for seeking sex with another man speaks to the fundamental confusion that characterized police efforts to regulate same-sex sexual activity.

Constructing the Venal Male Body

The lack of a clear regulatory apparatus governing men who sought sex with other men provided an opening for other self-proclaimed experts to intervene. The "worrying increase" in "pederasty and especially pederastic prostitution" justified the production of a set of discourses that strove to unite the act of pederasty with specific individuals in order to support police intervention.[56] By developing a system of sexual identification built around the detection of behavioral and physical signs, expert commentators tried to distinguish the pederast from other Parisians whether he was caught committing an act or not. In order to accomplish this feat, these doctors, sexologists, moral commentators, and police authorities drew on their confidence that they already possessed the ability to identify and categorize another sexual deviant: the prostitute. Just as the police distinguished between respectable and disreputable public womanhood—a distinction refracted through both a class-based ideological lens and a system of administration administered by the police—so too did they try to recognize the male pederast. The prostitute lacked the legal protections afforded to men, even those who deviated in their sexual behavior, in part because their very profession marked them as indecent.[57] By equating the male pederast with the female prostitute, indeed by constructing male-male sexual relations as forms of prostitution, the male body too could be made indecent. Even as the police remained wary of the limits of the law, then, they witnessed

---

56. Lacassagne, *Précis de médecine judiciaire,* 453–454.

57. Clyde Plumauzille, *Prostitution et révolution: Les femmes publiques dans la cité républicaine (1789–1804)* (Ceyzérieu, France: Champ Vallon, 2016), 138–139.

and promoted a discourse that justified violating it. Police attention to the problem of pederasty remained constantly in tension between these two poles.

Commentators who turned to pederasty were able to draw on an existing literature on prostitution and its regulation. Until the rise of the abolitionist movement against regulationism and then degeneration theory, the discourse around female prostitution remained relatively stable in France, with Parent-Duchâtelet's work remaining a touchstone.[58] Indeed, it is there that we perceive some initial efforts to relate female prostitution to same-sex sexual activity more broadly: Parent-Duchâtelet famously associated prostitution with the potential for "tribadism." Complementing Vidocq's claims regarding prison pederasty, Parent-Duchâtelet argued that prostitutes often became susceptible to this vice in prison communities.[59] As an acquired taste, tribadism was latent in all prostitutes: "One can therefore consider tribades as fallen into the final degree of vice in which a human creature can achieve."[60] The history of female same-sex desire in nineteenth-century France may indeed also be inscribed within the history of prostitution.[61] In fact, the police never devoted much attention to women's same-sex sexual activity, in part because they were already doing so through the regulation of prostitution.

The direct link between prostitution and tribadism did begin to break apart by the end of the century, when both the police and moral commentators began to notice the existence of female spaces catering to those with same-sex desires, as well as the existence of tribades who did not, in fact, belong to a prostitutional milieu.[62] In either case, lesbian relations never seemed as threatening

---

58. Nye, *Crime, Madness, and Politics,* 158–170; Alain Corbin, *Les filles de noce: Misère sexuelle et prostitution au XIXe siècle* (Paris: Flammarion, 1982), 37.

59. Alexandre Parent-Duchâtelet, *De la prostitution dans la ville de Paris, considérée sous le rapport de l'hygiène publique, de la morale et de l'administration,* 3rd ed. (Paris: J.-B. Baillière, 1857), 1:162–163.

60. Ibid., 1:167.

61. On the relationship between lesbianism and prostitution, see, for example, Catherine Van Casselaer, *Lot's Wife: Lesbian Paris, 1890–1914* (Liverpool: Janus Press, 1986), chap. 1; Leslie Choquette, "Degenerate or Degendered? Images of Prostitution and Homosexuality in the French Third Republic," *Historical Reflections/Réflexions Historiques* 23, no. 2 (1997): 205–228; Murat, *La loi du genre,* 68–78.

62. See, for instance, the dossier on the late nineteenth-century café, "Le Souris" at 29 rue Bréda, in JC 48, formerly BM2 31, and Ali Coffignon, *Paris-Vivant: La corruption à Paris* (Paris: Librairie Illustrée, 1888), chap. 21. On lesbian culture at the fin de siècle, see Francesca Canadé Sautman, "Invisible Women: Lesbian Working-Class Culture in Paris, 1880–1930," in *Homosexuality in Modern France,* ed. Jeffrey Merrick and Bryant T. Ragan Jr. (New York: Oxford University Press, 1996), 177–201; Nicole G. Albert, "De la topographie invisible à l'espace public et littéraire: Les lieux de plaisir lesbien dans le Paris de la Belle Époque," *Revue d'histoire moderne et contemporaine* 4, nos. 53–54 (2006): 87–105; Leslie Choquette, "Gay Paree: The Origins of Lesbian and Gay Commercial Culture in the French Third Republic," *Contemporary French Civilization* 41, no. 1 (2016): 1–24. On the broader expansion of lesbian representation at the end

to the police as male-male assignations. This lacuna was due to how women's same-sex sexual relations could serve as a kind of voyeuristic male pleasure, the notion that female same-sex sexual desire did not disrupt the family in the same way as male same-sex sexual desire, and the fact that the police themselves understood lesbian relations as part of an already regulated phenomenon.[63] Most important, in many European countries, the social approval of intense female friendships in the nineteenth century provided another kind of avenue for the expression of female same-sex sexual desire while also providing a kind of cover for those who did engage in same-sex sexual activity.[64]

The notion of lesbianism as a kind of ultimate vice, either a perversion of acceptable female-female relations or the culmination of the fall into calumny, parallels conceptions of male same-sex sexual activity during the period. Indeed, though the connection was never explicit, this nascent discourse on lesbianism could be seen as a precondition for using female prostitution to understand and justify attention to other forms of sexual deviancy. Female prostitution, in fact, seemed to be the very thing that enabled discussion and policing of men who sought sex with other men when experts turned to the subject in increasing numbers at the mid-century. This is not to say that French commentators had entirely ignored male same-sex sexual activity before this moment or that the link between same-sex sexual activity and prostitution was wholly new.[65] Rather, mid-century thinkers combined emerging criminological theories with older conceptions of sexual activity in order to define pederasts as prostitutes.

This process began with the most important French work on the subject, forensic pathologist Ambroise Tardieu's *Étude médico-légale sur les attentats*

of the century, see Lowry Gene Martin, "Desire, Fantasy, and the Writing of Lesbos-sur-Seine, 1880–1939" (Ph.D. diss., University of California, Berkeley, 2010); Gretchen Schultz, *Sapphic Fathers: Discourses of Same-Sex Desire from Nineteenth-Century France* (Toronto: University of Toronto Press, 2015); Nicole G. Albert, *Lesbian Decadence: Representations in Art and Literature of Fin-de-Siècle France,* trans. Nancy Erber and William Peniston (New York: Harrington Park Press, 2016).

63. On some of these themes in France and elsewhere, see Leila J. Rupp, "Sexual Fluidity 'Before Sex,'" *Signs* 37, no. 4 (2012): 849–856; Gabrielle Houbre, *Le livre des courtisanes: Archives secrètes de la police des mœurs, 1861–1876* (Paris: Tallandier, 2006), 31–33; Choquette, "Gay Paree," 2–3.

64. On female friendship, see esp. Lillian Faderman, *Surpassing the Love of Men: Romantic Friendship and Love between Women from the Renaissance to the Present* (New York: Morrow, 1981); Karen V. Hansen, "'No Kisses Is Like Youres': An Erotic Friendship between Two African-American Women during the Mid-Nineteenth Century," *Gender and History* 7, no. 2 (1995): 153–182; Martha Vicinus, *Intimate Friends: Women Who Loved Women, 1778–1928* (Chicago: University of Chicago Press, 2004); Sharon Marcus, *Between Women: Friendship, Desire, and Marriage in Victorian England* (Princeton, N.J.: Princeton University Press, 2007).

65. See, for example, Merrick, "Commissioner Foucault," 291.

aux mœurs (1857).[66] While not of the same scope as Parent-Duchâtelet's book on prostitution, Tardieu's was similarly influential regarding male same-sex sexual activity as it was revised and expanded until his death in 1879. Unlike Parent-Duchâtelet, who sought to legitimize a preexisting regulatory system centered on the female prostitution, Tardieu wanted to secure relatively new roles for the medical profession within the judicial system. Building on the work of alienists who claimed a role in determining the fault of an accused criminal, Tardieu saw the doctor as a final arbiter of the guilt or innocence of those who committed sexual crimes.[67] Medical expertise lent weight to the regulation of sex just as the use of that expertise by the authorities lent legitimacy to the doctors who participated in the system. Over the decades, medical authorities such as Tardieu accrued a great deal of cultural authority. Indeed, well after other doctors and sexologists challenged Tardieu's conclusions, more popular texts by moralists and retired police officers continued to cite and refer to his arguments—sometimes by simply reprinting long passages—through the end of the century.[68] Law courts as well, especially in the provinces, continued to use his ideas through the end of the century.[69]

---

66. Ambroise Tardieu, *Étude médico-légale sur les attentats aux mœurs* (Paris: J.-B. Baillière, 1857). On Tardieu's contribution to the study of pederasty, see Antony R. H. Copley, *Sexual Moralities in France, 1780–1980: New Ideas on the Family, Divorce, and Homosexuality* (London: Routledge, 1989), 105–107; Vernon A. Rosario, *The Erotic Imagination: French Histories of Perversity* (New York: Oxford University Press, 1997), 71–79; Murat, *La loi du genre,* 112–120.

67. The relationship between medical texts and the police was mutually reinforcing. Prefect of Police C. J. Lecour, for instance, began his 1870 defense of the regulationist system not with a description of his own experience as a police officer but by reporting on the conclusions of a medical conference on the subject held in 1867. C. J. Lecour, *La prostitution à Paris et à Londres, 1789–1870* (Paris: P. Asselin, 1870), chap. 1. On the relationship between sexology and the judicial system see Chaperon, *Les origines de la sexologie,* chap. 3. On the early nineteenth-century history of psychiatry, see esp. Jan Goldstein, *Console and Classify: The French Psychiatric Profession in the Nineteenth Century* (Cambridge: Cambridge University Press, 1987).

68. On Tardieu and his place in the broader development of French notions of homosexuality, see Robert Nye, "Sex Difference and Male Homosexuality in French Medical Discourse, 1830–1930," *Bulletin of the History of Medicine* 63, no. 1 (1989): 40; Rosario, "Pointy Penises," 152. Examples of reuse of Tardieu's work during this period include Léo Taxil, *La prostitution contemporaine: Étude d'une question sociale* (Paris: Librairie Populaire, 1884), 301–356; Caufeynon, *La pédérastie: Historique, causes, la prostitution pédéraste, mœurs des pédérastes, observations médico-légales* (Paris: Offenstadt, 1902), 60, 67. Tardieu's work, in fact, remains influential in certain areas of the world. It is still used in Egypt, for instance, to identify suspected homosexuals. See Scott Long, "When Doctors Torture: The Anus and the State in Egypt and Beyond," *Health and Human Rights* 7, no. 2 (2004): 114–140; Lizzie Dearden, "Egypt Still Using Anal Examinations to Detect and Imprison 'Chronic Homosexuals,'" *The Independent,* February 17, 2015, available at https://www.independent.co.uk/news/world/africa/egypt-still-using-anal-examinations-to-detect-and-imprison-chronic-homosexuals-10051103.html, accessed December 19, 2017.

69. Chaperon, *Les origines de la sexologie,* 77.

Tardieu's influence can be well understood in light of the argument of the text, which claimed that the victims and perpetrators of sexual crimes retained evidence of these acts on their bodies.[70] His emphasis on the acquired signs of pederasty underscores how his project stood between two poles: on the one hand, he understood pederasty as a vice into which one could fall; on the other hand, he grounded such a turn in physical features that revealed themselves well after the initial act. This tension reflects the position of the pederast within the law itself. While the public offense against decency revolved around specific behaviors, the effort to control same-sex sexual activity required knowledge of how to recognize a specific group of people.

To Tardieu, the public offense against decency was essentially a male act: "We well know the material and moral reasons that can prevent women from publicly committing acts capable of harming decency. Those that I have had the occasion to examine were all old women, almost septuagenarians, *rentiers,* retired shopkeepers, idlers, arrested in public places at the moment when they were indulging in obscene exhibitions and touching."[71] Tardieu's inability to envision many cases of women offending decency—omitting even prostitution from his list of examples—reflects an unwillingness to confront the possibility of female sexual agency even as he reinforces a hygienist discourse that associated publicity with masculinity.[72] Indeed, the second section of his book, the only one to feature women as its subject, focuses on cases of rape. Yet even there his interest in the signs of rape on women's bodies is not about them but about the guilt or innocence of the accused man. Tardieu's attention remains fixed on his true interest: male perpetrators. His own indulgence regarding male sexual violence—at one point he excuses a husband who had been abusing his wife during sex by indulging in "ardor that was a bit brutal," because he had not gone so far as to sodomize her—underscores his ultimate disinterest not only in women but also in intervening in male sexual privilege.[73] Instead he sought to place two kinds of men who threatened public order—rapists and sodomites—under his and the law's authority.

In Part 1, Tardieu distinguishes between the broad legal category of the

---

70. Ambroise Tardieu, *Étude médico-légale sur les attentats aux mœurs,* 3rd ed. (Paris: J.-B. Baillière, 1859), 141–156. All subsequent citations to Tardieu's *Étude médico-légale* refer to this edition of the text. On Tardieu's system, see esp. Rosario, "Pointy Penises," 148–153. See also A. Davidson, *Emergence of Sexuality,* 119–120.

71. Tardieu, *Étude médico-légale,* 4. Lacassagne agreed that those most likely to commit a public offense against decency were men. Lacassagne, *Précis de médecine judiciaire,* 453.

72. However, this is not to say that female prostitutes were not actually at risk of contravening Article 330. William Peniston and Lola Gonzalez-Quijano note that prostitutes could also be arrested for violating this law. Peniston, *Pederasts and Others,* 18; Lola Gonzalez-Quijano, *Capitale de l'amour: Filles et lieux de plaisir à Paris aux XIXe siècle* (Paris: Vendémiaire, 2015), 89.

73. Tardieu, *Étude médico-légale,* 124.

public offense against decency and the specific individuals so often caught up by it. For if, according to him, offenses against public decency were so obvious that "everyone knows what they mean," the same could hardly be said for male same-sex sexual activity specifically.[74] Indeed, this section of the book was "of only secondary importance," because the offense described was, by definition, one that took place "in the presence of witnesses," which meant that he and other pathologists were rarely needed.[75] Doctors did have a role to play—as we have seen in the case of urinals—when the accused made "excuses that could justify" having committed an offense, because only the doctor was in a position to confirm or deny the validity of the excuse.[76] Tardieu's book thus opens by implicitly reinforcing the notion that the very concept of "decency" was self-evident to all who possessed it. At the same time, Tardieu's willingness to countenance such excuses for behaving indecently in the first place speaks to his continuing concern that the indecent was not always so clear, a frustration more overtly expressed by his police allies.

If female prostitutes were, by definition, indecent, then men had to be placed into careful context in order for a similar determination to be made by the authorities. Tardieu thus concluded his brief discussion of the offense in general by declaring that doctors "must never neglect to see if traces of pederasty exist on individuals arrested for public offenses against decency; we must never forget that this legal qualification is almost the only one under which this shameful vice can, when it is possible, be repressed."[77] The tension within this discussion stems from Tardieu's evident faith that public offenses against decency were readily understood by those who witnessed them and his continuing conviction of the absolute need for doctors in order to locate evidence of pederasty. If the medical exam revealed "traces of pederasty" after an arrest, then the male suspect deserved to be prosecuted. The specific act for which the suspected pederast was arrested was irrelevant to his existence as such, which justified "repression." Tardieu's very project, then, was predicated on resolving a tension between the preservation of male authority and justifying medical and legal intervention into that authority under only precise circumstances.

Tardieu may be most remembered for declaring that active pederasts had "pointy penises" and passive pederasts had "flaccid buttocks" and for describing their effeminate characteristics, but his most effective move to justify

---

74. Ibid. 3.

75. Ibid. 3–4. In support of this claim, Tardieu quotes Alphonse Devergie, *Médecine légale, théorique et pratique*, 3rd ed. (Paris: Germer-Baillière. 1852), 1: 342. The quotation actually appears in Devergie, *Médecine légale*, 1:529.

76. Tardieu, *Étude médico-légale,* 4.

77. Ibid., 5–6.

subjecting pederasts to the police was to associate them with the dangers of female prostitution.[78] As he declared, in the third and final part of his book, "The most common and dangerous conditions under which pederasty is exercised are those of true prostitution, which, if it is not sheltered under the tolerance that protects female prostitution, is no less spread out, organized in some way like it, and constitutes in certain large cities the necessary complement."[79] The "most common" form of pederasty was simply prostitution "organized" in the same ways as its female counterpart. The informal organization of men who sought sex with other men may not benefit from police "protection," but it remained as "spread out" and "organized" as the tolerance system. As he continues to explain, like female prostitution, male prostitution had "its own special personnel, its own meeting places, its own particular habits."[80] The two were "necessary" complements, dependent on each other. They thus constituted a self-contained system that could, in theory, be addressed at one and the same time. Female prostitution may be regulated, but male prostitution—and male pederasty more broadly—too could be made amenable to such regulation by virtue of its similar organization and dependency on it.

Tardieu attempted to render pederasts amenable to sexual regulation by virtue of their participation in the venal economy. Even if this figure was biologically male, it would be as vulnerable to police arrest as any working-class woman. Tardieu emphasizes their union by incorporating the male prostitute within the tolerance economy itself. A prostitute once told Tardieu that "she often encounters on the streets young men who provoke men to debauchery as she does," and he reports that "a young man . . . was found to be bearing the card of a fille publique when he was arrested." In another case, Tardieu reports, a madam had young men dress as women for her clients: "The concert of the two prostitutions is so constant that we have seen pimps, in order to attract pederasts, use women dressed as men; and even more often young men have dressed as women in order to fool the police or hide the shameful preferences of the men who seek them out and take them with them."[81] Tardieu's conflation of male and female prostitution operated through two intersecting frameworks. On the one hand, he situated the business of male prostitution in terms of its female counterpart. He goes on to explain how men who sought sex with other men had constructed and appropriated spaces in which to engage in sexual encounters, even though it had no "tolerated

---

78. Rosario, "Pointy Penises," 149–151.
79. Tardieu, *Étude médico-légale,* 125.
80. Ibid., 128.
81. Ibid., 129.

refuge."[82] On the other hand, this business was essentially gendered female: "The metamorphosis is almost so complete" that a young pederast once claimed that the head of the morals police would be "quite embarrassed" if he had come across one of his compatriots in a "dress instead of pants," Tardieu reported.[83] The equation of the female prostitute with the pederast was thus so comprehensive that even those tasked with rooting them out would not be able to tell the difference. Hence, Tardieu implies—but never directly states—that perhaps the police should treat them as if there were no difference.

The Pederast as Prostitute

Tardieu's seminal text participated in and perpetuated a particular view of male same-sex sexual activity that linked it to the primary focus of the police: female prostitution. In doing so, he helped render such behavior understandable and recognizable to both the police and to other Parisians. The venal male body he enunciated entered both expert and popular discourse and remained a common reference point for both men who sought sex with other men and those who policed them through the 1880s. Indeed, the connection between female prostitution and male same-sex sexual activity more broadly provided the grounds on which nineteenth-century Parisians of all kinds came to understand the presence of public sexual activity in the city. Constructed as the target of a regulatory regime, the pederast as prostitute became a founding myth of mid- to late nineteenth-century understandings of male same-sex sexual activity in public.

Commentators and the police repeated Tardieu's claim that male and female prostitution formed "necessary complements" through the 1880s but expanded the association to incorporate all forms of male same-sex sexual desire. The "organization" not just of male prostitution but of pederasty more broadly, to these experts, took shape through social and sexual exchanges that were always venal. Félix Carlier, for example, drawing on the German sexologist Johann Ludwig Casper—both counterpart and opponent to Tardieu—wrote in his *Les deux prostitutions* (1887):

> The man who abandons himself to this sad passion enters a world entirely apart, that one could do no better than to compare it to a freemasonry of vice, having everywhere its affiliates, who recognize each other without ever being seen, who understand one another without

82. Ibid., 130–131.
83. Ibid., 129.

speaking the same language, and who take it upon themselves, as soon as one of them arrives in a country where they do not know anyone, to present him to their compatriots who welcome him with open arms into their society where, by paying for his favors, [they] procure for him the means of living if he is without resources; it's their manner of aiding one another.[84]

Although on one level this "freemasonry" could be understood as an emerging subculture—one reading of the passage would emphasize the ability of pederasts to recognize one another among strangers (see Chapter 4)—Carlier's description also erases same-sex sexual desire in favor of venality. First, by emphasizing the secrecy and separateness of this society, Carlier evokes descriptions of prostitution as a "world apart." Second, these men did not come together out of sexual attraction but rather out of a need for "resources." In this regard, sex between men transforms into a form of prostitutional exchange. The sexual relations taking place within the freemasonry make sense to Carlier only in light of the fact that some "pay" for the others' favors. That pederasts could recognize one another without—necessarily—being recognized only heightened the danger and necessitated greater intervention by the authorities.

The idea of a freemasonry of vice percolated through the discourse of the 1870s and 1880s. The writer Ali Coffignon, for instance, citing Carlier, declared, "It is not an exaggeration to say that pederasts of all nations form a kind of freemasonry."[85] Sometimes this notion was directly linked to prostitution. Published about a decade prior to Coffignon, Flévy d'Urville's *Les ordures de Paris* (1874) stated:

---

84. Carlier, *Les deux prostitutions*, 283. The idea also later emerges in slightly different terms in Marcel Proust's *Sodome et gomorrhe*, the fourth volume of *À la recherche du temps perdu*. Proust describes a "freemasonry far more extensive, more powerful and less suspected than that of the Lodges," made up of the dispersed "descendants of the Sodomites" who "have had access to every profession and pass so easily into the most exclusive clubs." However, unlike in the late nineteenth-century descriptions, the difficulty this community faced was not venality but shame. Describing the impossibility of rebuilding Sodom in order to provide a new home for them, Proust writes, "For, no sooner had they arrived there than the Sodomites would leave the town so as not to have the appearance of belonging to it, would take wives, keep mistresses in other cities, where they would find, incidentally, every diversion that appealed to them." Marcel Proust, *Remembrance of Things Past*, trans. C. K. Scott Moncrieff and Stephen Hudson, 2 vols. (London: Wordsworth Editions, 2006), 2:24, 37. On this passage and its relationship to the closet, see esp. Eve Kosofsky Sedgwick, *Epistemology of the Closet* (Berkeley: University of California Press, 1990), 222–223. Bruno Perreau's description of contemporary right-wing fears of "invasion" and "betrayal" of a "sexualist international" reflects the long duration of the fantasy of the freemasonry of vice. Bruno Perreau, *Queer Theory: The French Response* (Stanford, Calif.: Stanford University Press, 2016), 58–59. On Casper, see Spector, *Violent Sensations*, 82–89.

85. Coffignon, *La corruption à Paris*, 328.

They know how to recognize one another like freemasons, through certain physiological games and some external signs, by, for example, letting one see their handkerchief, and even serving as the go-between for a prostitute, because procurers unscrupulously occupy themselves with all forms of prostitution, and this new kind of business gives birth to a social plague that the police perhaps observe, but that they certainly cannot be ignorant of.[86]

D'Urville thus links the freemasonry directly to a "new kind" of prostitution that binds both men and women. That these books reveal the existence of a kind of community between desiring men is immediately disavowed in favor of the idea that they were all simply prostitutes and clients.

The freemasonry of vice included people from all backgrounds. Emphases on the diversity of the freemasonry showcased a growing concern not only that pederasty encouraged cross-class sociability but also that it effaced those distinctions. After directly quoting Tardieu's description of the pederast's physiognomy, Dr. Cox-Algit voiced this anxiety in his brief pamphlet on male prostitution: "Hideous sect! It counts the most disparate people among its numbers of affiliates: it's an agglomeration of shameful youth and ignoble old men, who occupy the most humble and the most brilliant positions in the world."[87] D'Urville too claimed, "One finds these *Gomorreans* among all ranks; some have university degrees, wracked by vices they contracted in college, forgetting themselves in order to satisfy their bestial passion until they live at the very heart of this Parisian mud that creates the notables of the prisons."[88] Sodomy and same-sex sexual desire between men of different stations ultimately brings them all down to the same level, erasing the distinction between client and prostitute as well. As Coffignon argued, "The shared vice effaces all social differences; the master and the *valet de chambre* are on the same footing; the millionaire and the tramp fraternize; the functionary and the ex-convict exchange their ignoble caresses."[89] If the implication was, on the one hand, that the rich were buying the poor, he also implied, on the other hand, that the exchange actually rendered the two as equals. The ten-

---

86. Flévy D'Urville, *Les ordures de Paris* (Paris: Librairie Sartorius, 1874), 69.

87. Dr. Cox-Algit, *Anthropophilie, ou étude sur la prostitution masculine à notre époque* (Nantes, France: Morel, 1881), 4.

88. Although we now often understand Gomorrah as referring to lesbians, d'Urville clearly meant it to refer to men who sought sex with other men. D'Urville, *Les ordures de Paris,* 69. On the association of Sodom and Gomorrah with Paris and with homosexuality, see Michael Sibalis, "Paris-Babylone/Paris-Sodome: Images of Homosexuality in the Nineteenth-Century City," in *Images of the City in Nineteenth-Century France,* ed. John West-Sooby, 13–22 (Moorooka, Queensland, Australia: Boombana Publications, 1998).

89. Coffignon, *La corruption à Paris,* 330.

sion between hierarchy and equality thus shaped this discourse as commentators strove to simultaneously emphasize its familiarity (it was hierarchical like prostitution) and its danger (it effaced difference). Female prostitution, for all its danger, maintained a certain social acceptability by virtue of the way it reinforced social and gender hierarchies so long as it occurred within the tolerated system. Male prostitution was particularly dangerous because it failed to uphold the distinction between buyer and seller.

One reason, therefore, that commentators emphasized the connections between male pederasty and female prostitution specifically was to reinforce recognizable distinctions. However, in doing so, these conceptualizations of male same-sex sexual behavior could also efface the difference between the male and the female prostitute. Gustave Macé argued that "their effeminate allures make them [pederasts] easy to recognize because they imitate the walk of *filles soumises* [registered prostitutes]" and "almost all are beardless or freshly shaved, never smoking, and walking in couples while laughing loudly like prostitutes."[90] Effeminacy in this description is made into a clear sign only by virtue of the taint of prostitution. It is the modifier of venality that makes the effeminate man recognizable as a pederast. The strongest language is that of Carlier, who conflated male and female prostitution in a chapter titled "Unity of the Two Prostitutions." He declared that "the solicitors, the *persilleuses* as one calls them, are true male prostitutes [*prostitués*] in all senses of the word. Between them and *filles publiques isolées,* there is an absolute identification of sentiments, of manner of being and of instincts."[91] This construction intersects with the gendered and classed dimensions of prostitution as well. Those men who sold themselves were most closely identified with their female counterparts. The poorest men who had sex with other men, the ones who rendered themselves available, were thus reconfigured as not only women but also the lowest class of woman.

One could argue that the very association of lower-class pederasts with female prostitution represented an attempt to reimpose a kind of hierarchy among them. However, by some lights, all forms of same-sex sexual behavior between men remained—in various forms—kinds of prostitution. The title of Carlier's book *Les deux prostitutions,* for instance, refers not to female and male prostitution but to female prostitution and to male pederasty as a whole. Those who solicit on the street, he argues, "especially represent conspicuous pederasty."[92] Furthermore, he later clarifies, "Pederasty and female prostitution are in fact the same thing; it's prostitution in the general sense of the

---

90. Gustave Macé, *La police parisienne: Mes lundis en prison* (Paris: G. Charpentier, 1889), 156.
91. Carlier, *Les deux prostitutions,* 354–355.
92. Ibid., 353.

word."[93] For Carlier, this relationship justified redefining the public offense against decency to encompass a broader range of behaviors that revealed the pederast. It was not just the sex act that was indecent but rather all the various ways men who sought sex with other men made themselves known on the streets: "It seems indispensable that the legislator protect, at least on the street, public decency; he should include solicitation, provocation, [and] cross-dressing as public offenses against decency. We should even prefer to go further . . . and make pederasty itself a special infraction."[94] The venal male body justified greater police intervention in the public lives of men.

These links may have been used primarily to justify police attention to men who sought sex with other men, but they did not circulate among merely moralists and police officers. The relatively limited number of sources makes generalization difficult, but police and moralist use of female prostitution to understand and rationalize attention to male same-sex sexuality percolated into the popular consciousness. For instance, in February 1869 the police received an anonymous letter complaining that on "rue Chauchat, between the rue de Provence and the Opera [in the ninth arrondissement], from 11:00 P.M. until midnight, there is a get-together of sodomites [who] solicit one another like female prostitutes." The letter goes on to describe a furnished hotel about a kilometer away on rue Notre Dame de Recouvrance in the second arrondissement where these men can go and, after "asking for the key in a certain manner," pay three francs for the opportunity to "do their nasty acts."[95] Unable to define the sodomite in its own terms, the letter writer instead reached for female prostitution as an apparently common reference point. The irony, of course, is that the letter itself reveals the author's own familiarity with the milieu, demonstrating that he understood the secret codes used to gain access to the hotel. The use of the female prostitute thus served a dual goal of unlocking those secrets and disavowing the author's own preexisting knowledge of them. The prostitute enabled the writer to speak of this other kind of sexual deviance, sodomy, without incriminating himself. The sodomites' attempt to hide floundered because they were really just another kind of prostitute even as prostitution enabled the (probable) sodomite to hide himself.

This discourse even had the potential to shape the self-conception of men who sought sex with other men themselves. Again, evidence limits broad generalization, but we can at least witness one possible outcome of the association of female prostitution with male same-sex sexual desire. In 1895 the doctor Henri Legludic published the memoirs of Arthur Belor-

---

93. Ibid., 467.
94. Ibid., 474.
95. Anonymous to Préfecture de Police, February 15, 1869, DA 230, doc. 355, APP.

get, who described their awakening to same-sex sexual desires and life as "the Countess," a cross-dressing café-concert performer during the Second Empire.[96] Legludic claimed to have received the document in 1874, and it stands as one of the few examples of same-sex sexual desire speaking for itself. As William Peniston and Nancy Erber point out, the text was written consciously as an autobiography and thus follows many of the tropes of the genre.[97] That said, it serves as one of the few ways to enter into the self-conception of someone attracted to members of their own sex during the mid-nineteenth century.

In the text, Belorget describes their gradual awareness of their same-sex sexual desires, their intense relationship with their mother, their transformation into the Countess through cross-dressing, and their eventual imprisonment for evading military service, during which they fell in love with another prisoner. Belorget may have understood their sexual desires as a defining characteristic, but those feelings remained acquired rather than innate: "At this point in my story, anyone who is reading these pages and paying attention at all must agree that, along with the innate tendencies of my character, chance had a significant role in developing in me that love of beauty and style that grew into a passion and would later degenerate into a frenzy and cause the disorders and the missteps that mark my life."[98] Although Belorget was somewhat predisposed to both same-sex sexual attraction and cross-dressing as a woman, it was only through their actual experiences that they realized such desires. Through their encounters with actresses and courtesans—met through their mother's seamstress business—they first developed their taste for "luxury." Belorget continues, directly: "There's no man on this earth, I'm convinced, who grew up surrounded by as much feminine beauty as I did, who gazed at so many pretty women's faces leaning over his cradle, smiling at him and promising him caresses, joys, and happiness."[99] Belorget thus comes to realize not simply their own desires, but the latent possibilities within all "men" through their encounters with women's fashion. It is thus that they became a "slave to beauty, luxury, and splendor."[100]

---

96. I use plural pronouns to refer to Belorget in order to emphasize their gender ambiguity. "Confidences et aveux d'un Parisien: La comtesse, Paris (1850–1861)," in *Notes et observations de médecine légal: Attentats aux mœurs,* ed. Henri Legludic (Paris: G. Masson, 1896), 237–349. The text was translated as Arthur W, "Secret Confessions of a Parisian," in *Queer Lives: Men's Autobiographies from Nineteenth-Century France,* ed. and trans. William A. Peniston and Nancy Erber (Lincoln: University of Nebraska Press, 2007), 7–72. Unless otherwise noted, citations to this text refer to Peniston and Erber's translation.

97. Peniston and Erber, *Queer Lives,* 1–2.

98. W, "Secret Confessions," 17–18.

99. Ibid., 18.

100. Ibid., 10.

Belorget's first encounters with men who sought sex with other men, including their first sexual experience, were couched in these terms as well. At boarding school, they found their first lover, Charles K:

> Having introduced me to the pleasures of the senses, Charles had destroyed all my good tendencies. This big step I had taken was irrevocable. I was lost forever—lost in my behavior and lost in my character. Having indulged in pleasure with someone older than myself, I had drunk deeply from the source of those predilections that make a man prostitute himself not by circumstance, nor by poverty, which a substantial amount of money might alleviate; no, by starting out with a boy four years older than myself, I was destined always to play the woman's role—the role of the *mignon*—that distinct and separate type among all men with similar passions.[101]

By having sex with Charles, Belorget became a "mignon," the "boy" or younger partner. Belorget understands this experience as fundamentally about pleasures that define them as "distinct and separate" even from those with "similar passions" (thus again combining their own difference with a sense of similarity from other men). Indeed, the following passage emphasizes the specific kinds of pleasures they felt in this experience: "And what pleasures for the eyes, especially the eyes, to devour someone of your own sex with the ravenous hunger of inexplicable, untranslatable looks!"[102]

The description is striking in its emphasis on the pleasures of same-sex sexual desire, but it ultimately follows the lines of the police and moral commentators by linking Belorget's actions to prostitution. Even if not out of a desire for money (in this case), their pleasures were precisely those that "make a man prostitute himself." Indeed, as Belorget increasingly participates in this milieu, they come closer to being a prostitute themselves: "Little by little I evolved into a machine for paid pleasures, and I began to lose my critical faculties by spending time exclusively with people who lived for and by pleasure."[103] Even as they express joy at finding pleasure with a man, Belorget fails to escape the confines placed around such activities that defined them as prostitution. If the ultimate decline of the female prostitute was her fall into lesbianism, then the final fall of the pederast was, perhaps, into female prostitution.

---

101. Ibid., 22.
102. Ibid.
103. Ibid., 31.

Conclusion

With the rise of a more mature field of sexology, the link between prostitution and pederasty began to lose purchase as experts increasingly focused their attention on the internal lives of those with same-sex sexual attraction. Alexandre Lacassagne's 1878 *Précis de médecine judiciaire* is a prime example of this transition. The book relied quite heavily on Tardieu for its discussion of male pederasty, quoting his description of male prostitution and emphasizing the link between same-sex sexual activity and crime.[104] And yet, despite being published during a period when the link between female prostitution and male same-sex sexual activity was well current, Lacassagne does not reference Tardieu's comments about the relationship between female prostitution and male same-sex sexual activity. Indeed, he argues that Tardieu's description of the exterior signs of pederasty "applies only to the exterior of men who prostitute themselves. But it does not apply to all individuals suffering from this complete deviation of the sexual instinct. For those there is often an original stain, and they are true moral hermaphrodites."[105] Even as Lacassagne goes on to approvingly cite Tardieu's physical signs of pederasty—while acknowledging that they had been recently challenged—he cannot help but emphasize the new language of inversion. Standing between two styles of reasoning around sex—the one venal and physical, the other internal but still vile—Lacassagne demonstrates how quickly and unevenly the discourse shifted during the early Third Republic. The emphasis on the venal male body provided a convincing discourse of male same-sex sexual activity at a particularly conservative moment in French governance and served as a unifying theory of public sexual deviance as, at heart, a form of female prostitution, but it began to fall away as new theories that emphasized innate difference emerged.

One explanation did not immediately replace the other. Doctor Louis Martineau, for instance, citing Tardieu, declared in 1881, "Pederasty constitutes a true prostitution that is like the necessary complement of feminine prostitution."[106] Especially dangerous because of its association with the practice of blackmail, male same-sex sexual activity could not entirely escape its venal associations. And yet Martineau also makes an interesting move by decoupling the sexual act most associated with pederasty—sodomy—from this conflation. Pederasty was a criminal enterprise, but "sodomy most ordi-

---

104. Lacassagne, *Précis de médecine judiciaire*, 455.

105. Ibid., 456.

106. Louis Martineau, "Leçons sur la sodomie," *L'union médicale* 31 (1881): 617.

narily appears under different circumstances. If I sometimes see it in ordinary prostitutes who, in order to augment their earnings, satisfy the depraved tastes of certain men who fear compromising themselves with pederasty, I see it more often in women who are ignorant of the abjection of an act imposed on them by their husband or lover."[107] The physical act of sodomy was thus detached from the being of the pederast. In its place remains the association with prostitution. Indeed, sodomy itself becomes more associated, in Martineau's telling, with heterosexual sexual acts rather than homosexual ones. The desire for anal sex thus no longer signifies the desire for the same sex.

This idea was later taken up by a Dr. Hayès, who, about ten years after Martineau, implied a link between the growth of pederastic prostitution and the spread of anal sex within the tolerated brothels and between spouses. Claiming that male prostitution had clearly increased—though not to the extent one saw in ancient Rome or Greece, he assured his reader—Hayès proceeds to note that "next to this genre of prostitution, there are those for whom the genital instinct seeks out satisfaction through acts against natural law, and, in this way, conjugal sodomy is very frequent."[108] Without arguing for a direct link between the rise of male prostitution and conjugal sodomy, Hayès nonetheless highlighted a more general increase in "unnatural" sexual acts. Presumably, the availability of the latter increased the desire among men for the former. Following Martineau, he claimed that sodomy was becoming more common between opposite-sex couples, even married ones, due to "three causes: ignorance, brutality, jealousy. We can explain this last by the fear of seeing the husband demand from a male or female prostitute the satisfaction of an abnormal genital desire."[109] The apparent recognition of prostitutes—whether male or female—as a source of and an outlet for particular sexual desires enforces a logic that saw prostitution as the root cause of other sexual ills. Hayès's reference to "abnormal genital desire," alongside his citations to both Tardieu and Carl Westphal, underscores how his text stands at a crossroads.[110] If work by doctors like Tardieu and police officers

---

107. Ibid., 618.

108. Dr. Hayès, *La pédérastie: Historique, conséquences funestes de ce vice honteux* (Paris: Librairie des publications modernes, 1891), 40–42. This argument was also made earlier by the official psychiatrist of the prefecture of police during the 1870s and 1880s. See Henri Legrand du Saulle, *Étude médico-légale sur la séparation de corps* (Paris: F. Savy, 1866), 6–9.

109. Hayès, *La pédérastie*, 46.

110. Carl Westphal's 1870 article on "contrary sexual sensations" is the moment Michel Foucault once pithily defined as the moment when "homosexuality was constituted . . . less by a type of sexual relations than by a certain quality of sexual sensibility, a certain way of inverting the masculine and the feminine in oneself." Carl Westphal, "Die Konträre Sexualempfindung, Symptom Eines Neuropathischen (psychopathischen) Zustandes," *Archiv für psychiatrie und*

like Carlier revealed a rather unstable sexual subject, Hayès's tentative move toward a new psychiatric sexology foreshadows later techniques of knowledge production that rooted sexual identity in the psyche.

Prostitution became the referent for other forms of social behavior that seemed "out of place," because female prostitution was the source of police authority over public sex. The effort to define these kinds of social and sexual activities thus depended on a kind of intermixture within the sexual discourse of the second half of the nineteenth century that also had social effects. Even as commentators emphasized the marginal character of female prostitution and discussed the so-called freemasonry of vice, composed of men who sought sex with other men, they also consciously brought the two together. The separation of the two groups was always both constructed and undercut by the very discourse that enunciated it. The construction of same-sex sexual activity as a form of prostitution may not have been a construction of a new subjectivity, but it was one of desire. Our ability to reconstruct how individuals felt about their encounters with one another is necessarily constrained by sources that explicitly sought to constrain and categorize people's experiences.[111]

By drawing on a preexisting discourse on female prostitution to render male same-sex sexual activity comprehensible, however, these authorities reshaped same-sex desire as necessarily venal. A new truth of public sex thus emerged at the moment that male same-sex sexual activity increasingly entered urban discourse. At the same time, this use of prostitution as a sign itself showcases how modes of sexual practice can float away from their initial referents. As the next chapter shows, public sex thus became less an act and more a way to make sense of the sights and sounds of the nineteenth-century city. Expert and police faith in their ability to "know" the prostitute was badly misplaced, but the overriding shadow of female prostitution provided a useful anchor for understanding other kinds of sexual "deviancy." This proliferation of discourse on male same-sex sexuality shared the preoccupations of preceding work on female prostitution and explicitly drew on that category of sexual activity in order to make sense of male same-sex sexual activity. Faced with a classed discourse that associated certain sexual acts by men with

---

nervenkrankheiten 2 (1870): 73–108; Michel Foucault, *The History of Sexuality,* vol. 1, *An Introduction,* trans. Robert Hurley (New York: Vintage, 1990), 43. See also A. Davidson, *Emergence of Sexuality,* 16; David M. Halperin, *How to Do the History of Homosexuality* (Chicago: University of Chicago Press, 2002), 127–130.

111. I was influenced on this point by María Elena Martínez, "Archives, Bodies, and Imagination: The Case of Juana Aguilar and Queer Approaches to History, Sexuality, and Politics," *Radical History Review* 2014, no. 120 (2014): 163–165.

debased women, the relationship between sex and gender itself was put into question as certain men were remade into certain women. Ultimately, the use of female prostitution to understand the dangers of other forms of public sexual activity provided the broader grounds for understanding the central role of sex in navigating a transforming urban environment.

4

CONSTRUCTING A PUBLIC
SEXUAL CULTURE

On November 18, 1850, a Monsieur Langangne decided he had had enough and took up his pen to write a letter to the police. Having the habit of taking an evening walk "*en flâneur*" from the Madeleine to the Faubourg Montmartre in what was then the first arrondissement (now the eighth), Langangne wrote that he had begun to notice "spectacles of shameful immorality that have painfully afflicted my sight and my spirit." These spectacles, he specified, were none other than "those offered by those beings without name, those hideous hermaphrodites!" He explained that so long as their behavior remained within "certain limits, he kept quiet, but that is impossible now that the activities of these unfortunates (who no doubt also portray themselves as advocates of the right to work, since bad examples are contagious) reach the alarming heights of organized blackmail." Indeed, Langangne proceeded to describe how, the previous day, he was "accosted" by two young men with "cheeks painted with makeup," who claimed to know him and who asked him to buy them some drinks. Surmising that the reason they approached him was that "he may have something in common with one of their brothers or friends," Langangne refused, which led the two men to launch a series of insults at him. This unpleasant encounter convinced this particular Parisian that "the boulevards are currently a veritable court of miracles planted in the middle of Sodom and Gomorrah, and soon all prom-enades on them will be forbidden not only to honest women who have not been able to show themselves for a long time, but also for men who should not have to be at odds with rascals."[1]

Langangne's complaint highlights how sexual encounters shaped mid-century urban life. As an employee within the Ministry of Finance, Langangne seemed to expect that the streets were in some ways "his." His right to them certainly outweighed that of those "hermaphrodites," a faith indicated by his self-identification as a "flâneur." The idea of the "flâneur" encapsulates a form of urban wandering predicated on class and gender privilege that permitted movement and observation of the attractions of modern city life.[2] The act of flânerie depended on the management and maintenance of perception, the clear control over what one saw and heard, as well as one's response.[3] More broadly, as Vanessa Schwartz has described it, the flâneur represents "a positionality of power—one through which the spectator assumes the position of being able to be part of the spectacle and yet command it at the same time."[4] By asserting himself as a "flâneur," then, Langangne referenced a whole host of assumptions about his place within the urban environment, all of which revolved around his ability to move about, look on, and assert himself within urban space as he wished.

In setting up this relationship, Langangne tried to distinguish himself

---

1. Langangne to Préfet de Police, November: 18, 1850, DA 230, doc. 206, APP. Luc Sante defines the *cour des miracles* as "a cluster of houses that by some mix of tradition, common accord, and benign neglect was deemed off-limits to the law and, as lore has it, where a sort of permanent feast of misrule persisted." Luc Sante, *The Other Paris* (New York: Farrar, Straus, and Giroux, 2015), 97.

2. Janet Wolff, "The Invisible *Flâneuse*: Women and the Literature of Modernity," *Theory, Culture, and Society* 2, no. 3 (1985): 37–46. Contemporary interest in the flâneur stems from the work of Charles Baudelaire and Walter Benjamin. See Charles Baudelaire, *The Painter of Modern Life and Other Essays,* trans. and ed. Jonathan Mayne (London: Phaidon Press, 1965), chap. 1; Walter Benjamin, *The Arcades Project,* ed. Rolf Tiedemann, trans. Howard Eiland and Kevin McLaughlin (Cambridge, Mass: Belknap Press, 1999), 416–455. On the flâneur, see also Keith Tester, ed. *The* Flâneur (New York: Routledge, 1994); Priscilla Parkhurst Ferguson, *Paris as Revolution: Writing the Nineteenth-Century City* (Berkeley: University of California Press, 1994), chap. 3; Catherine Nesci, *Le flâneur et les flâneuses: Les femmes et la ville à l'époque romantique* (Grenoble, France: Ellug, 2007); Mary Gluck, *Popular Bohemia: Modernism and Urban Culture in Nineteenth-Century Paris* (Cambridge, Mass.: Harvard University Press, 2005), esp. chap. 3; Gregory Shaya, "The Flâneur, the Badaud, and the Making of a Mass Public in France, circa 1860–1910," *American Historical Review* 109, no. 1 (2004): 41–77; Aruna D'Souza and Tom McDonough, eds., *The Invisible* Flâneuse? *Gender, Public Space, and Visual Culture in Nineteenth-Century Paris* (Manchester, U.K.: Manchester University Press, 2006).

3. Christopher Prendergast, *Paris and the Nineteenth Century* (Oxford, U.K.: Blackwell, 1992), 135. On the importance of sound to flânerie, see Aimée Boutin, *City of Noise: Sound and Nineteenth-Century Paris* (Urbana: University of Illinois Press, 2015). I address the senses more fully in the next chapter.

4. Vanessa R. Schwartz, *Spectacular Realities: Early Mass Culture in Fin-de-Siècle Paris* (Berkeley: University of California Press, 1998), 10.

(representative of the proper, the respectable, the *flâneur*) from those he encountered (the improper, the disreputable, the "hermaphrodite"). However, the letter ultimately reveals the difficulty in maintaining those boundaries: Langangne's encounter with the "hermaphrodites" constituted an "affliction on [his] vision and spirit." That the two men shifted from the formal (*vous*) to informal (*tu*) address in the course of their interaction highlights the threat Langangne felt. One way of reading the letter, then, is in terms of its oppositions; Langangne's letter attempted to (re)affirm an "other" against which the "respectable" could more clearly come into view, a binary supported by his brief but dismissive reference to the politics of the day and the battle over the right to work that had bloodied the Second Republic a year and a half earlier.[5]

Read against this interpretation, however, the letter reveals a social world in which the appearance of marginal figures functioned less to secure a privileged self than to sow confusion. This ambiguity rested on the relative legibility and illegibility of both the writer and the objects of his gaze. Like experts such as Tardieu, Langangne rested his legitimacy as a writer on his ability to know, delimit, and categorize those encountered. After all, although he initially declared that the men "had no name," he immediately followed up by identifying them as hermaphrodites. In fact, even as he emphasized his ability to name them, he implied that they were unable to do the same. Although they claimed to know him, they were unable to force him to cooperate.

However, Langangne was not entirely successful at asserting his own respectability against the disrepute of the men he encountered. The letter notes, after all, that he was only writing because the hermaphrodites' behavior had exceeded "certain limits." Presumably, in other words, they had been present before this moment, fixtures of a broader neighborhood culture that became an annoyance once they specifically targeted him. In addition, his admission that the "hermaphrodites" may have addressed him because "he may have something in common with" them highlights his difficulty in distinguishing his own identity from those who accosted him.[6] Although the letter may have tried to construct the writer's knowledge against the supposed ignorance of its objects, that knowledge was, in fact, premised on Langangne's own familiarity with his targets: he knew how to recognize them through their behavior and dress. That he may have "resembled" them reinforces the difficulty he faced in separating himself. He could know who they were only if he was in some sense already one of them. The "straight" flâneur thus becomes

---

5. Scott Spector has called this interpretation the "marginalization thesis." I follow his efforts to muddy this dichotomy. Scott Spector, *Violent Sensations: Sex, Crime, and Utopia in Vienna and Berlin, 1860–1914* (Chicago: University of Chicago Press, 2016), 2–3.

6. Langangne to Préfet de Police, November 18, 1850.

decidedly queer, because we can ultimately never know who he was: a victim or a participant in a culture of public sex.[7]

This chapter places the world of public sex at the center of nineteenth-century urban life. Whereas the previous chapter underscored how attempts to understand and manage same-sex sexual activity conflated such practices with female prostitution, this chapter explores how such confusion played out on the streets. In fact, the attempt to codify the kinds of sexual activity occurring on the streets spread it further by disseminating knowledge of such possibilities. That knowledge in turn shaped the use of the street by ensuring that Parisians understood the sexual implications of random encounters. This chapter therefore rejects the common distinction between marginalized prostitutes and "homosexuals" and a normative middle-class culture at mid-century. While I follow historians of both female prostitution and male homosexuality who have noted how the streets of Paris seemed to be increasingly sexualized in the wake of Haussmannization, I do not emphasize the threat of these practices to a normative urban culture.[8] Instead I highlight their centrality to nineteenth-century urban life more broadly.

In doing so, I follow work in literary criticism and queer studies that has questioned the separation between the sexual and asexual city. These studies have recognized how conceptions of the "urban" or the "modern" rest on mutually dependent notions of rational, public, asexual life and irrational, private, sexual experiences. As Rita Felski once argued, "Rather than being limited to an autonomous private sphere, affectivity and sexuality permeated nineteenth-century social space and were intimately intertwined with processes of commodification and rationalization often regarded as quintessentially modern."[9] Others have shown how the famous depictions of Charles Baudelaire and commentary by Walter Benjamin relied on supposedly marginal figures such as the lesbian and the prostitute to characterize urban modernity, a move that situates these figures at the center of understandings of the city, even as they remained disreputable.[10] Indeed, it is through that

---

7. Other considerations of the queer flâneur include Mark W. Turner, *Backward Glances: Cruising the Queer Streets of New York and London* (London: Reaktion Books, 2003), esp. chap. 2; and Dianne Chisholm, *Queer Constellations: Subcultural Space in the Wake of the City* (Minneapolis: Minnesota University Press, 2005), 46–49.

8. Alain Corbin, *Les filles de noce: Misère sexuelle et prostitution au XIXe siècle* (Paris: Flammarion, 1982), 301–303; Régis Revenin, *Homosexualité et prostitution masculines à Paris, 1870–1918* (Paris: L'Harmattan, 2005), 19.

9. Rita Felski, *The Gender of Modernity* (Cambridge, Mass: Harvard University Press, 1995), 57.

10. Deborah Parsons, *Streetwalking the Metropolis* (Oxford: Oxford University Press, 2000), 24; Julie Abraham, *Metropolitan Lovers: The Homosexuality of Cities* (Minneapolis: University of Minnesota Press, 2009), 30.

very tension between center and margin that public sex gained its power over urban space. The use of public space for sex should not be seen only in terms of anxiety by regulators and Parisians, but also as a practice that actively shaped the ways people encountered urban space.

I therefore follow the logic of Langangne's letter in order to show how sexual solicitation created a public sexual culture that threatened the distinction between sexual and nonsexual spaces and activities. The constitution of this public culture of sex was conditioned by struggles between those who sought out sexual opportunities and those who did not.[11] During this period, expert commentators, the police, and lay Parisians believed that sex was increasingly available and unavoidable on the streets of Paris. At the same time, the redevelopment of the city oriented it even more toward its image as a site of commercial "pleasure." This combination—an emphasis on the dangers of public sex and a social world that revolved around seeking out public pleasure—made sexual knowledge more essential to experiencing the city at the very time when it seemed that sex was escaping its boundaries. As the brothels failed and men who sought sex with other men were more apparent, the need to recognize the possibility of a sexual encounter, whether in order to pursue or avoid one, became more important. Public sex, therefore, should not be seen as an "other" practice against which "dominant" "norms" were defined, but rather as one way the city emerged in the first place. The need to know how to understand the possibility of encountering public sex disrupts any easy division between supposedly "illicit" forms of public sexuality and "licit" forms of social practice. Such a distinction, rarely named but often implied, never actually cohered.

Policing the "Pleasures" of Paris

New commercial enterprises, public parks, and boulevards offered opportunities for Parisians to participate in not only an emerging mass culture but also a culture of public sex. By the 1840s, Paris had already become the scene of a flourishing commercial culture centered on public amusement, especially in the western neighborhoods around the Champs-Élysées and the Grands Boulevards.[12] It is no coincidence that these were some of the spaces most associated with public sexual activity. The attempt to classify and denote the "deviant" users of Parisian space in the medical treatises and police memoirs

---

11. On "struggle" and public-making, see Michael Warner, *Publics and Counterpublics* (New York: Zone Books, 2002), 12–14.

12. H. Hazel Hahn, *Scenes of Parisian Modernity: Culture and Consumption in the Nineteenth Century* (New York: Palgrave Macmillan, 2009), 46.

examined in the previous chapter was a direct response to a shifting urban landscape explicitly designed to facilitate some pleasures and not others, for some Parisians and not others. The effort to denote a distinction between pleasure and deviance—often read as that between commerce and sex—often only revealed their mutual imbrication.

Efforts to manage commercial opportunities, therefore, were often also efforts to manage the city's sexual life. Unsurprisingly, the Palais-Royal became one of the first areas where the police tried to enforce the distinction between selling goods and selling sex.[13] In January 1840 the Commission Spéciale pour la Répression de la Prostitution turned its attention to press reports and complaints that shops and boutiques run by women were being increasingly used as sites of prostitution.[14] The commission was especially concerned that "nothing distinguished" the two kinds of establishments, those selling "useful objects" and those selling sex: "A young woman, even a man who would normally avoid places of debauchery, could confidently enter them in order to buy something." While the man, "whether he succumbs or resists," would come away from the incident lightly, "for the young girl, the test can be fatal and the evil irreparable."[15] In this instance, the commission's problem was less the actual physical presence of prostitution in the Palais-Royal than their lack of control over the way it appeared. So long as they remained incapable of ensuring that shoppers knew how to recognize spaces of prostitution, the authorities remained deeply conscious of their failure to manage the spaces of the city. At the end of the meeting, the prefect of police declared that he would redouble his efforts to use his existing administrative authority over prostitution to end the practice of using boutiques for prostitution.[16]

Matters came to a head in the fall of 1845 when the police organized a raid on these shops (or *comptoirs* as they were known) of the Palais-Royal. The report that followed explained that "these *filles de comptoir* receive no wages. . . . The advantage of their situation consists in being at the center of a continuous moving crowd, able to easily attract men and to have relative freedom of their time and their person. The *maitresses de comptoir* demand

13. Victoria Thompson, *The Virtuous Marketplace: Women and Men, Money and Politics in Paris, 1830–1870* (Baltimore: Johns Hopkins University Press, 2000), 22–23.

14. The commission specifically mentions an article from the November 9, 1839, edition of *Le National*. "Recueil des procès verbaux des séances de la Commission Spéciale pour la Répression de la Prostitution. Registre no. 2," 53e Séance du 7 Janvier 1840, DA 221, doc. 10, APP.

15. Ibid.

16. "Recueil des procès verbaux des séances de la Commission Spéciale pour la Répression de la Prostitution. Registre no. 2," 53e Séance du 7 Janvier 1840, DA 221, doc. 11, APP.

from them only that they refrain from accepting and completing a rendez-vous until some sales have been made at the shop."[17] Although the report explicitly asserts that prostitution was an ongoing problem, it also implicitly reveals that the two kinds of commerce complemented each other, as the shopgirls successfully attracted a clientele for both goods and sex. However, the police refused to acknowledge this reciprocal relationship and claimed it was not just out of a concern for morality that they intervened but for the sake of commerce itself. By "suppressing" these practices, the "scandal" that had affected "the freedom of circulation" would end, and the "monumental character" of these "beautiful" galleries would be more easily recognized.[18] Although the women arrested relied on the "movement of the crowd," the police sought to ensure a "freedom of movement" that could be exercised by only some Parisians and not others.

The ultimate failure of the police to prevent the appropriation of the Palais-Royal by women who sold sex—or men who sought sex with other men, for that matter—deeply concerned moral authorities. Police and moralist concern with sexual spaces outside the brothel became more acute after the revolutions of 1848, which, as we saw in Chapter 1, "interrupted" the regulationist system.[19] During the Second Empire, the authorities redoubled their attention to moral policing, efforts that simultaneously existed in response to, were a cause of, and stood in contrast with the Empire's reputation.[20] The Second Empire, for instance, was "the golden age" of the high-class courtesan, famously depicted in Émile Zola's *Nana* (1880).[21] In the novel, the eponymous protagonist ruins all men who come near her: Nana's "house seemed to have been built over an abyss in which men were swallowed up—their possessions, their bodies, their very names—without leaving even a trace of dust behind them."[22] Nana's thirst for "luxury" that so threatened the men who came to her was but the furthest extreme of what commentators feared was a general threat to Parisian women and men. In his *Les marchands de plaisir* (1856), the author Paul Auguez blames courtesans for degrading

---

17. Rapport, October 24, 1845, "Répression: Lieux interdits," DA 222, doc. 100, APP.

18. Ibid.

19. "Répression de la prostitution," April 27, 1848, "Répression. Voie publique. Circulaire du 27 Avril 1848. Circulation des filles publiques sur la voie publique et répression," DA 223, doc. 119, APP.

20. On some aspects of Second Empire moral concern around sexuality, see Pierre Hahn, *Nos ancêtres les pervers: La vie des homosexuels sous le Second Empire* (Béziers: H and O Éditions, 2006), 80–85.

21. Laure Adler, *Les maisons closes, 1830–1930* (Paris: Fayard/Pluriel, 2010), 24–25.

22. Émile Zola, *Les Rougon-Macquart: Histoire naturelle et sociale d'une famille sous le Second Empire,* 5 vols. (Paris: Gallimard, 1961), 2:1433; translation from Émile Zola, *Nana,* trans. George Holden (New York: Penguin, 1972), 410.

gender and sexual relations. These women were "without spirit, without principles and heart, without even a sex . . . [and] only seek out gold that they squander and material pleasures that they no longer know how to enjoy."[23] Again, the pursuit of wealth via sex risked disrupting the alignment between biological sex and gender, rendering the courtesan "without sex." However, Auguez complains, "here are the women for whom men of our century ruin themselves! Here are the women they prefer! Here are the women they love! / Oh, what moral progress!"[24] The rising commercial character of the city exacerbated fears that the pleasures of Paris were simply devolving into new forms of prostitution.[25]

As Haussmannization oriented the city around the flow of capital, commerce, and the middle classes, the congruence between sex and commercial pleasure became increasingly problematic as the police and expert commentators considered the regulation of urban space.[26] It was one thing to accept the presence of venal and immoral sex in areas of the city already associated with working-class debauchery as a necessary safety valve. It was another when such practices took center stage in spaces devoted to middle-class and elite Parisian consumption. The new department stores, for instance, seemed to offer not only a different scale of amusement to shoppers, both male and female, but also new kinds.[27] Even as the virtue of shopgirls remained up for debate, married middle-class women, some assumed, could use the gigantic stores for discreet encounters with their lovers. The very act of shopping thus became associated with adultery and, from there, with prostitution.[28] As Zola put it in his great department store novel, *Au bonheur des dames,* when describing one of the women who had been so drawn to the new shopping experience: "She didn't understand this nervous aversion to sales talk, because she was just the opposite, one of those women happy to be assaulted and to succumb to the caress of a public offer, with the pleasure of han-

23. Paul Auguez, *Les marchands de plaisir* (Paris: Dentu, 1856), 15.

24. Ibid., 17.

25. On this theme, see also Félix Carlier, *Etudes de pathologie sociale: Les deux prostitutions (1860–1870)* (Paris: E. Dentu, 1887), 27–29.

26. On the commercialization of Paris during Haussmannization, see Philip G. Nord, *Paris Shopkeepers and the Politics of Resentment* (Princeton, N.J.: Princeton University Press, 1986), chap. 3.

27. See, for instance, Michael B. Miller, *The Bon Marché: Bourgeois Culture and the Department Store, 1869–1920* (Princeton, N.J.: Princeton University Press, 1981), 192–193.

28. Ali Coffignon, *Paris-Vivant: La corruption à Paris* (Paris: Librairie Illustrée, 1888), 153–155. On gender anxiety and the department store, see Lisa Tiersten, *Marianne in the Market: Envisioning Consumer Society in Fin-de-Siècle France* (Berkeley: University of California Press, 2001), chap. 1. On adultery during the period, see Laure Adler, *Secrets d'alcôve: Histoire du couple de 1830 à 1930* (Paris: Hachette Littératures, 1983), chap. 5; Anne-Marie Sohn, "The Golden Age of Male Adultery: The Third Republic," *Journal of Social History* 28, no. 3 (1995): 469–490.

dling everything and wasting her time in pointless chatter."[29] The dangerous union of prostitution and commerce was simultaneously a process of gender discipline—associating women in public with disreputable urges—but also a recognition of the thin line between the two. Indeed, in Zola's depiction, the turn to prostitution by the middle-class shopper was precisely what she desired. "Prostitution," Dr. Martineau would argue in 1885, "is the commerce of pleasure. The generic term prostitution is applied to any immoral act accomplished in the spirit of lucre."[30] Every exchange could thus be a kind of prostitution. If Paris was a "city of pleasure," it was also a city of prostitution.

It was precisely this intersection of sexual opportunity and everyday life that enabled the emergence of a public sexual culture in mid-nineteenth-century Paris. Haussmannization facilitated movement about the city in ways that enabled both licit and illicit practices of pleasure that together produced a social world predicated on public sex. For instance, Alfred Delvau's guidebook published for the 1867 Universal Exposition, *Les plaisirs de Paris,* opens by defining its subject: "What is pleasure? Pleasure is nothing more than love, nothing more than wine, nothing more than music. . . . M. de la Palisse ['Captain Obvious'] would say: 'Pleasure is the art of amusing oneself'; and M. Prudhomme ['Mister Bourgeois'] would add: 'Without ruining your stomach, your heart, and your purse.'"[31] Paris, Delvau continues, is defined by these pleasures: "From the first step after debarking onto the asphalt of the boulevards, one hears the charming voices of those Parisian fairies sing: *Voilà l'plaisir, messieurs! Voilà l'plaisir!* And this voice, it is necessary to listen to it well,—unless one has cotton in their ears; they insinuate themselves softly into the heart so that they tickle and stir his most intimate depths."[32] Delvau here deploys a double entendre—a *plaisir* was also a pastry—to underscore the actual pleasures these "fairies" hawked to the newly arrived tourist.[33] Offering their wares, these sirens were irresistible to the unwary—the one

29. Zola, *Les Rougon-Macquart,* 3:621; translation from Émile Zola, *Au bonheur des dames (The Ladies' Delight),* ed. and trans. Robin Buss (New York: Penguin, 2001), 240.

30. Louis Martineau, *La prostitution clandestine* (Paris: Delahaye et Lecrosnier, 1885), 35.

31. Alfred Delvau, *Les plaisirs de Paris: Guide pratique et illustré* (Paris: Achille Faure, 1867), 3. M. De la Palisse is derived from the term *lapalissade.* See *Le dictionnaire de l'académie française,* 8th ed., vol. 2, *Dictionnaires d'autrefois, ARTFL* (Paris, 1932–1935), https://artflsrv03.uchica go.edu/philologic4/publicdicos/navigate/19/2894, accessed January 9, 2018. "M. Prudhomme" refers to a stereotypical bourgeois man made famous by Henry Monnier in the 1830s. See *Dictionnaire de la langue Française (Littré),* vol. 3, *Dictionnaires d'autrefois, ARTFL* (1873), https://artflsrv03.uchicago.edu/philologic4/publicdicos/query?report=bibliography&head=prud homme&start=0&end=0, accessed January 9, 2018.

32. Delvau, *Les plaisirs de Paris,* 4–5. Italics in the original.

33. Thanks go to Aimée Boutin for pointing out the double meaning of *plaisir* to me.

unprepared with earplugs—visitor to Paris. Once encountered, they "stirred" (read: aroused) him.

That such a guide was written for one of the most obvious attempts by the Second Empire to represent itself and, in particular, its industrial might—the Universal Exposition—reinforces the connection between the city, modernization, and not simply sexual, but specifically venal, pleasure. In fact, Maxime Du Camp made the connection explicit when he claimed that the 1867 exposition "attracted lost women from all four corners of the world."[34] Du Camp's handwringing highlights the link between representations of the city as an engine of modernity and its reputation as a space of sex.

In response to this apparent connection, the police attempted to draw a distinction between the sexual and other uses of the city, but they did so in ways that recognized the decline of the maison de tolérance. Although Prefect of Police C. J. Lecour still declared in 1870 that "tolerated *maisons de débauche* are the basis of the entire system of regulated prostitution," he seemed incapable of doing much but documenting their decline and lamenting a consequent rise in clandestine prostitution.[35] The cause of these changes can be attributed to a number of factors, not least the rise of new spaces for consummating a sexual exchange, powerful critiques of the system from government officials and the press, changing sexual tastes, and the physical destruction of tolerated brothels during Haussmannization, especially in the center of the city.[36] The decline of the maison de tolérance dispersed sex throughout the city, even as the need to recognize its signs remained. The gros numéro may have still been present, but it was increasingly replaced by solicitation on the streets.

The decline of the brothel increased the police's belief that the city was being overrun by clandestine prostitutes. Interactions between different groups of Parisians forced the police to recognize that the availability of public sex was reshaping how people understood their relationship to urban spaces and to other people they encountered in the city. In order to address the issue, the authorities focused on areas of the city where middle-class and elite Parisians were most at risk of encountering evidence of public sex, evidenced by a series of police reports from July 1868 regarding the Champs-Élysées. For instance, one lamented that the area "between the Chevaux de

34. Maxime du Camp, *Paris: Ses organs, ses fonctions et sa vie dans la second moitié du XIXe siècle,* 5th ed., 6 vols. (Paris: Hachette, 1875), 3:354.

35. C. J. Lecour, *La prostitution à Paris et à Londres, 1789–1870* (Paris: P. Asselin, 1870), 137, 256–257. See also Auguste Corlieu, *La prostitution à Paris* (Paris: J.-B. Baillière et Fils, 1887), 19–22.

36. Corbin, *Les filles de noce,* 174–178.

Marly and the Rond-Pont" was being used by a great number of prostitutes. "Repression is especially difficult," the report continues, "as this promenade is frequented in the evening only by people belonging for the most part to the elevated class of society, and the filles take advantage of the situation in order to solicit the passers-by openly in a manner that makes it impossible to promenade in this space."[37] On the one hand, this area served especially for Parisian elites; on the other hand, so many prostitutes took advantage of this fact that a promenade had become "impossible." The Champs-Élysées was thus torn between two contradictory notions: that elites and prostitutes were interacting but that such interactions were impossible. The negotiation between these two poles shaped the sexualization of Parisian space.

Indeed, public sex did not remain localized in specific spaces, such as parks and streets outside brothels, but rather moved about the city. Train and omnibus stations served as important spaces of sexual solicitation.[38] Travelers emphasized how prostitutes especially mingled with people going about their business and thus reinforced their inability to escape evidence of public sex. One complaint, for example, rhetorically asked whether the station's benches were intended for passengers or prostitutes.[39] Trains threatened to carry public sex through the city. One Parisian wrote to the police complaining about a prostitute who "exercised her profession" on a train and had accosted his son.[40] In another instance, *Le Petit Parisien* described the *caresses inexplicables* a young man performed on an eleven-year old boy in a train before assaulting him in another carriage and declared that "the singular epidemic [presumably, male same-sex sexual activity] that has reigned for some time in the Champs-Élysées has just made its appearance on the rail line that leads to the Montparnasse train station."[41] The article conflates sexual assault on an unwilling partner with the sexual liaisons taking place in the green spaces of the city. In doing so, the newspaper implies that public sex was no longer localized in particular areas of the city. Rather, carried by the train tracks,

37. "Rapport: Surveillance des filles prostituées aux Champs-Élysées," July 3, 1868, DA 223, doc. 36, APP.

38. See, for example, Martineau, *La prostitution clandestine*, 75. On the omnibus, see Masha Belenky, "From Transit to *Transitoire:* The Omnibus and Modernity," *Nineteenth-Century French Studies* 35, no 2 (2007): 414; Jennifer Terni, "The Omnibus and the Shaping of the Urban Quotidian: Paris, 1828–60," *Cultural and Social History* 11, no. 2 (2014): 227.

39. Letter to Préfet de Police, August 26, 1879, "Gare St. Lazare. Dossier general," JC 54, formerly BM2 60, APP.

40. Un abonné to Chef de Gare, March 16, 1876, "Gare St. Lazare. Dossier général," JC 54, formerly BM2 60, APP.

41. *Le Petit Parisien,* January 11, 1877.

the threat of public sex was everywhere.[42] Paris was not actually overrun by prostitutes—or pederasts—but their use of spaces of circulation and leisure made the "problem" appear greater than it actually was. In the imaginary of nineteenth-century Paris, it had become impossible to enjoy public space without confronting public sex.

Sexing the City

Interactions between Parisians, tourists, the police, and women and men seeking sex sexualized the spaces in which they took place. While it is difficult to precisely map the areas of the city where such encounters occurred—especially during the Second Empire, with the loss of so much archival material during the Commune of 1871—both the police and many Parisians began to see sex everywhere they looked.[43] Certainly the materials contained in the police archives emphasize specific spaces, such as parks and gardens like the Champs-Élysées and the bois de Boulogne, but they also reveal a more mobile vision of public sex that implicated the city as a whole. The police struggled to contain the sexual opportunities of the city; their efforts ultimately highlighted the ways public sexual activity seemed to be everywhere.

The management of public sex found new obstacles in Haussmannizing Paris as the existence of brothels seemed increasingly incongruent with modern city space. According to one letter writer, the transformation of the neighborhood around the new boulevard de Grenelle in the fifteenth arrondissement had made the streets into "a sanded promenade, lit up, decorated with trees and with benches," that contrasted with the "agglomeration" of brothels that still stood there, especially considering that the area was next to the future site of the 1867 Universal Exposition. The request that the police move at least some of the brothels, "in order to encourage construction and to breathe life into a neighborhood that appears to be destined to eternal prostitution," links the destruction of tolerated brothels to the redevelopment of the city.[44] The letter's deployment of the Universal Exposition—a shared reference point for those seeking to highlight the modernity of Second Empire Paris—to critique the existence of maisons de tolérance highlights the

---

42. Henning Bech also emphasizes the importance of train stations and rail lines to homosexual encounters in the modern city. See Henning Bech, *When Men Meet: Homosexuality and Modernity*, trans. Teresa Mesquit and Tim Davies (Chicago: University of Chicago Press, 1997), 158–159.

43. On the commune's destruction of archives, see Colette E. Wilson, *Paris and the Commune, 1871–78: The Politics of Forgetting* (Manchester, U.K.: Manchester University Press, 2007), 99–103.

44. Ch. Canday to Préfet de Police, July 1, 1865, DA 221, doc. 125, APP.

wide circulation of a discourse that associated regulated public sexuality with the urban disorder that Haussmannized Paris was supposed to eliminate.

The destruction of maisons de tolérance became a way to change the character of individual neighborhoods as they underwent redevelopment. In 1884 the police received a petition launched by a property owner, a Monsieur Peignot, who used the existence of a new market in the Montparnasse neighborhood to justify his complaint about the existence of three tolerated brothels in the area. Although the market inspector had never received "any complaint from the merchants or the public regarding the neighboring maisons de tolérance," Peignot "loudly complained against the keeping of tolerances in Paris, which, in principle, should be found only on the outskirts of the city and which, according to him, should have been transferred to the most faraway points long ago." Claiming that the brothels attracted both young local schoolboys and a bad crowd to the neighborhood, Peignot drew on the transforming city to justify his own claim. The increasing commercialization of the neighborhood demanded a different kind of policing, one that expelled even registered prostitutes. The police, it is worth noting, saw no reason to shut the tolerances down, though they agreed that they should not renew the licenses should any of the madams decide to depart on their own.[45] The brothel thus became a victim of a new image of urban space, one that depended on the clear contrast between its commercial life and its sexual life. The irony, of course, is that by reducing the number of tolerated brothels, evidence of public sex spread throughout the city.

In fact, it was precisely administrators' efforts to open the city to greater use, but still amenable to social control, that exacerbated the perception of a city overrun by illicit sex. The very qualities that recommended spaces such as boulevards, parks, and gardens for social display were precisely those that enabled sexual solicitation. The regular use of green spaces by female prostitutes was well known by both the police and the populace.[46] The very qualities that could favor forms of prostitution seemed to be precisely those that made a public park attractive to everyday use. For example, according to Carlier, the male prostitute needs "a fairly large area, neither too vast, nor too light, nor too obscure, little frequented, but also near sought-out promenades," as well as areas to hide and places that one could reappear frequently. Carlier claimed that spaces possessing "all these conditions at the same place in Paris are too rare for the *pétits jésus* [male prostitutes] and prudish gentle-

---

45. "Rapport: Au sujet des maisons de tolérance du Bd Edgar-Quinet," April 25, 1884, "Boulevard Edgar-Quinet. Dossier général," JC 76, formerly BM2 19, APP.

46. Richard S. Hopkins, *Planning the Greenspaces of Nineteenth-Century Paris* (Baton Rouge: Louisiana State University Press, 2015), 125–127.

men who, in the evening, go out looking for some fun, not to take advantage of these happy circumstances when they meet. Places so privileged inevitably become rendezvous spaces for them." And yet the one place that Carlier specifically mentions in this passage is none other than the Champs-Élysées, one of the most frequented areas of the city. Indeed, although Carlier places their activities between eleven and twelve o'clock at night, he also claims that "their coquetry attracts the extreme limit of ridicule."[47] The nightlife of the Champs-Élysées may not have been as active as that of other areas of the city during the Second Empire, but male prostitutes apparently still managed to attract attention.[48] The parks, gardens, cafés, and promenades built to serve a market culture based in part around social display also served as the ideal stage for proffering sex.

It was not just that clandestine prostitution and male same-sex sexual activity seemed increasingly evident. Rather, the very systems put into place to manage public sex tended to exacerbate the problem by moving evidence of public sex about the city. As Lecour describes, in order to ensure that registered prostitutes fulfilled their regulatory obligations, either sex workers had to travel to their required medical exam or a doctor would have to go to them. Under Prefect Debelleyme, doctors went to the women in the maisons de tolérance within Paris itself, while unregistered prostitutes caught by the police, filles isolées, and those who lived in the brothels in the *banlieue* (suburbs) came to the dispensary. In 1848 the police attempted to reform this system by requiring all prostitutes to have their exams at the dispensary, but they found this to be unworkable and returned to the old system in 1849. The annexation of the former banlieue in 1860 meant that some women in the brothels were brought to the dispensary while others were examined in the brothels themselves. In 1869 the police "extended" the visit at the brothel to all those maisons de tolérance in Paris.[49]

In part, this decision to have doctors go to the brothels owes to the difficulty in finding a way of moving female prostitutes about the city without being noticed. In the beginning, as Lecour put it, "the movement on foot of filles de maison who lived in the tolerances of the banlieue . . . caused a constant scandal." In response, the police required madams to hire transport that would take the women to their exam. However, "effectuated with the aid of omnibuses, *fiacres, chars à bancs* [long, horse-drawn carriages], the trans-

---

47. Carlier, *Les deux prostitutions,* 329–330.

48. On the nightlife of the Champs-Élysées, see Simone Delattre, *Les douzes heures noirs: La nuit à Paris au XIXe siècle* (Paris: Albin Michel, 2003), 227–228.

49. Lecour, *La prostitution à Paris et à Londres,* 79–83.

port of these femmes de débauche occasioned more disorder than when they walked." In response, the police required the use of "enclosed carriages."[50] These, however, attracted even more attention because of their unique appearance and the "cries and flashes of scandalous gaiety" that emerged from them.[51] When a dispensary doctor named Tavernier wrote a report recommending changes to this system, he also complained about the condition of the transports used to carry women working in the tolerances on the outskirts of Paris: "Their disgusting exteriors signal them as vehicles of the impure to passers-by."[52] Instead, the doctor suggested that a regular service should be organized for all registered prostitutes, using "expressly made carriages, well-kept, elegant, analogous (by form) to an omnibus, in a manner to be able to pass unperceived in the crowd of carriages of the same type."[53]

However, the opposite solution—having the doctors go to the brothels—also posed significant difficulties, as some of the dispensary doctors complained in the late 1850s. When Parent-Duchâtelet visited the brothels for his research, he always went with a police officer in order to make sure that no questions of impropriety were raised.[54] By the Second Empire, the doctor representing the authorities could not disassociate himself from the business of prostitution so easily without threatening his own respectability. As one report from 1858 declared, "The weekly visit of the doctor, going from house to house, in the middle of the day, is an outrage to public morality and to the dignity of the man who does it."[55] The doctor's physical appearance at the brothel, recognized by onlookers in the middle of the day, was itself evidence of the improper use of space. In part, this shift was due

---

50. Ibid., 80.

51. Ibid., 82–83.

52. Dr. Tavernier, "Mémoire sur les inconvénients des visites à domicile et sur les avantages qu'il y aurait à visiter toutes les femmes publiques au Dept. de la Seine, au Dispensaire," September 1857, DA 221, doc. 122, 5, APP.

53. Ibid., 7. Based on another memoir written by Tavernier addressing some concerns of the préfecture, it seems likely that the bureau remained skeptical of the plan to move prostitutes who lived within Paris to the dispensary. See Dr. Tavernier, "Discussion de quelques objections qui pourraient être fait, au point de vue de l'application du projet de transport des maisons tolérées," n.d. (c. 1857–1858), DA 221, doc. 123, APP. Throughout the period, the préfecture permitted private coachmen to transport prostitutes to and from the dispensary provided they prove that their carriage met existing conditions for privacy. See the dossiers in "Répression: Transport des filles publiques au dispensaire," DA 221. Carlier also noted that people complained about seeing prostitutes go to and from the dispensary and recommended making the medical visit more effective by increasing the number of doctors. Carlier, Les deux prostitutions, 256–257.

54. Charles Bernheimer, Figures of Ill Repute: Representing Prostitution in Nineteenth-Century France (Cambridge, Mass: Harvard University Press, 1989), 17.

55. Untitled report, June 23, 1858, DA 221, doc. 130, APP.

to the increasing professionalization of the medical profession.[56] As doctors raised their social status, the sight of them with prostitutes proved increasingly problematic, even as they were able to make greater and greater claims over them once the venereal panic truly took hold later in the century.[57] This shift in forbearance can also be attributed to the broader contrast being drawn between the changing city and the policing of sex. If, on the one hand, the medical examination of female prostitutes underscored the essential modernity of Parisian regulationism, it also, on the other hand, always revealed the incomplete nature of that project. The medical exam itself underscored the tangled web that linked city space to public sex.

The problem facing the Second Empire and early Third Republic police—joined by a shared moralist politics—was to reconcile contrasting goals: if the previous decades tended to emphasize the importance of regulated prostitution, the problems attendant with regulation tended to be more important from the 1860s until the end of the century. Indeed, Haussmannization made the task of sexual management more difficult, as it increased opportunities for sexual solicitation even as it made such encounters more fraught. The complaints and concerns regarding regulated as well as clandestine prostitution indicate how public sex was becoming less appropriate as it seemed to become more common. People's responses to sexual encounters were thus conditioned by a growing need to distinguish between appropriate and inappropriate urban pleasures, even as such efforts were precisely what highlighted the central place of sex in the city. Parisians were, in a sense, being trained to recognize evidence of sex by the very processes of sexual management put into place by the authorities.

The Signs of Sex

The constant back-and-forth between the police and those who sought sex on the streets created a public sexual culture on the streets of mid-century Paris. The production and dispersal of sexual knowledge combined with greater attention paid to street life by both the authorities and residents of the city

---

56. On medical professionalization in France, see George Weisz, "The Politics of Medical Professionalization in France, 1845–1848," *Journal of Social History* 12, no. 1 (1978): 3–30; Jan Goldstein, *Console and Classify: The Psychiatric Profession in the Nineteenth Century* (Cambridge: Cambridge University Press, 1987); Ian R. Dowbiggin, *Inheriting Madness: Professionalization and Psychiatric Knowledge in Nineteenth-Century France* (Berkeley: University of California Press, 1991).

57. Keely Stauter-Halsted describes this process in the Polish case in Keely Stauter-Halsted, *The Devil's Chain: Prostitution and Social Control in Partitioned Poland* (Ithaca, N.Y.: Cornell University Press, 2015), chap. 8.

to create novel sexual possibilities. Sexual solicitation put into question the distinctions the police relied upon, because it tended to also undercut the difference between the sexual and asexual lives of the city. Through speech, looks, and gestures that were sometimes directed at a subset of Parisians, sometimes directed at all Parisians, but always potentially both, women who sold sex and men sought sex with other men created a new audience of sexual commerce. As Parisians entered public space, they always risked meeting a prostitute or a pederast. The recognition of sexual possibility; the shared experience of sexual arousal, disgust, or something in between; and the mutual awareness of these possibilities created this public sexual culture. This public, then, revolved around not simply the call and response between solicitor and solicited but also muddying the waters between the two. In this respect, I expand the notion of "cruising" beyond its normal associations with same-sex sexual desire and invoke it to reflect how this "act of mutual recognition"—even if not always of mutual desire—reframed the everyday life of the city.[58]

Both the threat and power of solicitation were most overtly expressed by clandestine prostitutes. "Clandestine prostitution is legion," declared Lecour in 1870. "It displays itself loudly and attracts attention through its allures, its *toilettes,* its words, and its scandals." Unable to tell the difference between these women and registered prostitutes, he continued, the public could do nothing but complain.[59] By drawing attention to herself, then, the clandestine prostitute disrupted faith in the regulated system insofar as she put into doubt the difference between her and her registered compatriots. Moreover, she created possible clients out of those theatergoers who saw her against their will. The "attraction" of the "loud" prostitute makes something new out of the audience who recognized her.

To Lecour, the creation of potential clients out of unsuspecting men stood as a clear danger to those who wandered the city and put them at risk of blackmail. "Who has never," he asked, "while wandering [*flâner*] the streets in the evening, witnessed a small incident like the following: A somewhat older man, simply but carefully dressed, and whose attitude and manner are imprinted with a certain austerity who watched, and then followed with his eye, a woman, a *passante,* whose look crossed his own?" The passing woman, catching the eye of the apparently respectable Parisian, tempts him: "The visage of this woman

---

58. Turner, *Backward Glances,* 9. I am also influenced by Dianne Chisholm's conception of the "cruising flâneur" who sought out erotic pleasures that destroyed, rather than reinforced, the composure of the wanderer. See Chisholm, *Queer Constellations,* 46–47. For a more contemporary investigation of cruising, see Jamie S. Frankis and Paul Flowers, "Public Sexual Cultures: A Systematic Review of Qualitative Research Investigating Men's Sexual Behaviors with Men in Public Spaces," *Journal of Homosexuality* 56, no. 7 (2009): 861–893.

59. Lecour, *La prostitution à Paris et à Londres,* 18.

hit him; he watches her."[60] The transformation of the well-kept gentleman into a client relied on the effects of a mutual recognition much more subtle than that experienced in the theater but all the more powerful for being so innocuous. The signs of public sex remained subtle, which made them all the more present. "Who has never seen" such a moment? No one, apparently.

The distinction between various kinds of temptations—high-class courtesans, registered prostitutes, clandestine streetwalkers, and other criminals—proved difficult to sustain, even as its seeming omnipresence remade the spaces in which it took place. The police emphasized their growing concern during the latter part of the Second Empire. An 1868 report on the Champs-Élysées describes "unregistered and registered prostitutes, courtesans, and pederasts," who have, each night, rendered "this magnificent promenade forbidden to the honest classes." "Prostitutes of both sexes are as numerous as on the boulevards," the report continues, "but here the gardens and hedges make it so that even the most disgusting passions can be immediately satisfied on a bench, thanks to the obscurity they offer."[61] The report explains how the prostitutes of the neighborhood solicit sex: "The prostitutes who frequent this neighborhood are all elegantly and eccentrically dressed; their principal means of solicitation is to stay seated in the first row and to attract attention by their poses, their gestures, and their toilettes." The act of attracting attention is precisely what put into question the categories the police depended on—in particular that between honest and dishonest but also between kinds of prostitute. The report thus asks: "What distinguishes them [prostitutes] from women of the demimonde and even from certain women who call themselves honest seated next to them?"[62] The answer, the report implies, was nothing at all.

Although the police seemed concerned that solicitation by female prostitutes muddied the distinctions between honest and disreputable Parisians, they did not spend much time actually decoding them, because they refused to admit that they were anything but obvious. The apparent clarity of the methods women used to solicit sex therefore continued to provide a useful anchor for ensuring that Parisians knew how to recognize men who sought sex with other men as well. In his memoirs, the Second Empire police inspector Louis Canler drew explicitly on female prostitution as he described four groups of "antiphysicals," as he called men who sought sex with other men:

---

60. Ibid., 185–186. Lecour's description reflects some of the ambiguities in Baudelaire's famous poem "A une passante" (To a passer-by). Charles Baudelaire, *Œuvres complètes*, vol. 1 (Paris: Gallimard, 1975), 92-93.

61. "Rapport," July 4, 1868, DA 223, doc. 30, 1–2, APP.

62. Ibid., 3.

the *persilleuses,* the *honteuses,* the *travailleuses,* and the *rivettes.*[63] The first and third groups both came from the working class, but while the persilleuses were simply male prostitutes equated with female prostitutes (also called persilleuses in the slang of the day), the travailleuses were workers who engaged in male same-sex sexual activity out of "taste." Both groups, Canler assured his readers, were easy to spot. If the persilleuses made themselves apparent by acting like a prostitute—they "excited passers-by to libertinage on the streets . . . [and] differed entirely from other men by their figure, language, dress, manners, and demeanor"—the travailleuses were "perfectly recognizable by their languorous and drawling voice, as well as their gait, which does not at all differ from that of the persilleuses."[64]

The other two groups in Canler's physiology were more difficult to discern, because they belonged to all social ranks. The first, the honteuses (the ashamed), were in many senses the opposite of the persilleuses. While the latter displayed themselves, the former hid. While the latter earned their living through pederasty, the former sought only to indulge their "tastes." The honteuses, Canler claims, "belong to all classes of society, without any exception," and "since they dress like everyone, nothing could betray them, if not for their feminine voice."[65] The final group were the rivettes, who "have nothing that could distinguish them from other men, and it is necessary that the observer have the greatest attention joined to the greatest practice in order to discern them."[66] Although he claims that they too can be "encountered at all social ranks," these men most closely represent the trope of the aristocratic corrupter through their "preference for youth." The rivettes were the primary target for blackmailers, who used one of the members of the other groups to seduce them, and they were most concerned about the possibility of revelation. Although the "practiced eye" could recognize them as pederasts, they did all they could to blend in. Canler's emphasis on recognition situates his descriptions firmly within the street life of the city. As he draws upon female prostitution to make sense of the appearance of men who sought sex with other men, he taught his readers how to likewise recognize the evidence of same-sex sexual desire.

Canler's typology injects a class dimension into the mechanisms of rec-

---

63. Louis Canler, *Mémoirs de Canler, ancien chef du service de sûreté,* 2nd ed. (Paris: J. Hetzel, 1862), 265–266. On Canler's interest in pederasts, see Jean-Claude Féray, *"Pédés: Le premier registre infamant de la préfecture de police de Paris aux XIXe siècle suivi d'un dictionnaire des noms propres et noms communs les plus significatifs du registre, et d'annexes* (Paris: Quintes-feuilles, 2012), 13–15; Sibalis, "Palais-Royal," 123–124.

64. Canler, *Mémoirs,* 266–268.

65. Ibid., 267.

66. Ibid., 268.

ognition. Those most linked to female prostitution were those most associated with the working class and thus the most recognizable. Indeed, for these pederasts, the process of solicitation relied on addressing the public as female prostitutes. The more public the pederast, the more likely he was to be a worker and really just another prostitute. This discourse thus shaped the ways that Parisians could—if they so chose—identify a passing pederast. On the lookout, perhaps, for a female prostitute, Parisians also risked or enjoyed encountering men seeking sex with other men. Drawing on the scientific and moralist discourse that associated forms of male same-sex sexual activity with female prostitutes, Parisians learned how to recognize the availability of public sex with both women and men.

In fact, commentators and the police emphasized the mutual reliance of the two forms of prostitution as they described the ways they made themselves known on the streets. It remains difficult to determine just how often the two groups actually interacted, but they did so often enough that evidence remains in both published sources and police records. According to Félix Carlier, some male prostitutes paid their female counterparts in order to use their living quarters to turn tricks. Female prostitutes would sometimes signal to a pederast if she encountered a man seeking out another man during her rounds.[67] In addition, Gustave Macé recounted the story of a "pederast-pimp" who claimed that "certain prostitutes hold gatherings of lust by receiving, several times a week, depraved men who indulge themselves in unnatural acts with their [the prostitutes'] lovers."[68] These pimps, according to Macé's informant, tried to hide their own desires by attaching themselves to a female prostitute. This give-and-take reinforced the image of a fundamental interdependence between male and female prostitution. Moreover, it implies a broader connection between female prostitutes and men who sought sex with other men insofar as those seeking a male prostitute would have known that approaching a female prostitute or entering a brothel was one way to locate a sexual encounter with another man. In this sense, female prostitution became an axis around which an entire sexual economy revolved and provided the key to understanding the public signs of sex.

The emphasis on recognition and misrecognition, evident in the flurry of discourse that newly surrounded the pederast, highlights a major fear: that pederasts could hide from the unwary. For instance, an 1852 police report described a coterie of pederasts led by one "capable of changing his self-

---

67. Carlier, *Les deux prostitutions,* 359.
68. Gustave Macé, *La police parisienne: Mes lundis en prison* (Paris: G. Charpentier, 1889), 148.

presentation according to circumstances" who could fit in with men of both the upper and lower classes.[69] This ability to blend in while recognizing one another deeply concerned police commentators. The common metaphor of the freemasonry of vice therefore underscored not only their venality but also this very skill. Flévy d'Urville, for instance, claimed that pederasts "know how to meet one another like freemasons, through certain physiognomical games, through some exterior signs, in the manner of, for example, letting their handkerchief show, and even using the intermediary services of a woman."[70] Carlier agreed, describing "the antiphysical habits that suggest, to all who practice them, an obsequious and exaggerated politeness, an intonation of voice, a passion for striking jewelry . . . finally a je ne sais quoi. . . . He would never be noticed, at least if he is not pushed to exaggeration, by those who have never known this awful passion, but those who are its slaves will never miss it."[71] In addition, beginning in the late 1880s, women who desired other women were also spoken of in these terms, incorporating lesbian desire as well in a common discourse of public recognition: "Wherever they [saphists] go," Ali Coffignon declared in 1888, "they recognize one another through quasi-masonic signs, a rapid movement of the tongue and the lips."[72]

Although these techniques could provide the grounds for the emergence of a self-contained social world, they also enabled a broader system of recognition that pervaded the city. For the ability of men who sought sex with other men to identify one another implies the emergence of a system that could be learned, perhaps through the very books that warned of their danger. Indeed, Carlier provides a precise list of jewelry once carried by "an English pederast passing through Paris" almost as if it would be helpful to know what kind of button one should be on the lookout for. He further implies that the pederast could, "when pushed to exaggeration," be recognized even by those who did not share his proclivities.[73] Therefore, the very performance of these signals always contained the possibility of exceeding their immediate audience. These representations taught Parisians and visitors how to recognize the supposedly hidden signs of public sex.

The very confidence with which these commentators asserted their ability to decode the signs of pederasty demonstrates that these signs tended to float free of their immediate referents; already the vice that dare not speak its

---

69. "Rapport," January 23, 1852, 1, DA 230, doc. 247, 1, APP.

70. Flévy d' Urville, *Les ordures de Paris* (Paris: Librairie Sartorius, 1874), 69.

71. Carlier, *Les deux prostitutions,* 283–285.

72. Coffignon, *La corruption à Paris,* 309. See also Martineau, *La prostitution clandestine,* 94–95.

73. Carlier, *Les deux prostitutions,* 284–285.

name was also the "secret that always gave itself away."[74] The use of female prostitution to identify the common pederast highlights police confidence. If the clandestine prostitute was easily recognizable by virtue of her loud solicitation, the pederast could also be made visible by spreading knowledge of his signs. If one knew where to look, pederasty became quite visible indeed.[75] This emphasis on the ease with which the police could recognize either female prostitutes or male pederasts, and help others do so as well, conflicted with the supposed cause of concern: that both clandestine prostitutes and male pederasts could blend into the crowd. Ultimately, then, the circulation of sexual signs depended on a mutually reinforcing contradiction. On the one hand, neither the prostitute nor the pederast was entirely clear to the authorities; on the other hand, the authorities were constantly declaring their ability to discern both groups. The circulation of sexual knowledge rested on the constant assertion that such knowledge was hard to come by. This justification for the publication of forms of sexual knowledge provided both the means with which to recognize sexual opportunities and the ability to disavow one's ability or desire to do so.

Becoming Public

Encounters premised on these forms of sexual knowledge created a new sexual public. Because sexual solicitation required approaching strangers and, in fact, could be recognized whether one was the target or not, Parisians often had no choice but to become part of this public. Participation in a public sexual culture was not always a momentary experience, one that vanished after a single encounter. Rather, the public sexual culture put into the question some of the assumptions of public participation in the first place. If the urban culture of the Second Empire and early Third Republic was predicated on the preservation of social hierarchies, then it depended on the maintenance of a clear distinction between the proper and improper users of the city.[76]

---

74. The structuring device of the "closet" thus predates that of homosexuality per se. On the closet, the "open secret," and homosexuality, see esp. D. A. Miller, *The Novel and the Police* (Berkeley: University of California Press, 1988), chap. 6; Eve Kosofsky Sedgwick, *Epistemology of the Closet* (Berkeley: University of California Press, 1992), chap. 1.

75. Sibalis, "Palais-Royal," 117. See also Leslie Choquette, "Homosexuals in the City: Representations of Lesbian and Gay Space in Nineteenth-Century Paris," *Journal of Homosexuality* 41, nos. 3–4 (2002): 158.

76. Victoria Thompson, "Creating Boundaries: Homosexuality and the Changing Social Order in France, 1830–1870," in *Homosexuality in Modern France,* ed. Jeffrey Merrick and Bryant T. Ragan Jr. (Oxford: Oxford University Press, 1996), 113–120. This is not to say that such concerns were entirely new. See, for instance, Denise Z. Davidson, *France after Revolution: Urban Life, Gender, and the New Social Order* (Cambridge, Mass: Harvard University Press, 2007).

Efforts to ensure the clarity of these distinctions by describing prostitution and pederasty, however, only enabled more people to recognize them. Participation within a public sexual culture put these assumptions into doubt, then, as men and women were drawn to sexual experiences they may or may not have wanted. In doing so, sexual solicitation reshaped the possibilities of public encounter and what it meant to experience the city in the first place.

We have already seen how experts believed that some pederasts could be confused with female prostitutes on the streets, but sexual solicitation had wider ramifications for how users of public space understood their own role. For instance, an 1872 letter complained that "an honest man can no longer walk peacefully on the cours la Reine [near the Champs-Élysées] between 9 and 11 at night without being accosted by women who engage in revolting touches and direct the following verbatim proposition (Do you want me to jack you off?)."[77] The writer apologized for using such explicit language, "but it has been used by many of the ignoble creatures." That these encounters bothered him enough to write, that they stayed with him after he moved on, highlights the ways sexual solicitation created new feelings and emotions that were anything but momentary. The letter stands as evidence of the creation of a broader sexual public (who else heard these words?) even as it highlights how the individual writer's sense of self changed in some undefinable way in response to the encounter. In another instance, a man named G. Feuille wrote to the police in 1880 to complain: "It is scandalous . . . to see oneself attacked (*assaili*) and almost violated (*violenté*) by several prostitutes, who direct at you the most filthy remarks."[78] The violation implied here may not have actually been sexual assault as the French word *violenté* may imply, but the connotation remains significant. That this man felt sexually assaulted by women who put themselves at the service of male clients highlights the inversion at play as men were forced to reckon with their own sexual response. In both cases, the unwilling participation in a public sexual culture threatened the urban experience as imagined by privileged male pedestrians.

The "violation" felt by these two men at the attention of female prostitutes disrupted their ability to move about the city as they so chose, but it did not necessarily put into question their status as potential clients. Insofar as these "assaults" may have elicited a sexual response, they may have heightened their awareness of their status as sexual beings even as it challenged their gender privilege. Men who encountered other men seeking sex, however, could

---

77. G. D. to Préfet de Police, August 20, 1872, "Champs-Élysées. Dossier général," JC 208, formerly BM2 60, APP.

78. G. Feuille to Commissaire de Police, March 14, 1880, "Rue Monsieur-le-Prince, 65," JC 49, formerly BM2 45, APP.

find themselves even more deeply affected. Just like female prostitutes, men who sought sex with other men on the streets of Paris were not unknown on the streets; they drew the eyes of others even as this "cruising" was becoming more fraught with significance. Tardieu, for instance, argued that pederasts' dress and personal habits helped them "attract looks in public places."[79] In a police report, Carlier noted that his agents had been alerted to several groups of "individuals who go back and forth along the boulevards, walking with affectation, rubbing shoulders with men prowling around some urinals," who were "scandalizing everyone."[80] My emphasis on the public-ness of these men is not to deny the real constraints under which they lived. Rather, it is to emphasize how those very constraints helped shape the ways they still were able to make themselves quite known on the streets. As Carlier reports: police officers had heard passers-by ask "why the police do not remove these individuals from the boulevards."[81]

The circulation of a sexual discourse that taught Parisians how to recognize pederasts enabled participation in this culture of public sex, even if one were not actually interested in sex. For instance, the writer Pierre Delcourt described how to attract a pederast: "If you walk slowly, raising your nose distractedly, abandoning your hands to chance, you won't have long to wait before you see a slippery character before you, without sound on the pavement, swaying his hips in a bizarre manner, his hands generally crossed behind his back, dressed distinctly, shaved very closely."[82] The man's gaze, Delcourt continues, leaves no doubt as to his intentions, and if you stop at a shop window, "hands behind your back . . . you will soon feel the touch" of the other man.[83] In response, Delcourt continues, "you take away your hands, blushingly leave, without daring, for fear of scandal, to curse the gentleman whose impure self you had just recognized."[84] The exchange of looks, glances, and eye contact underscore the participatory nature of same-sex sexual cruising. It depended on displaying interest—perhaps even fake or accidental interest, as Delcourt's sarcastic description implies—being recognized and engendering a response. In doing so, the signs of sex make and remake new sexual publics as encounters occur and either dissipate or consummate; one always blushes, but perhaps one does not always leave.

---

79. Ambroise Tardieu, *Étude médico-légale sur les attentats aux mœurs,* 3rd ed. (Paris: J.-B. Baillière, 1859), 139.

80. [Félix] Carlier, "Extrait d'un rapport du service des mœurs joint au dossier de la 1ère section," November 24, 1864, DA 230, doc. 308, APP.

81. Ibid.

82. Pierre Delcourt, *Le vice à Paris* (Paris: Alphonse Piaget, 1887), 289–290.

83. Ibid., 290–291.

84. Ibid., 291

These encounters therefore contained the potential to reshape or confuse one's own sense of self. In their memoirs, for instance, Arthur Belorget describes an incident from their youth when "a well-dressed gentleman with his hands in the pockets of his overcoat walked up alongside me. If I stopped at a shop, he did too; if I crossed from one sidewalk to another, he did the same. Even though this gentleman seemed to be trustworthy, I don't know why he made me feel afraid to such an extent that I felt my legs losing all their strength and I trembled all over."[85] To the young Belorget, the man's outward appearance—his apparent trustworthiness, perhaps, underlined by the fact that he was "well-dressed"—clashed with his behavior, which affected them so much that they began to tremble. Fortunately, Belorget soon came across their friend Frédéric, who scared the gentleman off and warned Belorget to always seek help when a "filthy fellow" like that approached them. Frédéric, however, would not always be there, Belorget proceeds to explain, before awkwardly closing the chapter by explaining, "Among all the women I knew when I was growing up, there were some who didn't delude themselves about my nature."[86] Belorget thus concludes the story not by making any explicit claims about the nature of the man who followed them but rather about their own inner self. They reveal that a story of misrecognition was nothing of the sort. The stranger had actually recognized, in some unclear way, Belorget's own desires. Inclusion in the sexual culture contained the potential to blur the lines between passers-by and client and between hetero and homosexual desire, because it had the potential to awaken unexpected feelings within those who encountered it.

These possibilities often proved problematic for women who wished to also enjoy public space.[87] An 1872 letter signed by multiple residents of the boulevard de la Villette, for instance, claimed that the street was so encumbered that a wife and child could not exit their house without being taken as prostitutes by men who were constantly on the lookout.[88] The expectation that sex was available thus shaped how these residents were understood by those who saw them. As others have argued, the common assumption that a woman in public was a public woman placed all women, but especially

---

85. Arthur W, "Secret Confessions of a Parisian," in *Queer Lives: Men's Autobiographies from Nineteenth-Century France,* ed. William A. Peniston and Nancy Erber (Lincoln: University of Nebraska Press, 2007), 20.

86. Ibid., 21.

87. Lynda Nead, *Victorian Babylon: People, Streets, and Images in Nineteenth-Century London* (New Haven, Conn.: Yale University Press, 2000), 62–67. See also Julia Laite, *Common Prostitutes and Ordinary Citizens: Commercial Sex in London, 1885–1960* (Houndmills, U.K.: Palgrave Macmillan, 2012), chap. 4.

88. Letter to Préfet de Police, February 14, 1872, "Boulevard de la Villette. Dossier général," JC 95, formerly BM2 37, APP.

working-class women, in a vulnerable position.[89] The emphasis on the threat of the prostitute by the police and Paris residents tended to increase the association of public space with the possibility of venal sex, which, in turn, shaped how women encountered the life of the city. This is not to say that all women who appeared in public were assumed to be sexually available, nor that middle-class women were forbidden from the streets. As Temma Balducci has recently emphasized, the streets enabled a wide variety of encounters, dependent on the particular circumstances in which they occurred.[90]

In fact, rather than two possible categories—honest and dishonest—into which an unsuspecting woman could fall, movement about the city made such categorizations highly contingent. For example, on the evening of January 19, 1874, two police inspectors arrested a woman named Valerie Durand, a thirty-three-year-old piano teacher. According to the police, the officers were taking a prostitute to the station when they came across "a woman, alone, standing in the middle of the boulevard, next to a garden where they claimed to have seen her address several individuals." One of the officers then turned to his partner, "saying to him, 'Look over there, since you know the women of this neighborhood better than me, if that's an unregistered prostitute.'" The partner, so the police claimed, decided to approach the woman only after "recognizing that she was looking at men in a provocative manner." Asked what she was doing there, she responded by saying she was waiting for her husband and refused to give her name. She was then arrested and taken to the station, where she admitted to having lied about being married and "that in reality, she was waiting for a man who was employed in a factory, and, finally, that she was perfectly free to wait for whomever on the boulevard." She claimed that she was on her way home when she was arrested after stopping to button herself up. During the course of her arrest, the officers refused to check her story at her home, or even by asking an acquaintance living in the same building as the commissariat of police, before sending her off to the depot.[91] Police confidence in their ability to tell who was and who was not actually a prostitute, reliant on such vague attributes as a provocative glance, thus determined their will to act.

Durand's situation on the one hand highlights women's vulnerability. But on the other hand it illustrates the ways that the assumption of prostitution was never so stable as to totally delimit someone's ability to act. For

89. Harsin, *Policing Prostitution,* 248; Elizabeth Wilson, *The Sphinx in the City: Urban Life, the Control of Disorder, and Women* (Berkeley: University of California Press, 1992), 8.

90. Temma Balducci, *Gender, Space, and the Gaze in Post-Haussmann Visual Culture: Beyond the Flâneur* (London: Routledge, 2017), chap. 1.

91. "Rapport," January 23, 1874, "Dénonciations," DA 231, doc. 39, APP. See also "Mesure prise à regard de la nommée Durand," January 20, 1874, "Dénonciations," DA 231, doc. 38, APP.

Durand's actual identity was never fully determined in the police documents. Was she innocently returning home, as she claimed? Or was she waiting for a "male friend," as she also claimed? Perhaps the police were right and she was actually looking for a sexual client. The police eventually let her go, but despite having received "the most favorable information on her family," they still argued in favor of the "facts certified by the police agents." Indeed, the police superintendent took the opportunity to assure his superiors that he would "be even more circumspect regarding unregistered prostitutes who are vouched for by honorable persons."[92] This indeterminacy enabled Durand to be released to her family not only without being condemned as a registered prostitute but also without admitting to being totally honest. Perhaps Durand was an innocent working woman out for a date who got caught up in an awful situation. But perhaps she was actually a prostitute able to use the thin line between her own profession and that of other (honorable) women to her advantage to get off the hook.

Although far from typical, this case of apparently false arrest, a phenomenon that would receive much greater attention under the Third Republic as the abolitionist movement gained strength, demonstrates two essential aspects of the public sexual culture.[93] On the one hand, the moral discourse of prostitution did leave women vulnerable. The public sexual culture remained hierarchical, predicated on gendered and classed relationships. But it also provided, on the other hand, if not evidence of the opportunity for resistance, then at least the possibility of a different understanding of sex in the modern city outside the binaries of honest and dishonest, registered and unregistered. The administrative category of the prostitute struggled to remain solid in the face of the uses of the street. Valerie Durand's success at evading registration without falling into the category of the honest is but one example of the ways that late nineteenth-century sexual culture could not be slotted into a discrete set of categories.

The presence of public sexual opportunities on the streets of Paris therefore reshaped how men and women understood their interactions with one another. Sometimes these encounters caused a kind of crisis, understood as a form of assault rather than a creative act, as in the case of Feuille's encounter. And yet in his very protest, he highlighted his own understanding that the prostitute had revealed other kinds of publics beyond the one he sought to inhabit. For someone like Arthur Belorget, the sudden encounter obliquely revealed a "truth" they had not yet had the wherewithal to recognize. Their

---

92. Féré, Commissaire de Police, "Rapport," January 27, 1874, "Dénonciations," DA 231, doc. 43, APP.

93. Jean-Marc Berlière, *La police des mœurs sous la IIIe République* (Paris: Seuil, 1992), chap. 4.

momentary inclusion within a public sexual culture thus provided a founding myth for their own process of self-discovery into someone who enjoyed sex with other men and cross-dressing. For Valerie Durand, an encounter with the police placed her within the public sexual culture as they accused her of soliciting the public. And yet the fact that the sexual culture allowed people to move in and out enabled her to refuse being defined by the police. In all three cases, these men and women fall into a momentary identities that were ensured only by the encounter itself. They remained, therefore, highly mobile and in flux, able to be changed on the basis of whomever they next caught sight of on the streets.

Conclusion

By the middle of the nineteenth-century, the parks, boulevards, train stations, and theaters of Second Empire and early Third Republic Paris provided people with the means to create a different kind of public, constructed on the basis of social encounters predicated on the recognition of sexual desire, solicitation, and pleasure. Public sex, therefore, was not an "other" to a dominant vision of public space but instead provided one avenue for constructing how people understood those spaces in the first place. This argument positions marginalized figures back at the center of the story of Parisian life. The women who sold sex and men who sought sex with other men, and other Parisians, have often been treated as distinct groups. However, all three were in constant dialogue with one another, not simply through sexual encounters as clients but through chance recognition on the street. As the construction of the pederast as prostitute underscored the instability of attempts to codify public sex in the Second Empire and early Third Republic, the encounters between men and women illustrate a broader instability in defining sexual space and behavior. Shaped by those attempts to define prostitution as "other" to the "proper" pleasures of Paris and by attempts to lay out the signs of male same-sex sexual desire, everyday encounters became structured by sexual knowledge that emphasized the power of encountering "illicit" sex on the streets.

This interpretation not only highlights the place of lower-class women and men in the life of a city supposedly reconstructed for the growing middle class but also disrupts assumptions about the role of identity in this period. Sexual solicitation provided the means through which a broad public could emerge, grounded in its ability to blur, rather than create, social distinctions. Public sexual encounters did not create closed communities and oppositions but an open and unstable public. It constituted potentials for belonging and unbelonging, for identity formation or the lack of coherent identity. As Arthur Belorget declared in their memoir, their "vices were evident at a very young age, it's true, but they were neither more powerful nor more numerous than many other men's."[94] Their desires for other men did not make them unique; they gave them something in common with all other men. All who encountered a mysterious man in public, therefore, were at risk of recognizing something new within themselves.

By emphasizing the shared nature of this process I do not seek to underplay the inequalities that characterized how people could use public space. The ability to use the city continued to be shaped by differences of class and gender. The attempt to assert such distinctions is more fully explored in the next chapter. For now, however, I highlight how people used the city despite such restrictions. In doing so, I imagine a different kind of queer politics that not only encompasses both women and men but also encourages a loosening of identity overall, where people fell *between* rather than simply *within* the sexual categories of honest and dishonest. Urban development in the nineteenth century was part of a process intended to shore up social order through the maintenance of hierarchy and the control. Such developments also enabled new kinds of sexual uses that contrasted with such efforts. In this sense, this chapter has shown that it is not the form of urban space that determines our ability to build new kinds of sexual worlds but how we use and appropriate the spaces made available to us.

94. W, "Secret Confessions," 28.

PART III

5

PUBLIC SPHERE / PUBLIC SEX

On July 29, 1880, *Le Nouveau Journal* published a short article called "Coup de balai" (clean sweep), which was clipped and preserved by the prefecture of police. The article contrasts "brilliant, gay, playful Paris" with the "adjacent black and smoky streets where the heights seem to have unloaded a part of their sewers. It is there that the same indignities are seen, the same villainies are perpetrated; revolting vice bases itself there in all its hideousness." Calling on the city administration to complete a "clean sweep" of "our boulevards invaded by a swarm of prostitutes and procurers," the author had no doubt that "a number of my readers desire it alongside me." Indeed, the author deemed himself "Populus" (the people) and argued that he "insists . . . [on the] question of morality and public cleanliness" not "in his own name, because I do not, personally, have an indignant sense of decency: I am the echo of a considerable crowd of honest people whose letters I hold in my hands."[1]

Complaints about sex on the boulevards were thus endowed with the force of public opinion. The people, here amplified by the mass press, were situated against the common sight of sex on the streets of Paris. Personal proclivities and repulsions were explicitly disavowed in the name of the letters Populus had received from his readers, standing in for the public itself. The preservation of this public demanded state intervention: "We are today in a Republic, and the sovereign people do not accept that the agents that it pays should be employed

---

1. Populus, "Coup de balai," *Le Nouveau Journal,* July 29, 1880, "Boulevard de la Madeleine. Dossier général," JC 60, formerly BM2 16, APP.

for anything else but to protect them."[2] The people, of course, had been paying taxes since well before the founding of the Republic, but the meaning of those contributions had changed in the context of universal manhood suffrage. "Represented" rather than ruled by the authorities, the people now commanded. The state was thus called upon to preserve the arena of expression and bodily autonomy for the "public" against those sexual beings that threatened it—to separate, in other words, the public from the public sexual culture.

Whether or not Populus actually received any letters, the police really were the recipients of hundreds that complained about and denounced sexual impropriety, immorality, and crime in the city of Paris. Written largely by business owners and respectable *pères de famille* (good fathers), they show how mostly middle-class Parisians attempted to navigate and claim the city as their own. The writers ordinarily began with a formal solicitation, excusing themselves for taking up the prefect's time, and then proceeded with a description of the problem located in their neighborhood, in recreational spaces, or near their businesses. They usually closed by calling on the police to do their duty while assuring the prefect of their "most respectful consideration." A smaller cache of mostly anonymous letters denouncing male same-sex sexuality differ in tone and form but not in content. Both sets call on the police to purge the streets of evidence of sex and usually reference a particular moment that caused them distress or offense. An indiscreet touch, a forceful solicitation, a distasteful encounter, or a meeting gone wrong often led to a letter. The existence of the letters speaks to a certain deference to police power over the street, but their demands also highlight an effort to shape the prerogatives of the state to the authors' own ends.[3]

The letters reveal more than police procedures—a constant cycle of complaint, investigation, and report. They also stand, in the words of Arlette Farge, as "fragments of ethics. Fragments of ethics, in the sense that the stream of words each person used to describe herself and the events reflects an ethos, an aesthetic, a style, an imagination, and the personal link that connected the individual to the community."[4] The letters actively participated

2. Ibid.

3. The letters are contained in series JC at the APP; they were formerly in series BM2. Where possible, I provide both codes. Note, however, that the series is in the process of reclassification (as of spring 2018), and JC designations may change, as they did between 2016 and 2018. I viewed them under the original BM2 classification between 2009 and 2011, and I viewed selected dossiers under the new JC designation in 2016. I thank the archivists for providing me with updated codes in fall 2017 and summer 2018.

4. Arlette Farge, *The Allure of the Archives,* trans. Thomas Scott-Railton (New Haven, Conn.: Yale University Press, 2013), 91.

in the creation of particular modes of inhabiting the city, as the very act of writing creatively centered the author in a community and situated the body in relation to city space. In their focus on sex and sexuality, and their authors' response to it, they form part of the range of discourses that actively produced new kinds of sexual identities, experiences, and desires.[5] Although the letters often called for the repression of public sexual activity, they also enunciated new relations between sex and space. Indeed, they ironically made sex central to claims to citizenship in Third Republic Paris by emphasizing the need to reject it even as they highlighted their authors' inability to do so. One's reaction to an encounter with evidence of public sex provided the grounds on which to make a claim on the state.

The ethics that emerge from the letters, then, reflect the continuing preoccupation with purifying urban space through a logic of regulation, enunciated and put into practice during the early part of the century. But they also constitute a specific response to the emergence of a public sexual culture during the 1850s through the 1870s that threatened Parisians' ability to sustain the claim to their own respectability and honor, so central to emerging forms of both male and female citizenship.[6] Writing to the police provided Parisians with another way to take political action outside the crowd and voting booth.[7] In response to the apparent failure of the police to prevent the appropriation of streets, gardens, parks, train stations, and public urinals by prostitutes and pederasts, the letters presented an understanding of urban life premised on the ability of individual Parisians to maintain clear control over how they encountered their fellow citizens even as they revealed how incapable they were at doing so. Many claimed to represent a "public," but they often did so by virtue of their encounters with evidence of sex.

The authors, mostly though not exclusively men, who wrote to the police participated in a process whereby the prerogatives of citizenship became attached to specific masculine attributes, even as they were claimed as universal.[8] The letters were therefore written in the service of a specifically classed

---

5. Michel Foucault, *The History of Sexuality*, vol. 1, *An Introduction*, trans. Robert Hurley (New York: Vintage, 1990), 36–49.

6. Robert A. Nye, *Masculinity and Male Codes of Honor in Modern France* (Berkeley: University of California Press, 1998), 154–155, Andrea Mansker, *Sex, Honor, and Citizenship in Early Third Republic France* (New York: Palgrave Macmillan, 2011), 5.

7. The struggle to make voting the primary form of political expression is described in James R. Lehning, *To Be a Citizen: The Political Culture of the Early French Third Republic* (Ithaca, N.Y.: Cornell University Press, 2001).

8. As Harold Mah has emphasized, "The public sphere is a fiction. . . . The enabling condition of a successfully staged public sphere is the ability of certain groups to make their social or group particularity invisible so that they can then appear as abstract individuals and hence

and gendered end insofar as they articulated, from the bottom up, a view of who belonged to the city even as it should have—was claimed to—belong to everyone. As "Père le pudeur" (father morality), Senator René Bérenger, put it in 1895, "The street, public spaces, belong to everyone. Their monopolization by some to the detriment of all, would be an insupportable tyranny. The authorities have the obligation to prevent it."[9] The call to ensure that "all" were free to use the streets was thus actually a call to protect the rights of "some." "All," by definition, would have included everyone, even those who had a "dire influence on public morality through licentious exhibitions and excitations, which our streets too often serve as the spectacle," as Bérenger describes the problem.[10] Bérenger defines "everyone" as those not seeking out sex, ignoring the many ways Parisians did so in the course of their daily routines. And yet it is only through a discourse that acknowledged the seeming omnipresence of public sex that such a politics made sense. The letters were therefore less a reaction to the sexualization of Parisian space than a contributing factor.

This chapter shows how the struggle over space and sex contributed to the development of a specifically republican, participatory urban citizenship premised on a strict separation of the respectable individual from public sex that could never be fully put into practice. It was the recognition of that failure that led Parisians to turn to the police. Although they argued that the police had to be responsive to their concerns, their efforts to encourage state regulation of street life ultimately placed them at the mercy of the state as well. The extension of state surveillance and the application of the logic of regulation across city space thus emerged not against the development of republican citizenship but through it.[11] The contradiction between assertions of independent citizenship and the call for state intervention rendered the citizen vulnerable to the very same kinds of regulation that were supposed to be directed at those excluded from the public in the first place. The logic of regulation no longer applied to just prostitutes and pederasts; it applied to everyone.

---

universal." Harold Mah, "Phantasies of the Public Sphere: Rethinking the Habermas of Historians," *Journal of Modern History* 72, no. 1 (2000): 168. See also Judith Surkis, *Sexing the Citizen: Morality and Masculinity in France, 1870–1920* (Ithaca, N.Y.: Cornell University Press, 2006), 2.

9. René Bérenger, *Rapport fait au nom de la Commission chargée d'examiner la proposition de loi de M. Bérenger, sur la prostitution et les outrages aux bonnes mœurs* (Paris: Imprimerie du sénat, 1895), DB 408, 5, APP.

10. Ibid., 1.

11. The expansion of moral surveillance described by Marcela Iacub, therefore, came about not simply via the courts but through citizen action as well. See Marcela Iacub, *Through the Keyhole: A History of Sex, Space, and Public Modesty in Modern France,* trans. Vinay Swamy (Manchester, U.K.: Manchester University Press, 2016), pt. 1.

Constructing a Public

In 1881 a man named René Serrand wrote to the police asking them to arrest two prostitutes who had the habit of stationing themselves on the boulevard de la Madeleine and would "assault the passers-by and follow and insult them after they repel[led] their obscene propositions." One evening, one of the prostitutes took Serrand by the arm and claimed, "I have the right to do so; it's a free country [*nous sommes en republique*]!" After finding his complaint rebuffed by two *sergents de ville,* Serrand decided to write, arguing, "If honest men, paying a great deal in taxes and living a step from this boulevard, see themselves ignored by the sergents de ville, while they are chased, jeered, and insulted by prostitutes and their protectors, they will be forced, as you have been warned, to protect themselves." Finally, he points out that "there are enough maisons de tolérance that one could make these bareheaded women and these young men with effeminate voices who are the shame of our neighborhood disappear."[12]

This letter's rhetoric reflects the common themes of the cache of complaints contained in the Archives de la Préfecture of Police of Paris. Gradually expanding from the particular to the general, the letter opens by describing a specific encounter and concludes with a broader call for the morals police to intercede in the city. In between, the writer asserts his own contribution, in the form of his tax payments, which should justify his claims in the eyes of the police. In addition, he acknowledges—indeed supports—the existence of a system of public moral regulation that relegated female prostitutes to the city's brothels. In fact, he even extends that logic to encompass men who sought sex with other men as well, reflecting the continuing association of the two. At the same time, he reveals his own knowledge of how to recognize the presence of both (bareheaded) women who sold sex and (effeminate) men who sought sex with other men. The preservation of Serrand's identity as an honest man therefore necessitated not simply his continued contribution to the commonwealth but also his freedom of movement on the streets, secured through state action that would ensure his separation from the public sexual culture even as he knew how to recognize it.

The letter is relatively unique, however, in that it gives mediated voice to one of the women so targeted, who declared that she had the right to act in public, to address passers-by, and to make herself otherwise known. Her

---

12. René Serrand to Préfet de Police, April 14, 1881, "Boulevard de la Madeleine. Dossier général," JC 60, formerly BM2 16, APP. Regulations forbade registered prostitutes from going bareheaded, but one doctor, at least, argued that doing so was the habit of some classes of prostitutes. See L. Reuss, *La prostitution au point de vue de l'hygiène et de l'administration en France et à l'étranger* (Paris: J.-B. Baillière, 1889), 269.

reference to the Republic, ironic perhaps, lays bare the contradictory promises at play. On purely ideological grounds, attempts to simply ban certain classes of women from the streets of Paris were no longer wholly tenable. By arguing that she too had the right to a public existence, now that she lived in a republic, this woman underscored a possible shift in how Parisians perceived police toleration of prostitution. Indeed, this encounter took place during a moment of heightened tension within the prefecture of police regarding these precise issues.

Beginning in the mid-1870s, a movement of abolitionists against regulated prostitution showed increasing confidence levying critiques at the police. Under the influence of Josephine Butler's campaigns against the British Contagious Diseases Acts, men such as the politician Yves Guyot and the doctor Louis Fiaux engaged a sustained campaign against what they argued—correctly—were constant violations of women's right to liberty.[13] Under the brunt of these attacks, the prefect of police actually disbanded the morals brigade in 1881, bringing it under the auspices of the Paris Sûreté, the city's detective bureau.[14] A public relations move rather than a real change in policy, this moment nonetheless stands as an important milestone in the development of neo-regulationism, a shift away from enclosure to one of surveillance that culminated in the police's official recognition in the very early part of the twentieth century of maisons de rendezvous, brothels within larger apartment buildings that did not house those who worked within them but served as the meeting point for prostitution, often for a higher class of clientele than that intended for the maisons de tolérance or who would frequent a clandestine hotel.[15] These debates over the proper role of the state in regulating women's public sexuality were reflected in this 1881 letter. The woman lays claim to "liberty" and to the right to access public space and interact with others, while the writer asserts the continuing need for state intervention into the sexual life of the city.

The letters were ultimately less concerned with actual policy than they were with using policy to frame public opinion and produce a reaction by the police. By speaking in the name of all "honest" men and women, the letters constructed a general public threatened by the outrages of the public sexual culture. Therefore, letter writers strove to subordinate their individual

---

13. Alain Corbin, *Les filles de noce: Misère sexuelle et prostitution au XIXe siècle* (Paris: Flammarion, 1982), 316–324; Charles Bernheimer, *Figures of Ill Repute: Representing Prostitution in Nineteenth-Century France* (Cambridge, Mass: Harvard University Press, 1989), 211–212.

14. Jill Harsin, *Policing Prostitution in Nineteenth-Century Paris* (Princeton, N.J.: Princeton University Press, 1985), 337–338.

15. Corbin, *Les filles de noce,* 257–273, 470–473.

interest to a general good. In doing so, the writers performed the necessary fiction of "[rising] above, or set[ting] aside, one's private interests" in order to justify participation in a "critical public."[16] Specifically, letters often situated particular grievances within a broader frame while also using various shorthand—"good father" was the most common—that signified one's ability to represent the public interest (even as these terms underscored how such a concept actually relied on particular characteristics). The display of sex and sexual solicitation threatened the ability of these Parisians to maintain this fiction, as it revealed their own inability to leave sex in the private sphere and to escape its public existence. One's own public desires—elicited by a passing prostitute or pederast—therefore threatened one's ability to speak for this public in the first place. The weakness of the claim helps explain why the letters seem so willing to call on the state in the first place. The justification for state intervention into public space and private lives relied on the notion of a public sphere that was increasingly coextensive with the state itself, because absent such power the public sphere's fictive character seemed increasingly apparent.[17]

First, many writers simply asserted that they spoke in the name of the larger community. Letters from individuals used their claims to construct an "honest" public in whose name they spoke. Individual encounters were reconfigured into possible threats to anyone who wandered the city. For instance, at the very end of the century, after arguing that the presence of prostitutes was hurting his business, a porcelain and crystal dealer on the rue de Provence asked, "What, therefore, is to be done to ensure that the rights of honest people are respected?" No longer were his specific business interests at risk; instead, the rights of all "honest people" were under attack. The broader community was thus constructed in opposition to the prostitutes who also happened to be using that particular space. He closes his letter by claiming that his "complaint is that of the entire working neighborhood which has aspired for a long time to breathe clean air."[18] The letter thus builds a constituency in whose name it speaks by virtue of its opposition to the evidence of public sex, even as he wrote out of his own specific interest.

16. Michael Warner, *Publics and Counterpublics* (New York: Zone Books, 2002), 40–41.

17. Jürgen Habermas describes the "structural transformation" of the public sphere as a process where on the one hand, once-public functions came to be carried out by private institutions and, on the other hand, the state increasingly extended into society. Jürgen Habermas, *The Structural Transformation of the Public Sphere: An Inquiry into a Category of Bourgeois Society*, trans. Thomas Burger (Cambridge, Mass: MIT Press, 1991), 142. On this claim, see esp. Craig Calhoun, "Introduction: Habermas and the Public Sphere," in *Habermas and the Public Sphere*, ed. Craig Calhoun (Cambridge, Mass: MIT Press, 1992), 21.

18. Louis Borelli to Préfet de Police, August 4, 1899, "Rue de Provence. Dossier général," JC 61, formerly BM2 32, APP.

Petitions signed by multiple people represented the shared concerns of entire neighborhoods rather than those of the individual signatories. One petition sent to the police on September 20, 1876, claimed that the passage Raguinot off the rue de Chalons in the twelfth arrondissement "was inhabited by a great deal of *femmes de mauvaise vie.*" The petition was sent in the name of a group of shopkeepers who complained that the presence of prostitutes prevented them from making a profit; they argued that "this arcade would be inhabited by many honest employees of little resources who have wives and children, because the location is not very expensive, and who are unable to stay here in view of the immorality that reigns here." The petition accuses the police of not caring about their plight, even though their agents' salaries are paid by "we taxpayers," and that they should "protect the weak against the strong and the moral against the immoral." Further, the petition claimed, good fathers were unable to bring their wives and children to the area "without often witnessing the most immoral acts and hearing words that should not be uttered in good society." The petition closes by claiming to speak for not only those who had signed but the greater community as well: "These exploiters of human flesh, numbering as they do no more than three in the arcade, the demands of the majority should take priority over those of the minority."[19] The petition thus expands from speaking in the name of the shopkeepers of the passage Raguinot, to their employees, to taxpayers, to the honest men of the city, to, simply, "the majority." This latter term refers, of course, to the ten or so signatories to the petition, but it also alludes to the democratic promise of the Republic more broadly. The single community of the arcade becomes, in this sense, the one true public, in whose name the police had a duty to act. The small "minority" of prostitutes lose their right to the city in the face of this constructed majority.

Second, the construction of universality relied on a certain kind of particularity: heterosexual reproduction. Writers linked the terms "honorable" and "honest" to their familial roles, usually as fathers but occasionally as mothers. The protection of children stands as the representative practice of the honorable Parisian and necessitated the control of public space. Indeed, contemporaneous developments in public health discourse, combined with pronatalist impulses that emerged after the Franco-Prussian War (1870), emphasized the importance of ensuring that children had access to fresh air and public space.[20] Writers drew on this discourse as they complained

---

19. Petition to Commissaire de Police du 12 arrondissement, Paris, September 20, 1876, "Passage Raguinot. Dossier général," JC 74, formerly BM2 14, APP.

20. Third Republic pronatalism encouraged the opening of green space for children's health. See Richard Hopkins, *Planning the Greenspaces of Nineteenth-Century Paris* (Baton Rouge: Louisiana State University Press, 2015), 54–58.

that the presence of women who sold sex prevented them from taking their children outside. One mother wrote to the police to complain that she was forced to "cloister" her young son and daughter in their apartment, keeping the blinds and windows closed, so that they not witness the prostitute who solicited from her window and the "to and fro of men entering the house."[21] In another case, a man wrote to the police to describe "the deplorable things that take place in our neighborhood, especially being a good father," after going for a walk with his children and witnessing "a drunk woman showing her nudity to them."[22] The emphasis on the safety and security of children helped transform the idea of speaking for a wider public into speaking in the name of a general interest connected to one of the most important issues of the day.[23]

Even those who were not necessarily themselves fathers drew on the connection. In 1873, for example, the police received a letter from a B. Lecrivain, the "president of an association of apprentices and young workers in Paris." The letter complains that "for some weeks, the area around our building has been frequented by corrupted beings, both men and women, who provoke our children." In particular, the previous Friday, "a worker around 35 years old appeared to place the hand of a child of fourteen years old on his uncovered genitals." He notes that no crime had seemingly been committed, because their apprentices were older than thirteen and no violence had occurred, but "it remains profoundly regrettable to see these young men, minors for the most part, so exposed to corruption."[24] Lecrivain situates himself as the protector of "his" children, which justifies the complaint in the face of a law code that saw no victim, even if the child himself may have been quite disturbed by the incident.[25] Of course, making an arrest was not always the

---

21. Letter to Préfet de Police, March 28, 1892, "Rue Pigalle, 63," JC 61, formerly BM2 10, APP. For another example of mothers writing to the police, see Un groupe de Mères de Famille to Préfet de Police, August 2, 1898, "Boulevard de la Villette, 123bis," JC 95, formerly BM2 58, APP.

22. Letter to Préfet de Police, May 21, 1882, "Rue de Villejuif, 15. Hôtel. Vve Buisson," JC 71, formerly BM2 28, APP.

23. On French pronatalism during this period, see, for example, Karen Offen, "Depopulation, Nationalism, and Feminism in Fin-de-Siècle France," *American Historical Review* 89, no. 3 (1984): 648–676; Jean Elisabeth Pedersen, "Regulating Abortion and Birth Control: Gender, Medicine, and Republican Politics in France, 1870–1920," *French Historical Studies* 19, no. 3 (1996): 673–698; Joshua Cole, *The Power of Large Numbers: Population, Politics, and Gender in Nineteenth-Century France* (Ithaca, N.Y.: Cornell University Press, 2000), chap. 6.

24. B. Lecrivain to Préfet de Police, November 24, 1873, DA 230, doc. 366, APP.

25. Lecrivain was referring to Article 331 of the penal code, "Attentat à la pudeur sans violence," which defined statutory rape at the age of thirteen. On the age of consent in this context, see Régis Revenin, *Homosexualité et prostitution masculines à Paris, 1870–1914* (Paris: L'Harmattan, 2005), 169–171.

point of moral policing, and the authorities did respond by sending officers to keep an eye on the young man as he left the workshop. A few weeks after the incident, having not seen anyone bother him and having been assured by the child himself that he "no longer worried," the police let the matter go, "although this area will continue to receive the attention of the service."[26]

Third, the letters situate their authors in a particular relationship with the police, asserting that the police worked for them and not the other way around. Constituting a public of taxpaying citizens, letter writers' opposition to the state was a process of democratic subordination. This shift is particularly important in the context of a shift from the police state of Napoleon III to the Third Republic. Although the new regime kept in place most of the police apparatus that predated it, the prefecture found itself increasingly responsive to a public it now served.[27] For instance, one 1892 letter, from a B. Rousseau, could only express astonishment "that the police don't watch the entrance to the bois de Boulogne in the area of the pavilion d'Armenonville [near the Porte Maillot in the northeastern section of the park]," where "no less than 40 prostitutes and at least as many pimps" hung out. According to Rousseau, those who lived in the area were tired of complaining and being ignored by the prefecture. He threatens to write directly to the prefect, warning that influential people as well as the newspapers will take notice of the superintendent's lack of progress regarding the problem, before asking, "Where is our money going, if we are ourselves reduced to playing police?"[28] More than a simple threat, Rousseau's rhetoric establishes him and those whose voices he amplifies as the proper source of authority. The prefect of police has been rendered subordinate to the demands of the citizenry, in this letter at least, reflecting a broader shift from the time when all police agents were simply seen as spies.[29]

These requests were fraught because by writing Parisians revealed their own participation—even if unwilling—in the culture of public sex. The let-

26. "Rapport: Au sujet d'excitation à la débauche de jeunes apprentis du patronage de la rue Stanislas, no. 11," December 15, 1873, DA 230, doc. 368, APP.

27. Jean-Marc Berlière attributes the survival of the prefecture of police under republican rule to the government's fear of social disorder, combined a willingness of well-professionalized police force to follow orders irrespective of politics. Jean-Marc Berlière, *Le monde des polices en France: XIXe–XXe siècles* (Paris: Éditions Complexe, 1996), 91–95. On the police and public opinion, see Malcolm Anderson, *In Thrall to Political Change: Police and Gendarmerie in France* (Oxford: Oxford University Press, 2011), chap 3.

28. B. Rousseau to Commissaire de Police, August 29, 1892, "Bois de boulogne. Dossier général," JC 82, formerly BM2 42, APP.

29. One reason why the police began wearing uniforms in the late Restoration era was "to convince the public that the police were there to help and were not all spies." Clive Emsley, "Policing the Streets of Early Nineteenth-Century Paris," *French History* 1, no. 2 (1987): 261.

ters therefore had to negotiate the precise relationship between revealing that participation and disavowing it. The decision whether to sign one's name highlights this issue. As we have seen, many of those who wrote to the police in order to complain about female prostitution signed their letters; some who wrote regarding men seeking sex with other men did so as well. Although no absolute rule governed whether or not a letter was signed, many did so because they remained confident that they stood for the general interest. In this way, particular characteristics—namely, class privilege—became the avenue for membership in a public that required one to leave private interest behind. Signing one's name, ironically, thus signified the ability of that singular individual to represent the general public. In contrast, the anonymous denunciation came to represent the writer's inability to abstract themselves. Fear of being revealed, itself rooted in a self-interest, came to be associated with the public sexual culture, particularly male same-sex sexual activity. The need to hide one's identity had the ironic effect of associating one's complaint with particular and personal interests.

The police and moral commentators explicitly associated the anonymous denunciation with sexual perversion, because they believed that it was used for petty interests or blackmail. Félix Carlier, for instance, declared, "The anonymous letter is the most exact expression of [pederasts'] courage; they turn to it in every circumstance," such as when they would denounce someone who rebuffed their advances or used it against a rival.[30] Ali Coffignon agreed, declaring, "For pederasts, the anonymous letter is their greatest weapon; these individuals always incarnate cowardice allied with ferocity."[31] The anonymous denunciation highlighted a writer's difference; it provided the measure of their distance from those who actually possessed the right to address the state. Anonymity drew attention to one's involvement with the public sexual culture and highlighted the writer's knowledge of the signs of public sex. For instance, while an anonymous letter sent to the prefecture in September 1876 claimed to be sent out of "duty," its precise description of two men, both named and described in detail, reveals the writer's intimate familiarity with at least some men who sought sex with other men. Indeed, this almost illegible letter asks the prefect to excuse the writer's desire to "remain incognito . . . despite wanting to render service to society."[32] The anonymous letter thus tries, but fails, to accomplish the same kind of generalization as those that featured signatures. It explicitly recognizes the suspicion drawn by

---

30. Félix Carlier, *Études de pathologie sociale: Les deux prostitutions (1860–1870)* (Paris: E. Dentu, 1887), 287.

31. Ali Coffignon, *Paris-Vivant: La corruption à Paris* (Paris: Librairie Illustrée, 1888), 335.

32. Anonymous to Préfet de Police, September 21, 1876, DA 230, doc. 390, APP.

an unwillingness to attribute one's claim to a specific person, even as it cannot resist noting the particular targets of its venom. Here, then, is an irony: only those letters that directly identified the specific writer successfully performed participation in the public sphere; those that remained anonymous were precisely those most likely to have actually emerged from the public sexual culture itself.

That the letters, whether anonymous or not, always revealed the writers' participation in the public sexual culture proved problematic for those seeking to speak against it, especially in reference to men who sought sex with other men. For instance, a letter sent by L. Ravaday in August 1876 described a "band of vagabond young men between 15 and 18 years old, without means of existence other than blackmail and a shameful métier against morals," who had harassed him. These young men, he explained, "frequent the puppet theater of the Champs-Élysées during the day and the perimeter of the cafés-concerts during the evening, where they exercise their culpable work." These details, he concludes, "had been given to me by a well-informed person," but he wrote in the name of "honest people" who "should be able to return home without being bothered."[33] Although he signed his name and referenced the broader public, this writer still felt the need to displace his own knowledge onto another, anonymous person. The information itself, therefore, remained anonymous, which undercut the letter's claim to universality. This example highlights the difficulty men had in speaking of same-sex sexual activity. No one would assume that the men who signed their names to complaints about female prostitutes were prostitutes, but to mention male same-sex sexual desire was to reference their own knowledge of same-sex sexual activity. Perhaps, too, it speaks to the fear that such desires needed merely the right spark of "curiosity" to find themselves awakened. Therefore, having tried to separate himself from these pederasts, the writer succeeded only in putting his own claims and social place into doubt. By referencing same-sex sexual activity, the male writers of these letters put their own desires into question; their understanding of the signs of same-sex sexuality placed them as participants in the public sexual culture.

Bodies and Boundaries

The arena of public opinion represented by the letters depended on a dual move of asserting one's ability to speak for the populace in general terms while also distinguishing oneself from the very acts that gave content to the letters. The discourse enunciated in the letters strove to assert and maintain

---

33. L. Ravaday to Préfet de Police, August 21, 1876, DA 230, doc. 389, APP.

the autonomy of particular classed and sexed bodies in the city. As Elizabeth Grosz has argued, "The city provides the order and organization that automatically links otherwise unrelated bodies," which produces particular kinds of "corporeality."[34] As men and women used urban space, encountered one another, and interacted with objects and other people, their sense of who they were in their very skin shifted and remade itself. To exit the ostensibly "private" sphere and enter the public necessitated everyday interaction between strangers that remained fraught as middle-class Parisians became committed to a sense of personal autonomy. This form of self-fashioning stood as an attempt not only to ensure control over the experience of urban life but also to assume an inviolable body, one impermeable to the sights, sounds, and textures of sex in the city. And yet the letters also reveal, unsurprisingly perhaps, a consistent anxiety that bodies were always susceptible to invasion by the public sexual culture. The imposition—if one can call it that—of arousal, so often outside our control, threatened the ability to control how one experienced the transforming urban landscape.[35]

Parisians called on the state to preserve new relations between the senses and the self in order to protect a particular vision of class and urban belonging. Alain Corbin has famously described a process whereby the bourgeoisie, by controlling and managing both its own smells and those of others, distinguished itself from the "putrid" working classes.[36] The reconfiguration of urban smell—through individual practices, such as the use of perfume, and state action, such as the removal of excrement—formed one part of a broader process whereby experts and individuals strove to manage the experience of the city. Less a process of "deodorization" and more a new kind of management, the successful conditioning of bodily experience and bodily odor enabled individual Parisians to separate themselves from the urban crowd even as they moved about the city.[37] Others, however, failed at this project: men who sought sex with other men were linked with "animal fetidity," through

34. Elizabeth Grosz, "Bodies-Cities," in *Sexuality and Space,* ed. Beatriz Colomina (Princeton, N.J.: Princeton Architectural Press, 1992), 243.

35. Keely Stauter-Halsted makes a similar point in her study of Poland. See Keely Stauter-Halsted, *The Devil's Chain: Prostitution and Social Control in Partitioned Poland* (Ithaca, N.Y.: Cornell University Press, 2015), 34.

36. Alain Corbin, *Le miasme et la jonquille: L'odorat et l'imaginaire social, XVIIIe–XIXe siècles* (Paris: Flammarion, 1986), 168.

37. Mark S. R. Jenner underlines that "to suggest that nineteenth- and twentieth-century sanitary developments amounted to a 'total war against smells' on the part of modernity is thoroughly misleading, because the modern (however defined) embraced and emitted so many of them." Mark S. R. Jenner, "Follow Your Nose? Smell, Smelling, and Their Histories," *American Historical Review* 116, no. 2 (2011): 340.

their association with anality and the public urinal.[38] Those who wrote to the police asserted their need for bodily integrity in order to use the city while at the same time underscoring the fragility of their attempts to achieve this aim.

The complaints sent to the police emphasized how prostitutes shattered faith in police ability to control the urban experience through vivid descriptions of the sights, sounds, and textures of public sex.[39] These solicitations, whether referencing a look, a touch, or a sound, threatened the walker's control over his own body. Prostitutes were adept at taking advantage of men's desires. As one commentator wrote, prostitutes stopped men "in the middle of the street" in order to "torment, excite, and lead them to debauchery."[40] The "torment" of solicitation threatened to dissolve the innocent walker's self-control, which signified his ability to safely move about the modern city.

The letters underscore the importance of visual solicitation as a way of seeking sexual encounters during the second half of the nineteenth century. They reveal at the same time, however, that the female prostitute had not simply become another *femme-spectacle* to be consumed by the male bourgeois.[41] Instead, as we have seen, her embodiment of sexual commerce served as a major challenge to the division between the licit and illicit and thus the control of one's own body. Her ability to attract the gaze—sometimes despite itself—emphasizes the importance of sex in how people conceived of modern urban life. Although privileged walkers gazed on objects, the letters reveal that supposed objects of those looks frequently attracted an unwilling gaze as well. For instance, one writer complained that while taking a walk with his children, an inebriated prostitute "showed her nakedness" to them.[42] Another anonymous letter, sent in the name of "all honest inhabitants," claimed that prostitutes were exhibiting themselves to honest women in the bois de Boulogne.[43] In yet another instance, B. Rousseau wrote to the police again to complain that he and a friend's family had come upon a prostitute engaging

---

38. Corbin, *Le miasme et la jonquille,* 172.

39. Although expert discourse such as that studied by Corbin refers to the smells of illicit sexuality, the letters I have examined do not. For instance, in 1856 Paul Auguez described the "robust young girls, lively and fresh, sporty and pink, exhaling love from all the pores of their alabaster bodies." Similarly, Ambroise Tardieu declared that pederasts' bodies "exhaled the most penetrating perfumes." Paul Auguez, *Les marchands de plaisir* (Paris: Dentu, 1856), 17; Ambroise Tardieu, *Étude médico-légale sur les attentats aux mœurs,* 3rd ed. (Paris: J.-B. Baillière, 1859), 138.

40. A. Granveau, *La prostitution dans Paris* (Paris: 1868), 28.

41. Corbin uses this term to underscore the importance of visual solicitation in an "extroverted" city. See Corbin, *Les filles de noce,* 301–303.

42. Letter to Préfet de Police, May 21, 1882, "Rue de Villejuif, 15," JC 71, formerly BM2 28, APP.

43. Letter to Directeur de la Sûrêté publique, March 1, 1879, "Bois de Boulogne. Dossier général," JC 82, formerly BM2 42, APP.

in "the most obscene acts" with a client in the same park, who proceeded to shout "invectives at us, saying that we had bothered her client."[44]

These visual affronts disrupted writers' faith in their ability to move about the city and maintain their control of the experience, but the challenges the public sexual culture posed entailed more than the sight of sexual solicitation.[45] Women who sold sex disrupted the confidence of the imaginary typical (read: middle-class and respectable) walker. Touching could be an especially intense experience.[46] Combined with the possibility of sex, an indiscreet touch could stand for a dangerous invasion of personal space. By touching or inviting the touch of men in public, prostitutes and men who sought sex with other men defied social convention and revealed their power to shape the male walker's experience of public space. Recall the letter writer who complained that "an honest man can no longer walk peacefully on the cours la Reine [near the Champs-Élysées] between 9 and 11 at night without being accosted by women who engage in revolting touches and direct the following verbatim proposition (Do you want me to jack you off)."[47] Both actual touching and the invitation to be touched disrupted this person's ability to enjoy his promenade. The writer excuses himself for using such visceral language but explains that he had been propositioned in such a way several times. Why he insisted on roaming the area at night, when such encounters were more common, is left unexplained.

A wrong touch could be precisely what brought down the police. An 1869 police report on men "pretending to urinate" in some public facilities notes that they have not been arrested, because "they do not indulge in any touching."[48] In the urinal, men could touch themselves but not others. They had to learn to both avoid the touch of and resist touching the other men. To do otherwise created the wrong kind of connection, tacitly confirmed through skin-to-skin contact or even just its possibility. No wonder that the prospect of touch could give rise to unusually vehement letters. As seen in the above complaint, the threat of touch enabled the writer to break some of

---

44. B. Rousseau to Préfecture de Police, September 14, 1892, "Bois de Boulogne. Dossier général," JC 82, formerly BM2 42, APP.

45. The letters underscore Aimée Boutin's emphasis on the need to incorporate other senses, in addition to the visual, in our interpretations of nineteenth-century urban life. Aimée Boutin, *City of Noise: Sound and Nineteenth-Century Paris* (Urbana: University of Illinois Press, 2015), 12–13.

46. Elizabeth D. Harvey, "The Portal of Touch," *American Historical Review* 116, no. 2 (2011): 386.

47. G. D. to Préfet de Police, August 20, 1872, "Champs-Élysées. Dossier général," JC 208, formerly BM2 60, APP.

48. "Rapport: Réponses à des lettres signalant des rendez-vous de pédérastes," March 23, 1869, DA 230, doc. 356, APP.

the conventions when writing to the authorities; in fact, it is extremely rare for the letter writers to express themselves by quoting the vulgarities of the public sexual culture.

The "honest" men who managed to avoid the presence of prostitutes and pederasts sought to protect their status as such by avoiding their physical presence. However, the letters reveal how prostitutes especially subverted such strategies. When C. J. Lecour, for instance, declared in 1870 that the clandestine prostitute "displays herself loudly and attracts attention by her allures, her *toilettes,* her words and her scandals," he underscored the ways prostitutes sought to reveal themselves not only through sight but also through sound.[49] Lecour's mixed metaphor of a "loud" display highlights the importance of the aural to anxieties over the presence of prostitutes in public space. To Lecour, the display of sex could be expressed in terms of volume. The prostitute's offense thus escapes her body to shape the sensory experience of both those who witness her with their eyes and those who are simply nearby. No longer localized on her clothing or her behavior, her presence expresses itself in a way that carries it through the city. Once she appears in public, the danger of the prostitute is no longer restricted to her specific location. Returning to this example highlights the intersection between the creation of a public sexual culture and the emergence of a clear threat to bourgeois self-respect while also showcasing the ways that sex seemed unavoidable.

The sounds of solicitation intersected uneasily with those of a modernizing city. Although possessed of content, writers classified solicitation as noise.[50] Indeed, they implicitly followed writer Maxime Du Camp, who once said that prostitutes "literally do not know how to speak, not that they cannot articulate the sounds, but because they do not possess the number of words necessary to form an idea."[51] Noise, however, can mean different things depending on the context. For example, an 1892 letter complained that a group of prostitutes were in the habit of stationing themselves at the corner of boulevard Barbès and rue Labat, a rather busy intersection in northern Paris, at the base of Montmartre. Between nine and eleven o'clock, "the animation of the boulevard and the noise of the carriages deaden the scandalous noises of these . . . women [ellipsis in the original]." Later, however, "toward midnight, when a relative silence reigns, the situation becomes intolerable" as they launch invectives "that would make a dragon blush" and "full-throatedly converse with their pimps on the lookout *on the other side of the boulevard!*

---

49. C. J. Lecour, *La prostitution à Paris et à Londres, 1789–1870* (Paris: P. Asselin, 1870), 18.

50. For a definition of noise in this context, see Boutin, *City of Noise,* 5–6.

51. Maxime Du Camp, *Paris: Ses organes, ses fonctions et sa vie dans la second moitié du XIXe siècle,* 5th ed., 6 vols. (Paris: Hachette, 1875), 3:336.

[emphasis in the original]."[52] While both the city and solicitation qualified as noise, only the latter proved problematic. Indeed, the sense of the city's movement effectively hid the source of the other problem. When the street noise died down, however, the writer found himself caged in; he complained that he had not been able to open his windows during the evening for about three months. The quiet of the night was supposed to guarantee the ability of people to work during the day. By disrupting people's sleep, prostitutes managed to intrude themselves on people's most private moments. The break of repose signified how sex threatened to invade the interior spaces of well-behaved citizens.

The preservation of internal quiet could be a way of signaling one's class position. For the upwardly mobile Parisian—whether in fact or in fantasy—the struggle with sex could be a way to make a claim for a particular status. In 1888, for instance, J. Collet twice wrote to the police to complain about the prostitutes using the building that abutted his apartment, where he also had a clock-making shop. Specifically, his bedroom was next to one of the neighboring hotels, separated by a "light board partition" used to repair the separation before he was there, which "was rented out several times by day and by night." Unable to sleep before three or four o'clock each morning, he and his family could "hear everything that happened there." After complaining to the proprietress, asking her to find someone "tranquil" for the room, "she responded that it was a *chambre de passe* [a furnished room let out for prostitution] that brought in money and that the people, once inside, were free to make whatever ruckus pleased them."[53]

If modern bourgeois society depended on the interior as a scene of familial reproduction (Collet specifically mentions the presence of his young children) to signify one's membership in a privileged elite with the right to call upon the state, then the violation of that interior space by the sounds of illicit sexual pleasure—decoupled from the familial drive—deeply troubled the ability of those affected to confidently claim the attention of the authorities. At the same time, the brothel keeper next door relied on those very principles insofar as she depended on the inviolability of private space to perpetuate her business. That sound moved between two different "private" spaces highlights the ultimate permeability of the category, even as both relied on the presumption of its security. The act of writing the letter to the police signifies Collet's attempt to assert his right to call on the state in the face of a threat to

---

52. Antoni Frapasnik to Préfet de Police, June 23, 1892, "Boulevard Barbès. Dossier général," JC 86, formerly BM2 15, APP.

53. J. Collet to Préfet de Police, April 7, 1888, "Passage Brady, 74," JC 64, formerly BM2 45, APP.

his ability to adequately protect his home and his bodily need for sleep—to say nothing of his business interests. That he had to "renew" his entreaties to the police emphasizes his ultimate weakness, a class-based weakness represented best by the fact that he lived next to a chambre de passe.

Vocal solicitation forced Parisian walkers to face their apparent lack of personal space while wandering the streets of Paris. By verbally addressing those not seeking sexual gratification, prostitutes undermined the sense of control these men assumed in public. For instance, in 1900 Charles Maniget de Ponté wrote to the prefect of police and complained that "every walker who finds himself . . . passing by the avenue [du bois de Boulogne] is accosted by women who offer them certain things not necessary to describe." However, he described them anyway: "Come here, honey," a woman once invited de Ponté, "come make love a little. You [tu] aren't coming to spend a few moments next to me[? W]e would have fun together." And another time: "You [tu] will see what it's like, put your hands under my skirt."[54] The prostitute's use of the informal second person in addressing de Ponté—whose use of the particle "de" signifies, if not aristocratic blood, at least aristocratic pretension—underscores her verbal inversion of social order as she brings him into the public sexual culture by inviting his sexual touch.

Indeed, this particular prostitute seemed to relish her ability to discombobulate de Ponté. Refusing his entreaties to be quiet, "she began insulting me, and every day she called me a name." Why de Ponté did not simply find another place to walk remains unsaid, but his underlying faith that urban space belonged to him and not her was reflected in his conviction that these encounters remained out of the ordinary, unexpected, and ultimately aberrant, despite their apparent regularity. Indeed, unable to effectively shut her up, de Ponté grabbed hold of the visual and, in doing so, asserted his ability to objectify her through his own gaze. The letter ends, therefore, with a curt description:

Brown hair.
Figure, a little wrinkled.
Aged in the 40s. 45 years old.
Medium height, rather tall.
Fairly correctly dressed.
Always wearing a white boa.[55]

---

54. Maniget de Ponté to Préfet de Police, September 27, 1900, "Bois de Boulogne. Dossier général," JC 82, formerly BM2 42, APP.
55. Ibid.

De Ponté thus asserts his ultimate superiority by reducing this woman to a list of measurements. And yet he also reveals his final insecurity not only in his inability to pinpoint her age or height but also in his focus on her "fairly correct" accoutrements. Although this woman revealed herself verbally as a prostitute, visually she could have been respectable. She thus maintained final control of the situation, revealing her profession by conscious choice rather than passive signification.

The idea that sexual solicitation entailed a loss of bodily integrity drew upon a complementary discourse that emphasized its threat to physical health. Many letters evoke themes of contamination and illness—not simply the specter of venereal disease but also of the larger metaphors of decay and putrefaction that attached themselves to certain forms of public sexual activity. An anonymous complaint regarding a "male brothel" declared, "It's horrible what is disgustingly done in this infected hellhole." This almost incoherent letter associated these infections with anal sex, specifically declaring that the patron and his employee were "sodomites" and "buggerer and buggered." Concluding by simply lamenting "dirty house dirty world," the infected brothel here threatened to overrun the public world.[56]

Reflecting broader concerns over venereal disease that gripped the medical profession at the turn of the century, Parisians feared the potential for infection and grounded the threat in the bodies of those they came across. An anonymous writer, for instance, echoed Gustave Macé's description of pederasts as "infected beings" when he wrote that prostitutes were "living epidemics" after he contracted a "certain malady" from a young woman who had "twisted" him.[57] One mother from Niort, in the west of France, wrote to the Paris police and described the fall of her son in the city. After arriving in Paris, her son "fell into the hands of a woman who, after using him up to his last sous, afflicted him with one of those shameful maladies from which he will suffer his entire life."[58] Although few people seemed willing to admit having a sexually transmitted disease, the archives feature some examples of those who just happened to know people infected by a prostitute. One young man complained that several of his friends had contracted venereal diseases

56. Anonymous to Commissaire de Police, August 14, 1890, "Rue St. Denis, 289," JC 38, formerly BM2 47, APP.

57. Gustave Macé, *La police parisienne: Mes lundis en prison* (Paris: G. Charpentier, 1889), 172; Anonymous to Préfet de Police, February 21, 1901, "Rue Mazarine, 68," JC 49, formerly BM2 17, APP.

58. Richemond to Préfet de Police, December 12, 1895, "Rue de la Fidélité, 3," JC 66, formerly BM2 33, APP.

from the prostitutes at the Wagram dance hall.[59] In another instance, a woman wrote and complained that a prostitute living in a *garni*, a cheap dive hotel, had infected her husband.[60]

The fear of disease led back from the body to the spaces where one encountered sex. As the doctor Louis Martineau argued, "Syphilis loves these little Parisian corners; there, it makes fine nests of silk and velvet, but it has many disagreeable surprises for the imprudent explorer!"[61] Space itself had become infected with the effects of illicit sex; disease did not threaten just those foolish enough to patronize a prostitute but also those who sought to seek out "little Parisian corners." One Parisian echoed this discourse when he lamented that should the administration simply demolish a hotel near Les Halles, "the ground would still be infected." Nevertheless, the note still emphasized the need for the police to "clean" the streets of Paris: it lauds the "vigilance taken to clean up the neighborhood of les Halle [*sic*] Centrales, but much remained to do."[62] The "clean sweep" demanded by these letters therefore demanded the cleansing of both the city and the body in order to render public space sanitary and safe. The letters show not only how the venereal panic of the later decades of the nineteenth century permeated popular consciousness but also how sex enabled the construction of a common link between the sanctity of the city and that of the body. Preserving one necessitated protecting the other.

The Police and the Public

The union of bodily and spatial integrity was drawn from the very policing practices that the letters critiqued, especially those of neo-regulationism. Neo-regulationism entailed new strategies of sexual management that emphasized surveillance over enclosure but ultimately served to perpetuate the existing regime with a more humanizing veneer against the claims of a rising abolitionist movement.[63] Abolitionists, however, were not the only ones able

---

59. L. Trouin to Directeur du Bureau des Mœurs, May 4, 1893, "Avenue de Wagram. Dossier général," JC 85, formerly BM2 32, APP.

60. Anonymous to Préfet de Police, n.d., "Rue Rampon, 14," JC 70, formerly BM2 63, APP.

61. Louis Martineau, *La prostitution clandestine* (Paris: Delahaye et Lecrosnier, 1885), 83.

62. Anonymous to Préfet de Police, August 5, 1895, "Rue du Plat d'Etain, 3," JC 34, formerly BM2 33, APP.

63. Abolitionism in France was influenced by the public campaigns of Josephine Butler against the British Contagious Diseases Acts. She published her French speeches in Joséphine Butler, Aimé Humbert, and Armand Després, *La police des mœurs et la morale: Discours prononcés à Paris, en Janvier et Février 1877 par Mme Joséphine Butler et MM. A. Humbert, Butler, Donat Sautter, et le Dr. Després avec un appendice contenant le compte rendu sommaire des études du Conseil Municipal de Paris sur le Service des Mœurs* (Paris: Sandoz et Fischbacher, 1877). Anti-

to point to public opinion in support of their cause.[64] The letters of the late nineteenth century that demanded more, not less, police activity also constitute demands on the state explicitly made in the name of the public. Ironically, though, by arguing in favor of greater surveillance, those who wrote to the police tended to undercut their own claims to autonomy in favor of ever increasing state power.

Assessing the precise relationship between police practice and public opinion is necessarily difficult in a context where the police possessed arbitrary power over those they suspected of selling sex, to say nothing of the lack of public polling.[65] We have already seen that the police took at least some care in how they enforced their mandate, aware of both legal restrictions and the possibility of public outcry. Whatever restrictions the police placed on themselves, however, were never sufficient guarantee against abuse. As Harsin has argued, "The [regulationist] system was vulnerable to the good or bad intentions of the men who put it into operation; there were no structural, built-in safeguards for the women who were caught up in the system, and even the prefecture had to admit that abuses had occurred."[66]

As early as 1853, the police wrestled with how they should treat women who appeared in public. That year, during the evening of July 21, two women were arrested on the rue St. Antoine because "they were seen walking together . . . and one of them was a prostitute."[67] The arresting officers admitted that the women had not been caught soliciting—in fact, the "innocent" woman explained that she had hired the other woman to make a dress and they were out looking for supplies. The officers explained that they had assumed both were prostitutes and that they had "orders to arrest any filles appearing in public during the day, even when not committing any infraction." In response, their superiors requested that they be ordered to fulfill these duties in a more "rational manner": "We cannot allow two filles to be arrested

---

regulationist propaganda circulated about the mass press in France after her visit to Paris, most famously in the anonymous letters of Yves Guyot, republished as *La police des mœurs: Lettres adressées au journal* La Lanterne *par un ex-agent des mœurs et un médecin* (Paris: Administration du Journal La Lanterne, 1879).

64. Abolitionist attempts to turn the public against the regulationist system are described in Corbin, *Les filles de noce,* 453–460; Harsin, *Policing Prostitution,* 324–330. See also Berlière, *La police des mœurs,* chap. 4.

65. Some informal surveys were taken of medical professions and local administrators' views of regulation. See Corbin, *Les filles de noce,* 458–460.

66. Harsin, *Policing Prostitution,* 269.

67. This woman was referred to as a "fille publique" in the report and was most likely registered with the police. At the very least, she was probably known to the arresting officers. "Rapport: Arrestation sur la voie publique de la femme Dumaine logeuse, et de la fille Marcon, en cela parce qu'elles se trouvaient ensemble et que la femme Dumaine était supposée inscrite à la Préfecture," July 21, 1853, "Répression: Instructions," DA 223, APP.

because they find themselves together on a public street, and not having done anything to attract the attention of passers-by." The two women were set free by the superintendent.[68]

This incident highlights the contradictory impulses at the heart of the regulationist project. On the one hand, these women's lives were easily and summarily interrupted at the whim of two police officers; on the other hand, the chagrin of their superiors indicates their concern with their public image, if not with the rights of the women accused of being prostitutes. A note written by the prefect and the head of the morals police a few days later regarding this arrest argues that "this way of proceeding could give rise to the most regrettable errors, such as happened today, when a married woman having nothing to do with prostitution was arrested simply for appearing with a prostitute."[69] The specter of the false arrest proved a useful conceit for abolitionists for precisely this reason. In addition to highlighting the risk the police invited by arresting women in public, it played on a concern that was internal to the police themselves, even during the Second Empire. The supposedly absolute and arbitrary authority of the police was thus always at least partly circumscribed by an ongoing attention to public relations.

Many letters encouraged the police to ignore these qualms. They may have been sharp in their critique, but they also provided cover for the perpetuation of police power. Some writers expressed disbelief at the police's apparent incompetence at managing public sex. One 1868 letter, for instance, claimed that "if the police care about good morals, they will purge the Palais-Royal, the arcades and areas around the theatres of the mischief-makers who exploit their behind" and concludes by pointedly asking if "the Empire's police, who are so worried about political opinions, [should] be a little more active regarding morality." According to the anonymous writer, the police's priorities had been misplaced. The root of instability lay not with political dissidence but with public immorality, and the police proved incapable of telling the difference: "Are the police so blind," the letter writer asks, "that they cannot recognize all these mischief-makers, because they are well dressed by the price of their prostitution and swindling?"[70] Alluding to pederasts' supposed ability to hide their proclivities, the writer proclaims the police incapable of telling the difference between a respectable bourgeois and

---

68. Ibid.

69. "Note pour M. le Chef de la Police Municipale. Au sujet d'une arrestation opérée sur la voie publique," July 25, 1853, "Répression: Instructions," DA 223, doc. 86, APP.

70. Anonymous to Commissaire de Police du Palais-Royal, June 18, 1868, DA 230, doc. 350, APP. The writer pointed in particular to a tailor, but the police responded by saying that this individual had never been brought to their attention before. "Rapport: Transmission d'une lettre anonyme," June 18, 1868, DA 230, doc. 351, APP.

someone "well dressed" through male prostitution. Left unsaid is what would happen should the police make a different kind of mistake and accuse the respectable walker of being a pederast.

By the time the majority of the letters were written, the police had largely given up on their attempts to eliminate evidence of public sexual activity from the public spaces of Paris. The shift from enclosure to surveillance entailed a subsequent change in the meaning of "tolerance" whereby streets and other informal spaces could be more readily used for sexual solicitation and sexual activity, so long as the police had access to them. These shifting strategies of sexual management reshaped the justifications that underwrote the system in the first place. The very phrase "necessary evil" entered the popular discourse as an encouragement to police action. One letter claimed that "it would be truly useful to sweep the area around the Gare Saint-Lazare, which is infected by female prostitutes, especially when children are leaving the Lycée Condorcet." The writer goes on to explain, "We know that prostitution can be a necessary thing, but is it not still necessary to surveil it? Would it not be possible to confine it to a set area[?]"[71] The letter thus threw back at the police the very terms that justified regulation in the first place—not only the language of infection but also the accusation that while the police declared prostitution to be a "necessary evil," they did little to secure it. The slippage between prostitution as necessary evil and the system as necessary evil reemerges as the writer encourages the expansion of the later in order to contain the former.

In fact, these writers were asking the police to extend the logic of regulationism over the entire city. The desire to surveil prostitutes became a demand to watch for the potential for public sex everywhere, even in supposedly "private" spaces. The attempt to secure bodily coherence and autonomy therefore necessitated accepting greater state involvement in everyday life. In 1879, during one of the early abolitionist debates, a municipal councillor of Paris asked the prefect of police whether he had the authority to arrest all women during a raid. The question emerged out of the increasing concern that the police risked arresting innocent women taken for prostitutes. In response, the prefect admitted, "The administration is asked from time to time to make a special surveillance of areas which serve as a gather[ing] place for many clandestine prostitutes . . . and some[times] regrettable and involuntary errors are committed." Harsin has argued that this moment reveals that the police lacked any great concern over the possibility of making a false arrest,

---

71. "Un père de famille" to Préfet de Police, October 21, 1891, "Gare St. Lazare: Dossier général," JC 54, formerly BM2 60, APP. This letter also claims that a man was offering "obscene" material to the students as they left the school at night.

but it also highlights the complicity of Parisians in encouraging such risky activity.[72] As the prefect explained, they were asked to conduct these raids.

These interventions sometimes did occur following a request from the populace. For example, in 1891 the manager of Société du Passage Jouffroy—a group of proprietors located in the famous arcade not far from the Folies Bergère and the Grands Boulevards—and a number of residents wrote to the police complaining of the "excess of prostitution in the neighborhood" and explaining that they had hired two guards to keep the prostitutes out of the arcade and to "forbid access to those who are personally known to them and expel those whose looks leave no doubt to them."[73] The women so affected did not leave quietly, which drew a crowd and sometimes their pimps as well, who would insult the guards. The apparently public space of the arcade was anything but. Such an attitude may have been self-defeating, and removing prostitutes actually hurt business.[74] In any case, the problems that the private guards encountered were such that the société decided to ask the police to conduct "periodic raids" of the arcade in order to secure the space for "honorable clientele" by "aiding them in cleaning the passage Jouffroy and its surrounding areas." In order to do so, the association gave the police "advance authorization . . . to proceed in the galleries of this private property."[75] These men thus opened their homes and businesses to the eyes of the police. The presence of sex placed them not in opposition to, nor really coextensive with, the state, but rather subservient to it.

This problematic of policing was especially acute in precisely the kinds of spaces where the public/private distinction blurred or could not really be assumed. The garni provides a case in point. The police frequently targeted these retreats of both surreptitious lovers and prostitutes with their clients, as they sought out as well "people *sans aveu* [literally meaning 'people without profession' but referring to the perpetually unemployed and indigent] or in a state of vagabondage, *filles de débauche,* etc.," as one record of a raid describes the instructions given to the police.[76] The police attempted to distinguish between those who deserved privacy and those who did not: "A private act of debauchery not being sufficient for authorizing an arrest, it is necessary, in

---

72. Quoted in Harsin, *Policing Prostitution,* 4–5.

73. A. Brénard et al. to Préfet de Police, April 28, 1891, "Passage Jouffroy. Dossier général," JC 59, formerly BM2 65, APP.

74. Walter Benjamin claimed that a "ban on prostitution" was among the "reasons for the decline of the arcades. Walter Benjamin, *The Arcades Project,* ed. Rolf Tiedemann, trans. Howard Eiland and Kevin McLaughlin (Cambridge, Mass: Belknap Press, 1999), 88.

75. Brénard et al. to Préfet de Police, April 28, 1891.

76. Gustave Percha, "Visite de nuit dans le garni: Boulevard [de la] Chapelle, 88," September 15, 1881, "Boulevard de la Chapelle, 88," JC 88, formerly BM2 34, APP.

order to confirm habitual acts of public debauchery, to engage in the most fastidious research in order to verify if the resident . . . is the one sought. This is why a woman, found in a garni with a man, does not court an arrest, if she is in a habitual relation with he who accompanies her."[77] The author of this text, one in a series of books largely replicating information published elsewhere on a variety of sexual crimes and activities aimed at a popular audience, attempted to soothe reader concerns that they could ever find themselves under the gun of the police in a garni. And yet this very effort at reinforcing the care the police took—namely, their fastidious research—served to highlight the need to break everyone's privacy within the hotel, even if not everyone was at risk of arrest. How else, in other words, could one confirm habitual debauchery but via habitual surveillance? The hotel had become a brothel because of its use by prostitutes and its invasion by the authorities.

Moral commentator Jules Davray once declared of furnished hotels that "at each keyhole an ear listens, eyes watch, and all of their [otherwise innocent lovers'] beautiful love speeches, their caresses sighing languorously, are the prey of attentive servants."[78] The fictive privacy of the garni could not be sustained. Indeed, one lodger wrote to the police in order to complain that the police were harassing his tenants, making it so that they "could no longer go home without being remarked upon." He goes on to note, "I am a lodger and I think therefore that I have the right to receive a couple who comes to demand a room for the night, unless I am unaware of something."[79] This proprietor, arguing, of course, that he did not receive prostitutes, recognized how the request for surveillance not only put the city under constant watch but also turned innocent couples into sexual suspects. The letter of complaint served the men who wrote to the police so long as they escaped the repercussions, but such escape was never really possible. The very confidence that the letter writers would be able to maintain their own privacy in a city of surveillance highlights how the panoptic city emerged as much from the bottom up as from the top down. The letter writers had rendered themselves into prisoners, unaware of when the state was watching, but apparently glad it was, even as they seemed barely cognizant of the fact that it always could. The construction of "privacy" in this sense rendered everyone simultaneously—and perpetually—public.

77. Dr. Caufeynon [Jean Fauconney], *La prostitution: La débauche à Paris—les maisons de tolérance—la prostitution clandestine—règlements de police—caractère des prostituées* (Paris: Offenstadt, 1902), 40.

78. Jules Davray, *L'amour à Paris* (Paris: J.-B. Ferreyrol, 1890), 20.

79. Simonin to Préfet de Police, June 8, 1890, "Rue St. Denis, 71," JC 35, formerly BM2 34, APP.

Conclusion

The people who wrote to the police in order to complain about public sexual activity believed that the state had a responsibility to respond to their concerns. This faith relied on the emergence of a public capable of speaking in its own interests. Members of this public relied on the sanctity of their private lives to justify their public roles. The failure to separate their lives from the public sexual culture threatened that premise, because it undercut their sense of autonomy, the sanctity of their interior self. In response, writers encouraged the police to actively and aggressively police public space, even if that response required the invasion of the private. Sex became both the source of a discourse that supported the public sphere and the extension of state power over that realm at the same time. The strength of neo-regulationism can be sourced to this conjuncture of a public sphere constituted through a discourse of sexual regulation that named it as central and also disavowed it. While it is true that the abolitionist movement relied on republican notions of liberty that also laid claim to public opinion, such arguments ultimately floundered in the face of the apparent need to manage sex. Public support for police activity buttressed the emergence of this continuing regulation of illicit sex. Regulationism did not persist despite Third Republic discourses of liberty but because such discourses seemed to require delimiting who could and could not use public space.

Public sex therefore stood as an important axis around which essential questions of bodily autonomy and state power were worked out. Encounters with the public sexual culture put into question the ability of Parisians to justify their participation in republican politics. The reassertion of that role required abstracting oneself as representative of a general public with the right to call on the state. But the very surveillance this strategy required put that autonomy back into question, because nothing could guarantee that the government would respect it. The instability inherent in the public sphere highlights how it ultimately failed to separate from the public sexual culture. Reliant on it as a convenient other, Parisians used evidence of public sex to generate a common understanding of urban space. In the name of their right to freely circulate about Paris, the writers called on the police to curtail that right to others. There could be no true privacy in the modern city, because that would lead to the freedom to use and enjoy it. These men had such little faith in their own secure identities that they could not risk allowing anyone and everyone to freely move about alongside them. Indeed, the application of the regulationist logic beyond the brothel reinforced the central place of public sex in the way people understood and used the city.

6

SELLING THE PLEASURES OF PARIS

On April 27, 1894, René Bérenger rose in the French Senate to defend his proposed law on "prostitution and offenses against morals." His effort to place prostitution under clear legal authority for the first time complemented his resistance to Third Republic liberalization more broadly. Bérenger therefore made sure to couch his proposal in those terms, acknowledging, "It is no doubt impermissible . . . to encroach upon the domain of liberty or exercise any constraint on private life." However, he continued, "If each person has the right to express his thoughts and to regulate his actions with complete freedom, no person has the right to inflict on others spectacles likely to harm, disturb, or especially corrupt them. It is therefore in the name of liberty itself that the law must intervene, because no society would be possible without reciprocal respect for the rights of others."[1] Thus argued, Bérenger's proposed restrictions would actually guarantee greater freedom rather than less.

Bérenger proposed a new crime of solicitation, but much of his ire was directed at the spaces and people that enabled prostitution in the first place. In 1880 Third Republic legislators shifted the legal foundation under which drinking establishments could open. Rather than requiring "authorization" from the police, café proprietors could now open with "a simple declaration"

---

1. [René] Bérenger, "Proposition de loi: Sur la prostitution et les outrages aux bonnes mœurs," *Sénat Session 1894* (Paris: P. Mouillot, 1894), 2.

of intent to do so.[2] This new freedom, according to politicians, the police, and other moralists, was being abused. In particular, quoting an unspecified government proposition previously sent to the Chamber of Deputies, Bérenger pointed his finger at those who, "abusing the liberty granted by the law of 18 July 1880, operate veritable maisons de tolérance under the guise of drinking establishments."[3]

Bérenger specifically targeted drinking establishments that featured women servers, known as *brasseries à femmes*.[4] These places encouraged their employees to flirt with, touch, and otherwise entice customers to drink. Such modes of sexual play made it so the customers could always believe that the servers were also for sale. In support of his moral outrage, Bérenger presented a sampling of leaflets advertising these institutions: "Today, the inauguration of the Temple of Venus. Everyone will want to admire the marvelous goddesses in the graciousness of their outfits." Another: "Auberge de Cupidon [Cupid's Inn] . . . Service performed by priests of the god of love in the most original costumes. Come once more to worship at their altars." And a poem: "On their mischievous lips / Are joyous kisses [*baisers*] / Which can, one guesses, / Gather lovers." Although Bérenger claims that these advertisements were "the most explicit," they actually rely on a certain ambiguity, implying the sexual wares they made available while never confirming them.[5]

Historians, literary critics, and art historians have long recognized the role of ambiguity in the new sexual economy of the late nineteenth century, but they have usually followed Bérenger in assuming their essential heterosexuality.[6] This chapter takes up the indecipherability of the new sexual

---

2. W. Scott Haine, *The World of the Paris Café: Sociability among the French Working Class, 1789–1914* (Baltimore: Johns Hopkins University Press, 1996), 20. For the text of the law, see *Instruction sur la police des cafés, cabarets, auberges et de tous les lieux publics: Avec la jurisprudence de la Cour de cassation sur tous les cas particuliers* (Paris: Léautey, 1896), 5–8.

3. Bérenger, "Proposition de loi," 11.

4. On the brasseries à femmes, see Alain Corbin, *Les filles de noce: Misère sexuelle et prostitution au XIXe siècle* (Paris: Flammarion, 1982), 250–254; Theresa Ann Gronberg, "Femmes de Brasseries," *Art History* 7, no. 3 (1984): 329–344; Hollis Clayson, *Painted Love: Prostitution in French Art of the Impressionist Era* (Los Angeles: Getty Publications, 2003), 133–152; Jessica Tanner, "Turning Tricks, Turning the Tables: Plotting the Brasserie à femmes in Tabarant's *Virus d'Amour*," *Nineteenth-Century French Studies* 41, nos. 3–4 (2013): 255–271; Lola Gonzales-Quijano, *Capitale de l'amour: Filles et lieux de plaisir à Paris aux XIXe siècle* (Paris: Vendémiaire, 2015), 119–128; Andrew Israel Ross, "Serving Sex: Playing with Prostitution in the *Brasseries à femmes* of Late Nineteenth-Century Paris," *Journal of the History of Sexuality* 24, no. 2 (2015): 288–313.

5. Bérenger, "Proposition de loi," 12–13.

6. Corbin, *Les filles de noce,* 296; Gronberg, "Femmes de Brasserie," 339–340; Clayson, *Painted Love,* 150–152; Tanner, "Turning Tricks," 256–257; Ross, "Serving Sex," 293–294.

entertainments of the fin de siècle but places it in a broader context in order to show that sexual play was not simply a function of "heterosexual" desire. Rather, the assumption of heterosexuality also enabled men to meet other men, and sometimes women to meet other women, under cover. However, by drawing on heterosexuality, placing the power to sell sex in the hands of male entrepreneurs, and enabling distinct group spaces, these trends tended to undermine the fundamental instabilities inherent within the public sexual culture of the street that had characterized Paris in the prior decades.

By emphasizing the importance of sexual play in fin de siècle consumer culture, I complicate our understanding of the relationship between gender and consumption in the late nineteenth century. Jules Michelet's statement in 1860 about the place of single women in the city has shaped how we understand the gendered nature of urban space: A single woman "can hardly go out in the evening; she would be taken for a prostitute. . . . She would never dare enter a restaurant. She would be an event; she would be a spectacle. She would constantly have all the eyes fixed on her, hearing impertinent and unkind conjectures."[7] The bourgeois woman who entered these public spaces risked association with the lower classes, who were, in turn, linked to moral decay in general and to prostitution in particular.[8] This argument, however, not only stabilizes an imaginary bourgeois "norm" but also reifies the position of working-class women, whose own relationship to prostitution and "the male gaze" was not always so clear.

Recently scholars have recuperated the possibility of women's public enjoyment free from the stigma of prostitution. Ruth Iskin, for instance, has emphasized the increasing importance of women's presence in spaces of modern consumption toward the end of the century, which allowed them to "participate as members of the modern public" while keeping their bourgeois status.[9] In their attempt to recover "respectable" womanhood in the public spaces of the city, these analyses displace working-class women—who did indeed sometimes engage in sexual transactions—as somehow less indicative of women's place in modern society while also reinforcing a clear divide between the two. That the possibility of being confused for a working-class

---

7. Jules Michelet, *La Femme* (Paris: Hachette, 1860), xxxiv.

8. Griselda Pollock, *Vision and Difference: Femininity, Feminism, and Histories of Art* (London: Routledge, 1988), 69.

9. Ruth E. Iskin, *Modern Women and Parisian Consumer Culture in Impressionist Painting* (Cambridge: Cambridge University Press, 2007), 51. See also Temma Balducci, "Aller à pied: Bourgeois Women on the Streets of Paris," in *Women, Femininity, and Public Space in European Visual Culture, 1789–1914,* ed. Temma Balducci and Heather Belnap Jensen (Burlington, Vt.: Ashgate, 2014), 151–166.

woman is often presented as a moral and legal danger—or, at best, in terms of slumming—understates how such mixing was precisely what those who entered these spaces sought out.

This is not to say that middle-class women ultimately wanted to be confused with their working-class counterparts. Rather, urban entertainment revolved around the temporary abeyance of such clear distinctions. It is therefore a mistake to declare that women found ways of maintaining their bourgeois status while still going to the dance hall, because losing that status, temporarily, was sometimes precisely the point. Indeed, Holly Grout has recently argued that bourgeois women appropriated some of the stylings of working-class, commercial sexuality as they participated in an emerging beauty industry during the early Third Republic. The images of feminine beauty, such as the Venus and the grand coquette, provided models for respectable women that nonetheless emphasized sexual power and pleasure outside the domestic sphere.[10] Grout's analysis complements other historians' emphasis on the shifting opportunities for women's political, social, and sexual emancipation during the period.[11] Here I draw on these histories in order to emphasize how otherwise respectable Parisians sought sexual pleasure in the public spaces of Paris. Where I differ, however, is in my displacement of the assumption of heterosexuality. I take that assumption itself as an object of analysis by arguing that it stood as a strategy deployed by businessmen, prostitutes, and pederasts in order to offer otherwise forbidden pleasures to a wide public.

Attempting to evade a police crackdown, businesses negotiated a fine line between emphasizing their sexual nature and hiding it. In doing so, they deployed the strategies of solicitation that circulated about the street so as to put the public sexual culture under their own imprimatur. Proprietors and customers thereby participated in broader trends within Parisian consumer culture that emphasized the deployment of seductive spectacle in the service of consumption. Institutions such as department stores, panoramas, and music halls created a new kind of mass culture through the deployment of "dream worlds of mass consumption."[12] If these institutions encouraged the development of the participatory, shared urban culture described by Vanessa

10. Holly Grout, *The Force of Beauty: Transforming French Ideas of Femininity in the Third Republic* (Baton Rouge: Louisiana State University Press, 2015), chap. 2.

11. See Lenard R. Berlanstein, *Daughters of Eve: A Cultural History of French Theater Women from the Old Regime to the Fin de Siècle* (Cambridge, Mass: Harvard University Press, 2001); Mary Louise Roberts, *Disruptive Acts: The New Woman in Fin-de-Siècle France* (Chicago: University of Chicago Press, 2002).

12. Rosalind Williams, *Dream Worlds: Mass Consumption in Late Nineteenth-Century France* (Berkeley: University of California Press, 1982), chap. 3.

Schwartz, they did so by crafting specific strategies that spoke to different kinds of sexual desire even as they created the necessary conditions for interaction between them.[13] In doing so, public sex became more fully commercialized and available to a wider range of clients and participants than those who would have entered a brothel or who enjoyed an unexpected street encounter. By placing sex on display, these canny businessmen not only took it out of the hands of pimps and madams but also domesticated it, enabling people to enjoy it without permanently tarnishing their reputation.

These institutions of early mass consumption took control of sexual publicity in order to produce male desire. Businessmen drew on, while also undermining, the initial impulses of regulationist attempts to manipulate the sexual economy of the city by crafting their own ways of signaling the availability of sex in interior spaces. In this sense, these processes represent a return to an earlier form of regulationism, as commercial enterprises provided new outlets for male (hetero)sexual desire under the watch of the police that only sometimes included the possibilities of same-sex sexual encounter. At the same time, however, those who ran these establishments took up the ways that street solicitation tended to muddle the hierarchies of respectable and disreputable, honest and dishonest, and homo and hetero. By crafting new entertainments that purposefully undercut the distinction between client and prostitute and hetero and homosexual desire, the entertainments of the 1880s and 1890s sold the very objects of bourgeois anxiety as a source of pleasure. They placed public sex at the center of an emerging mass culture but also weakened the ability of sex workers and men who sought sex with other men themselves to shape the meaning of sexual encounter. While these businesses enabled the emergence of new publics and eventually new identities, they did so at the expense of the more fluid publics of the nineteenth century. Ironically, the selling of ambiguous identities ultimately hardened them by cordoning off space where one could be or encounter a prostitute or seek out same-sex sexual pleasure from the wider life of the city. Consequently, new spaces emerged for like-minded individuals to interact with one another, but they did so increasingly out of view of the general public.

The Moral Regulation of Spaces of Sociability

The supposed increase in public sexual activity identified in the 1850s encouraged greater attention by politicians, state authorities, and moralists on

---

13. Vanessa R. Schwartz, *Spectacular Realities: Early Mass Culture in Fin-de-Siècle Paris* (Berkeley: University of California Press, 1998), esp. chap. 1.

spaces of sociability as the source of moral decline.[14] Regulationists had long argued that cafés and other drinking establishments—by which I mean any commercial establishment open to the public that provided space for socializing and refreshments—facilitated clandestine prostitution. Alexandre Parent-Duchâtelet, for instance, claimed that a variety of drink shops existed "all over Paris . . . but especially in areas where workers and low-class people gather" that "received prostitutes, for whom they opened private rooms intended for exercising their profession."[15] This association between sex, drinking establishments, and the working class percolated through the course of the century.

However, efforts to regulate drinking establishments often said little about moral concerns. Instead, they more often concerned the preservation of social and political order. In the wake of Louis-Napoléon Bonaparte's December 2, 1851, coup against the Second Republic, the government passed a law that endowed the police with the responsibility for approving any cafés that wished to open and with the power to close them at will. It said nothing explicitly about morality and instead referred to "public safety."[16] Historians generally agree that the law's goals were essentially political; at the same time, it had clear moral inflections and implications. During the "Moral Order" government of the 1870s, the police increasingly "conflated" political and moral concerns and "presumed to enforce not simply political but, at least in principle, total control over one's public comportment."[17] The *cabinets noirs* (private or back rooms) that so concerned Parent-Duchâtelet, for instance, largely closed down in the wake of the new regulation.[18]

Despite the authority granted to the police, almost twenty thousand drinking establishments had opened in Paris by the end of the Second Empire.[19] By the 1870s, the police were already fighting an essentially rearguard

---

14. On nineteenth-century approaches to the regulation of café life, see esp. Haine, *World of the Paris Café,* chap. 1.

15. Alexandre Parent-Duchâtelet, *De la prostitution dans la ville de Paris, considérée sous le rapport de l'hygiène publique de la morale et de l'administration,* 3rd ed. (Paris: J.-B. Baillière, 1857), 1:510–511.

16. "No. 3481 Décret sur les Cafés, Cabarets, et Débits de boissons du 29 Décembre 1851," in *Bulletin des lois de la République française* 8, no. 475 (Paris: Imprimerie Nationale, 1852), 1266–1267. On this law, see esp. Haine, *World of the Paris Café,* 17; Susanna Barrows, "'Parliaments of the People': The Political Culture of Cafés in the Early Third Republic," in *Drinking: Behavior and Belief in Modern History,* ed. Susanna Barrows and Robin Room (Berkeley: University of California Press, 1991), 88.

17. Barrows, "'Parliaments of the People,'" 89.

18. Félix Carlier, *Études de pathologie sociale: Les deux prostitutions* (Paris: E. Dentu, 1887), 94–96. See also Jill Harsin, *Policing Prostitution in Nineteenth-Century Paris* (Princeton, N.J.: Princeton University Press), 32–33.

19. Haine, *World of the Paris Café,* 28.

action against their spread, preferring to surveil them than shut them down on a great scale. For example, in 1876 the prefect of police wrote to the minister of beaux arts in order to explain why he was having difficulty preventing the growth of café-concerts, which offered performances alongside drink, in Paris.[20] He explained, first, that "since the taste of the Parisian public for these establishments has become generalized, their frequentation has become normal," which had increased the demand for new establishments. Second, the prefect continued, he refused permission to any prospective owner who "does not offer serious moral guarantees." Third, he concluded that, barring a failure to adhere to these conditions, there was little he could do to prevent new café-concerts from opening and, moreover, that doing so would open him up to accusations that he was protecting already existing establishments. In the end, although the prefect promised to "redouble the attention and severity of the inspections made when a request to open a café-concert was made and to observe more closely those already established," he washed his hands of the matter by inviting the minister to provide him with contrary instructions.[21]

The minister responded by accepting the prefect's arguments and promising to support new legislation that was "more in conformity with the general interests and more suited to this matter."[22] However, they were shortly handed quite the opposite. The final collapse of the Moral Order government in 1879 brought to power a group of dedicated republicans who, in 1880, repealed the 1851 law and granted Parisians the right to open a drinking establishment by writing to the police and declaring their intent to do so at least fifteen days in advance. Local authorities throughout France, however, retained the authority to regulate the distance of cafés from certain public institutions, such as churches, hospitals, and schools, similar to the rules that governed the maisons de tolérance.[23] The police thus lost their ability to arbitrarily close down drinking establishments but still maintained a measure

---

20. For a contemporary definition of the café-concert, see Émile Mathieu, *Les cafés-concerts* (Paris: 1863), 5. See also Elisabeth Pillet, "Cafés-concerts et cabarets," *Romantisme*, no. 75 (1992): 43. On cafés-concerts as a space of sexual pleasure and eroticism, see, for instance, Lise Manin, "Perverses promiscuités? Bains publics et cafés-concerts parisiens au second XIXe siècle," *Genre, sexualité et société* 10 (2013), http://journals.openedition.org/gss/2955, accessed April 9, 2018. On the regulation of cafés-concerts in the nineteenth century, see Kelley Conway, *Chanteuse in the City: The Realist Singer in French Film* (Berkeley: University of California Press, 2004), 29–30.

21. Préfet de Police to Ministre de l'Instruction publique et des Beaux-arts, June 17, 1876, F21 1338, AN.

22. Ministre de l'Instruction publique et des Beaux-arts to Préfet de Police, June 30, 1876, F21 1338, AN.

23. *Instruction sur la police des cafés*, 5–8.

of responsibility to manage them, even though few actually took advantage of the law's restrictive powers.[24] The results of repeal were as expected: by the 1880s, the number of drinking establishments in Paris had skyrocketed to over forty thousand. This number then decreased to just under thirty thousand by the end of the century.[25]

Critics blamed the liberalization of the Third Republic generally and the 1880 law specifically for encouraging moral license and especially prostitution. The police inspector and chief of the morals police under the Second Empire, Félix Carlier, couched his concerns in a broader critique of economic liberalism. He lamented that "as the appetite for comforts and the taste for luxurious pleasures have developed and become the norm, [the authorities have] become just as liberal in regard to spaces of pleasure."[26] He associated these changes with the growth of Paris, which drew "travelers and foreigners hoping eagerly to live outside their daily life, [and] from this agglomeration of people in search of pleasure arose an invincible current that took the administration by surprise and against which it has not sufficiently reacted."[27] Those who owned and managed cafés, restaurants, taverns, and dance halls were especially to blame as they "overtly speculated on public debauchery." Capitalism itself seemed to be at fault. As Carlier declared immediately after his condemnation of these sites of sociability, "The stock market which . . . has raised so many rapid fortunes has also been one of the elements of a general demoralization. . . . The stomach and the prostitute, outside of financial fiddling, are their [financiers'] only preoccupations."[28] For Carlier, the failure of the Second Empire and then the Third Republic to manage the moral life of the city entailed more than an abrogation of their responsibility over specific spaces of social life. Rather, it indicated a more fundamental crisis facing late nineteenth-century society that could be blamed on an unwillingness of the authorities to exercise their power and rein in people's desires.

The liberalization of regulations that governed drinking establishments served as a specific example of this general trend. In 1887 the doctor and moral commentator August Corlieu argued that "since taverns are opened with a simple declaration, the administration no longer has rights over these establishments: it cannot withdraw an authorization which it had not granted."[29] Another doctor, Alfred-Jean-Marie Pierrot, put it similarly in his 1895 study of the relationship between alcoholism and prostitution: "The law

24. Haine, *World of the Paris Café,* 20–21.
25. Ibid., 29.
26. Carlier, *Les deux prostitutions,* 27.
27. Ibid.
28. Ibid., 29.
29. Auguste Corlieu, *La prostitution à Paris* (Paris: J.-B. Baillière, 1887), 118.

of 1880 constitutes not only an encouragement to debauchery and drunkenness for those who frequent cabarets, but it is even more frequently an incentive to idleness for those who keep them."[30] According to these men, by relaxing state regulation, the authorities had, in effect, encouraged café proprietors to appeal to society's lowest common denominator. Despite the very real ability of the police to monitor and regulate drinking establishments, the process of liberalization brought forth moralist nightmares of a culture unmoored from imagined moral ideals of respectability and sobriety. As the doctor Armand Laurent declared in 1893, "The increase in the number of clandestine prostitutes is due to the great liberty accorded to prostitutes who do not live in the maisons de tolérance: liberty on the street, liberty in the taverns, cafés-concerts, nocturnal bars, etc. . . . [l]iberty of all kinds . . . largely aided by the insufficiency, inaptitude, weakness—voluntary or not—of the police and those who direct them."[31]

The police obviously disagreed that they were to blame but largely accepted the premise that selling drink and selling sex were mutually reliant. On March 2, 1880, for instance, the police complained about two wine merchants on the rue de Provence who "receive prostitutes and their pimps and alert them to the presence of police officers on the street." After eating, the report continues, the women "exit onto the street, cigarettes in their mouth, and as soon as they see an officer they escape into the interior and the manager refuses to bring them out."[32] Some proprietors, Carlier claimed, encouraged prostitution in their establishments by "turning their bars into hotels or bringing the two industries together in the same building. . . . The furnished hotel and wine-sellers are, in sum, the two most useful auxiliaries to the development of clandestine prostitution."[33] These testimonies asserted that the profits of wine sellers and café proprietors depended more on sex than on drink. As the doctor Louis Martineau claimed, some wine merchants "close their eyes to the traffic in flesh that goes on around [them], sometimes en-

30. Alfred-Jean-Marie Pierrot, *Essai d'étude sur l'atténuation de l'alcoolisme et de la prostitution par la modification de la loi du 17 juillet 1880 sur les cafés, cabarets et débits de boissons* (Montmédy: P. Pierrot, 1895), 19. On the connection between the 1880 law and the increasing popularity of drinking establishments for sexual encounters, see Corbin, *Les filles de noce,* 216–220; and Régis Revenin, *Homosexualité et prostitution masculines à Paris: 1870–1918* (Paris: L'Harmattan, 2005), 50–51.

31. Quoted in Charles Virmaître, *Trottoirs et lupanars,* vol. 4, Paris Documentaire (Mœurs) (Paris: Henri Perrot, 1893), 13. The source is listed as Armand Laurent, *De la fréquence des maladies vénériennes* (Paris: J.-B. Baillière, 1893), 73, 83. This book is cited elsewhere, but a reference could not be located in the catalog of the Bibliothèque Nationale de France.

32. "Rapport: Au sujet de la rue de Provence," March 2, 1880, "Rue de Provence. Dossier général," JC 61, formerly BM2 32, APP.

33. Carlier, *Les deux prostitutions,* 266.

couraging and profiting from it," since the clandestine prostitute "encourages consumption" in their establishments.[34]

The link between public sociability and public sex in the drinking establishments of late nineteenth-century Paris was also perpetuated by a flourishing tourism industry. By the end of the century, rather explicit guidebooks began to circulate that instructed their audience in how to find sexual pleasure in the city. These books shared a common purpose with their more staid counterparts that sent visitors to museums, parks, and monuments insofar as they struggled to reduce the various opportunities for pleasure—sexual or otherwise—to a manageable, disciplined list of possibilities that rendered the new metropolis essentially knowable even to the temporary visitor.[35] The *Guide secret de l'étranger célibataire à Paris,* for instance, promised to "satisfy the curiosity of bachelors who, masters of their desire and free to go wherever their fantasies take them, have an interest in knowing exactly which are, of all the taverns, places of pleasure, or special establishments, those that most merit attracting their fancy and awaken their attention."[36] The guidebook thus simultaneously revealed "secret" information to anyone who purchased it while also constructing an audience of those respectable men who were able to "master their desire" and had the leisure time to enjoy their own "fantasies." In doing so, the guidebook built on earlier links between the city and its pleasures (see Chapter 4) while also reducing their essential spontaneity and limiting—supposedly, at least—their audience.

These books tended to integrate the world of venal sex with that of leisure more generally and thus participated in the creation of a new commercial culture that linked sociability and sex, oriented around the assumption of heterosexual desire that was safe for the young, middle-class, and male tourist to enjoy. Another *Guide secret* opened with an advertisement for "*guide-gentlemen,* who the agency promises have perfect respectability, which the tourist or traveler in Paris knows to be of the utmost importance," and who will, unlike "ordinary interpreters," take the visitor through "secret Paris."[37] The role of sexual play in the provision of tourist attractions was at the center of this form of Parisian self-advertising. The multilingual *Guide complet des plaisirs mondains et des plaisirs secrets à Paris,* for instance, contrasted Paris with London: while Paris may have shared with London its ability to ren-

34. Louis Martineau, *La prostitution clandestine* (Paris: Delahaye et Lecrosnier, 1885), 75. See also C. J. Lecour, *La prostitution à Paris et à Londres, 1789–1870* (Paris: P. Asselin, 1870), 213.

35. Rudy Koshar, "'What Ought to Be Seen': Tourists' Guidebooks and National Identities in Modern Germany and Europe," *Journal of Contemporary History* 33, no. 3 (1998): 326–328.

36. *Guide secret de l'étranger célibataire à Paris* (Paris: L. Gabillaud, n.d. [1889]), 3.

37. *Seul et véritable guide secret des étrangers à Paris* (Sceaux, France: Charaire, n.d.), 2.

der one "free, independent, and incognito," only Paris had "those beautiful women whose beauty is too complex to analyze and who, when they pass, despite themselves and despite everything, make the world's head turn and leave their image in an eternal photograph on the eyes."[38]

Even a more traditional guidebook, such as the 1899 *Guide des plaisirs à Paris,* which features neither brothels nor explicit mention of prostitution, couches its pleasures in terms of heterosexual sex. It promises "portraits of the prettiest women of Paris," and its one-page description of the brasseries à femmes, for instance, reminds its reader that "in these establishments . . . one drinks like elsewhere, but one also makes conquests, and what conquests! An entire harem of gaunt and withered girls, recruited by a matron who is usually a former prostitute retired from the business!"[39] As the guides provided the knowledge necessary to enjoy these pleasures, they constructed Paris as a site of commercial sex—somewhat displaced, here, onto the orientalist image of the "harem"—and maintained the illusion of respectability by those who sought them out. The guides both responded to and produced the "tastes" of those who read them.[40]

It is difficult, if not impossible, to precisely determine the readership of these books. Although intended for both French and foreign visitors, there is no reason to suppose that Parisians themselves did not find pleasure within their pages as well. The circulation of the guidebooks complemented a moralist discourse that produced new kinds of sexual knowledge that placed public sex—especially, but not exclusively, female prostitution—at the center of a burgeoning leisure industry. These texts did more than reflect a preexisting reality; they also made the very connection that they claimed to either describe or declaim. Both guidebooks advocating the use of public space for locating sex and moralists decrying such activity participated in the same process that remade spaces of sociability into spaces of sex. Both genres taught Parisians and visitors how to locate and solicit sex in novel public spaces. They trained visitors to recognize the difference between a bar offering sex and one offering only drink. At the same time, by providing sites of police surveillance and sites for male pleasure, the space of the café provided a useful complement for the regulated brothel. In this sense, the rise of prostitution within cafés should be seen less as an aberrant effect of a

38. *Guide complet des plaisirs mondains et des plaisirs secrets à Paris* (Paris: André Hall, n.d.), 20. Two editions of this book exist, one entirely in French and the other with English, German, and Spanish translations. Citations refer to the former edition.

39. *Guide des plaisirs à Paris* (Paris: Édition Photographique, n.d. [1899]), 107.

40. Jan Palmowski, "Travels with Baedeker: The Guidebook and the Middle Classes in Victorian and Edwardian England," in *Histories of Leisure,* ed. Rudy Koshar (Oxford, U.K.: Berg, 2002), 105–106.

consumer culture spiraling out of control, as the moralists claimed, and more as a disciplinary strategy for both regulators and entrepreneurs who would be able to monitor, control, and benefit from the provision of sex. By inciting sexual desire among Parisians, these discourses and spaces provided the means for the police and businessmen to shape when and how sex would be made available to a consuming public.[41]

Brasseries à (et pour) Femmes, Brasseries à (et pour) Hommes

Clever entrepreneurs capitalized on the association of drink with sex. The brasseries à femmes stand as the most explicit example of this general trend. While other cafés invited prostitutes in as customers, brasseries à femmes took the logic of sexual enticement even further by having serving girls emphasize their apparent sexual availability. As one 1880 police report claimed, the manager of a café in the Latin Quarter "sent away the serving boys and replaced them with serving girls, hoping that their presence would attract clients and that his takings would be higher."[42] The long-standing moral discourse that decried the symbiotic relationship between prostitution and drink became a business strategy in the hands of clever managers. While the police elaborated a system of public sex and surveillance in order to render public desire amenable to forms of discipline, proprietors took advantage of this system in ways that made desire amenable to forms of consumption.

In a brasserie à femmes, serving girls flirted and drank with the customers, sometimes inviting the men to touch them as well, in order to provide a fantasy of sexual play. A police report from December 1879 noted that the serving girls at La Cigarette, "as in all establishments of this type," carried out their duties by "sitting with the clientele, being informal with them, encouraging them to buy, and having dirty and gross conversations with them."[43] Serving girls took customers' orders but also acted as their friendly companions throughout the evening. They did so in order to sell drink by convincing the customers that they were buying more than just a beer. As an 1882 article in Le Petit Parisien described it, "Young men, sometimes children, lean on wooden tables, struggle to swallow without grimacing some infected beverage, smoke cigarettes and try to earn the approval of the venue's god-

---

41. Michel Foucault, *The History of Sexuality,* vol. 1, *An Introduction,* trans. Robert Hurley (New York: Vintage, 1990), 23.

42. "Rapport: Au sujet du café situé Boulevard St. Germain, 166," November 22, 1880, "Boulevard St. Germain, 166," JC 46, formerly BM2 16, APP.

43. "Rapport: Au sujet du café de la Cigarette," December 12, 1879, "Rue Racine, 3," JC 50, formerly BM2 24, APP.

desses." These women, the article explains, "move about, pouring the venue's poisoned ambrosia, sitting next to this one, provoking that one" in an effort to sell as much drink as possible.[44]

The servers constructed a fantasy of seduction so compelling that the customers sometimes forgot it was not real. As the paper asked in another article in response to evidence that the cafés were distributing pictures of their serving girls to attract customers: "How many young men, so attracted, went and lost their money, their honor, their health, and their life in these dives! We have seen children of twenty years blow their brains out for a serving girl!"[45] Relying on the men's desire for love, serving girls offered only fantasy, illusions that were actively encouraged by the discourse that surrounded them. The theme of young men falling in love with unattainable serving girls proliferated in newspaper articles and moralist commentaries. According to Dr. Louis Martineau, the relationship between customer and serving girl often took on "the appearance of young and crazy love, which gives the exchange a naiveté and makes him voluntarily believe in a driving force, when there is only calculation."[46] Martineau believed that these women cynically manipulated male sexual desire and created a new kind of sexual economy premised not simply on selling sex but also on the interaction, in public view, between customer and server.

These concerns remained premised on some of the same assumptions that animated regulationism. The presumption of male desire as essentially uncontrollable and easily excited enabled the brasseries à femmes even as they relied on the performance of sex as much as the sexual act. The precise outlet may have changed, but the underlying goal of providing outlets for male sexual desire through the control and surveillance of women's bodies remained the same. In fact, for all the outcry regarding the prevalence of prostitution in these kinds of institutions, the police often preferred to keep them under surveillance, allowing them to operate so long as they did not cross largely unspoken boundaries. For example, an 1881 police report described a brasserie on the boulevard St. Germain that was "frequented partially by students and workers of the neighborhood. As in most houses of this type, the women drink with the customers, but . . . they do not make more of a spectacle of themselves than elsewhere and, if they accept propositions it's only after closing, because there is no evidence of prostitution in this establishment, which

---

44. Jean Frollo, "Le 'Mauvais Oeil,'" *Le Petit Parisien,* November 13, 1882.

45. Jean Frollo, "Filles de Brasserie," *Le Petit Parisien,* December 13, 1881.

46. Martineau, *La prostitution clandestine,* 78. See also Coffignon's description of a man's suicide after falling in love with a serving girl, recounted by *Le Temps.* Ali Coffignon, *Paris-vivant: La corruption à Paris* (Paris: Librairie Illustrée, 1888), 106.

is not, furthermore, set up for it."[47] Here, the police accepted the behavior of the servers as ordinary, within the bounds of acceptability, if not of propriety. By behaving in particular ways, these women protected their livelihood, even as they promoted the play between themselves and their customers under the eyes of the police who declined to otherwise intervene at this moment.

The promotion of ambiguous sexual availability by serving girls produced other opportunities for Parisians to take advantage of commercial establishments to seek out or provide sexual opportunities. The indeterminacy of the position of serving girls implied a more general problematic for determining who was and was not selling sex in drinking establishments. In 1892, for example, a wine seller wrote to the police requesting a meeting with the prefect regarding recent accusations that prostitutes frequented his establishment, arguing (somewhat unconvincingly), "I do not keep a hotel, so I cannot facilitate prostitution. If I receive prostitutes in my establishment, I am unaware of it and those who I know I send away. . . . However, I pay for the right to sell. I cannot refuse the sale of my drinks when everything is happening in good order."[48] The distinction between the (presumably working-class) women who frequented his establishment and prostitutes was anything but clear. While the association of drink with prostitution drew police attention to this establishment, the instability in the categories at play provided a measure of protection at the same time. Indeed, this proprietor could simultaneously declare that he was unaware of prostitutes in his establishment and that he knew of some. This kind of plausible deniability—here meant not as an ironic wink that we know who these women "really" were but as continuing evidence of our inability to know—shaped the business of drink and sex in the nineteenth century.

The relative instability in knowing just who and what was being sold in these establishments enabled other kinds of drinking establishments targeted at men who sought sex with other men and women who desired other women as well. Other historians have documented the growth of institutions catering to both groups, often rooted within working-class and prostitutional milieus.[49] The role of spaces specifically intended to produce heterosexual de-

---

47. "Rapport: Au sujet de la brasserie situé boulevard St. Germain, 166," February 14, 1881, "Boulevard St. Germain, 166," JC 46, formerly BM2 16, APP.

48. Letter to Préfet de Police, September 15, 1892, "Boulevard de la Chapelle, 74," JC 87, formerly BM2 65, APP.

49. On late nineteenth-century drinking establishments catering to nascent homosexual subcultures, see Régis Revenin, *Homosexualité et prostitution masculines à Paris, 1870–1918* (Paris: L'Harmattan, 2005), 46–64; Nicole G. Albert, "De la topographie invisible à l'espace public et littéraire: Les lieux de plaisir lesbien dans le Paris de la Belle Époque," *Revue d'histoire moderne et contemporaine* 4, nos. 53–54 (2006): 87–105; Leslie Choquette, "Gay Paree: The Origins of Lesbian and Gay Commercial Culture in the French Third Republic," *Contemporary French Civilization* 41, no. 1 (2016): 1–24.

sire in enabling same-sex sexual activity, however, has been understated. For example, reporter and moral commentator Jules Davray blamed the brasseries à femmes for the rise of these other spaces: "The greatest danger constituted by the brasseries à femmes, according to us, is that they enable the development of antiphysical prostitution and endow it with the same security as in an ordinary brasserie."[50] Supposedly fearing that sites of same-sex sexual prostitution would gain as much notoriety as brasseries à femmes, Davray nonetheless assists in this development as he informs his readers that "the brasseries à hommes—since it is impossible to otherwise designate them—are located, by preference, in the general neighborhood of prostitution, that of Notre-Dame-de-Lorette."[51]

Relative police tolerance for sites of heterosexual liaisons enabled heterosexuality to offer a kind of protection to other forms of sexual activity. In 1893, for instance, the police received an anonymous letter accusing a café near the Hôtel de Ville patronized by pederasts of hiding itself under the guise of being an ordinary brasserie à femme. The letter claimed that in the early evening "men-women come to dine" and that he learned of what was happening after he was invited by a friend of his.[52] The letter's attempt to disavow the reason the writer was present highlights the success of the business at its masquerade. The innocent man would only have accepted the invitation if the brasserie truly seemed to be a brasserie à femmes. Therefore, the men who patronized this café relied on their privilege as men to freely enter otherwise suspect spaces. The assumption that men out on the town sought certain kinds of pleasures and not others—those offered by the serving girl rather than the serving boy—enabled them to socialize in the hope of going unnoticed. By playing at established sexual hierarchies, men who sought sex with other men presented themselves as fellow travelers in the enjoyment of public space.

This strategy was only partially successful. Even before they had received this denunciation, the police had conducted surveillance during the first half of 1892, which ended in July after an undercover visit failed to confirm reports of pederasty or any other infraction.[53] However, in response to the letter, the police initiated another round of surveillance in November 1893. According to them, the mostly, but not exclusively, working-class men usually "indulge in only some touching and provocation toward some young men of their sort, but with great reserve, always fearing being watched."

---

50. Jules Davray, *L'amour à Paris* (Paris: J.-B. Ferreyrol, 1890), 108–109.

51. Ibid., 109.

52. Anonymous, October 26, 1893, "Quai de l'Hôtel de Ville, 16," JC 42, formerly BM2 15, APP.

53. "Rapport: Débit quai de l'Hôtel de Ville, 16 (Bar mal famé)," July 26, 1892, "Quai de l'Hôtel de Ville, 16," JC 42, formerly BM2 15, APP.

However, through the course of several nights of observation, the police were able to recognize several known pederasts, saw several enter a nearby hotel together, and even witnessed a champagne raffle where two of them kissed. These facts provided enough evidence for the police to recommend a raid, but whether one actually occurred is left unclear in the remaining documents.[54] The police thus faced a unique difficulty in dealing with spaces of male-male sociability. The strategy employed by these brasseries and cafés was to combine elements of the brasseries à femmes with those of the public sexual culture by feigning participation in the heterosexual sexual economy while also providing opportunities for same-sex sexual activity.

Similar strategies of incitement, disavowal, and ambiguity were also followed by late nineteenth-century lesbian restaurants and cafés. The reporter Charles Virmaître, for instance, divided brasseries into two categories: "brasseries de femmes for women and brasseries de femmes for both sexes."[55] To Virmaître, even those brasseries opened for the pleasures of men could also provide for the pleasures of women: the dividing line between the brasseries à femmes and the brasseries pour femmes was never entirely clear. For example, opened in 1892, "La Souris," at 29 rue Bréda in Montmartre, was a converted brasseries à femmes that catered to women.[56] The police noted in 1897 that the clientele was mostly composed of "former courtesans, lesbians it is said, and it is absolutely forbidden to the pimps of the neighborhood." This is not to say that men were forbidden from the café, as it employed waiters as servers.[57] Indeed, this inversion of the gendered hierarchy of the brasseries à femmes—women customers and men as servers—in some ways indicates how these institutions were able to play with heterosexual assumptions, even as the space enabled women to interact with one another, and forbade those men who once profited from the business of prostitutes. The police con-

---

54. "Rapport. Au sujet du débit de vin sit, 16, quai de l'Hôtel de Ville," November 3, 1893, 3, "Quai de l'Hôtel de Ville, 16," JC 42, formerly BM2 15, APP. A report from two weeks later notes that the police arrested two men, one of whom had been previously mentioned in the November 3 report, who had injured the proprietor during a fight in the establishment the previous Saturday. Saturday is when the previous report recommended a raid; that this report concludes by requesting orders for "an eventual raid in this establishment" also indicates that one had not taken place in the meantime. "Rapport: Au sujet du débit de boissons, 16 quai de l'Hôtel de Ville," November 20, 1893, "Quai de l'Hôtel de Ville, 16," JC 42, formerly BM2 15, APP. The same request was made three days later. "Rapport: Au sujet de l'établissement sis, quai de l'Hôtel de Ville, 16," November 23, 1893, "Quai de l'Hôtel de Ville, 16," JC 42, formerly BM2 15, APP.

55. Virmaître, *Trottoirs et lupanars,* 158.

56. Choquette, "Gay Paree," 5.

57. "Rapport: Au sujet de la brasseries de 'La Souris,'" July 20, 1897, "Rue Bréda, 29," JC 48, formerly BM2 31, APP.

cluded their report by arguing against any intervention, because "the women do not indulge in any immoral act."[58]

Even the guidebooks addressed to young and single men underscore how heterosexuality provided one path through which same-sex sexual spaces emerged. The *Guide complet,* for instance, did not limit itself to heterosexual sexual opportunities. In its exclusively French edition, it included a brief description of the Rat Mort, a "café restaurant, one of the most famous of Montmartre. . . . The reputation of the Rat Mort is above all due to the women who frequent it, many of whom, incidentally, have only female lovers, at least as long as they have no need of money."[59] The inclusion of this lesbian space in this guidebook indicates how the precise pleasures of Paris blurred. The book's reference to the Rat Mort was certainly intended as a kind of voyeuristic opportunity for its presumed male readership. The perpetuation of the link between female prostitution and women's same-sex sexual desire not only points to the continuing overlap between those two categories but also represents an attempt to reduce this women's space to a kind of brothel as well and thus accessible to male desire. And yet it also provides quite the opposite. For the interested female reader, the book reveals the existence of lesbian space available to them too. By promoting lesbian space as the source of heterosexual pleasure, the book also perpetuates and enables its continued use by the women clientele themselves.

Although these three kinds of institutions all directed themselves at specific desires—heterosexual, homosexual, for men, for women—they tended to rely on similar premises. The first was that sexual desire provided an ordinary mode of selling drinks. The attraction of sexual enticements to café proprietors, customers, and male and female prostitutes did not generally undercut their position within the urban economy, despite the wishes of the aggravated Parisians described in the previous chapter, to say nothing of the recriminations of the police and published moralism. Second, although premised on the acceptability of heterosexual desire, all three relied on forms of ambiguity to provide not only pleasure for men who sought out venal sex but also opportunities for the waitresses and queer women and men who used these spaces. Put differently, heterosexual desire may have provided the avenue to deploying sexual desire in commercial establishments, predicated on the availability of working-class women to middle-class men, but it also enabled other kinds of desire to enter that economy. In light of the emergence

---

58. Ibid.

59. *Guide complet des plaisirs mondains,* 74. This passage does not exist in the multilingual edition, though it does still list the Rat Mort.

of a public sexual culture on the streets of Second Empire Paris, these Third Republic developments should not be terribly surprising. The appropriation of public spaces in ways that simultaneously reinforced aspects of familial, heterosexual, conservative sexual politics and enabled the emergence of subversive forms of sexual address, practice, and discourse also shaped the rise of commercial life. However, by providing interior spaces for men to meet men, women to meet women, and women to play the prostitute, these establishments risked providing ready-made sites of surveillance separated from the wider sexual culture, through which these three groups would eventually solidify into their now-distinguishable sexual identities.

Dance and Music Halls

Late nineteenth-century Paris featured a wide variety of spaces of sociability, of which the brasseries were only a part. Other kinds of establishments not only made performance even more central to the transformation of sex into an ordinary consumer object; they also more explicitly offered participation in sexual ambiguity. Bars and cafés that deployed sexual play tended to be directed at a particular audience—men seeking sex with women, women seeking sex with women, men seeking sex with men. Music and dance halls also used heterosexual pleasure to draw in male customers, but they also encouraged those customers to enjoy the fantasy of being something else and of encountering people they could not quite place. That these establishments generally offered their entertainments at a higher price than bars or cafés demonstrates that as such play entered mainstream consumer culture, it also exited the working-class milieu in which it emerged and became one more thing for others to purchase.[60] As the century came to a close, the culture of sex that grew up on the street, rooted in the activities of female prostitutes and men who sought sex with other men became repackaged as middle- and upper-class entertainment. This final section addresses two of the most famous spaces of mass consumption during the period—the Folies Bergère and the Opera Ball—to show how modern consumer spectacle sold the public sexual culture but managed to successfully restrict it to those who could afford to pay.

One of the most popular entertainment venues of the early Third Republic was the Folies Bergère. Opened in 1869, this music and dance hall originally served "a 'true public' of husbands and wives, provincials and Parisians

---

60. On class formation in leisure spaces, see esp. T. J. Clark, *The Painting of Modern Life: Paris in the Art of Manet and His Followers,* rev. ed. (Princeton, N.J.: Princeton University Press, 1999), 234–239.

from skilled worker to aristocrat."[61] Although the clientele would become more exclusive after 1900, during the nineteenth century spaces such as the Folies Bergère were one of the few in which a cross-class public interacted with those offering sex.[62] The Folies Bergère was a music hall that presented a multitude of spectacles all at once, wonderfully evoked by Charles Rearick:

> Under an ochre and gold ceiling of ruffled and tasseled fabric, amid allegorical statuary and rattan divans, customers could watch a trapeze duo, ballet dances, a juggler, a snake charmer, wrestlers, clowns, and such novelty acts as a kangaroo boxing a man . . . or an array of other spectators throughout the well-lighted hall. No matter where one sat or stood, one's ears were filled with a medley of waltzes and polkas and finale chords blaring over the cries of program hawkers and shoe shiners, audience chatter and applause. Everywhere the air was laden with perfume scents and the acrid odors of cigar smoke, beer, and dusty rugs. The miscellany of sensations mixed together as promiscuously as the prostitutes, *mondaines,* and their admirers in the famous *promenoir* (gallery-lounge) with its elegant bar that Manet's painting has immortalized.[63]

The experience centered not on what occurred on stage but on the various interactions within the "audience," which the police sometimes described as too large for the space.[64] As one 1877 report noted, "The program of the show is insignificant."[65] Those who paid attention to the stage had missed the point. As a character in Guy de Maupassant's *Bel-Ami* (1885) exclaimed in showing off the scene to the protagonist Duroy, who was then new to Paris, "Take a look at the orchestra: nothing but solid citizens with their wives and children, well-meaning nitwits who've come to watch the show."[66]

Sex stood as one of the main selling points of the Folies Bergère during the 1870s and 1880s. In late 1878, for instance, the manager, seeing the number of prostitutes attending the Folies decline, gave out free entries in

---

61. Charles Rearick, *Pleasures of the Belle Époque: Entertainment and Festivity in Turn-of-the-Century France* (New Haven, Conn.: Yale University Press, 1985), 84.

62. The working poor, of course, remained largely excluded. Ibid., 94–95.

63. Ibid., 84.

64. "Rapport: Surveillance exercée aux Folies-Bergère," September 16, 1877, "Rue Richer, 32," JC 62, formerly BM2 7, APP.

65. Ibid. See also Rearick, *Pleasures of the Belle Époque,* 153.

66. Guy de Maupassant, *Bel-Ami* (Paris: Victor-Havard, 1885), 17. Translation is from Guy de Maupassant, *Bel-Ami,* trans. Margaret Mauldon (New York: Oxford University Press, 2008), 13.

order to draw them back in.[67] Indeed, police reports speak to the importance of sexual solicitation within the Folies Bergère: "As always, the prostitutes of the Boulevard can be found in great numbers, addressing obscene remarks to men—even those they do not know—who then respond in the same tone. . . . This space is treated by habitués like a brothel. . . . Honest people could no longer enter this theater."[68] And yet the very emphasis these reports make on the huge crowd moving about the Folies Bergère undercuts that claim: "honest" people continued to go and enjoy themselves in great numbers. The Folies thus represented a mirror image of the discourse of those who complained to the police. The very pleasures that so discomfited the middle class on the street were eagerly purchased at the Folies Bergère. No wonder then that Virmaître simply declared the music hall to be a "meat market."[69]

Female prostitution was not the only sexual activity taking place at the Folies Bergère. A short note from 1873 claimed that the Folies Bergère was the haunt of both prostitutes and pederasts who "publicly indulge in obscene touching there."[70] Another report from November 1876 notes the presence of pederasts as well as prostitutes in the Folies Bergère, a couple of whom were already known to the police.[71] Both men and women could indulge in same-sex sexual flirtation at the Folies Bergère: another police report from the same period noted the "disgusting scene" of two drunken prostitutes embracing and "flaunting with the greatest cynicism their passions against nature."[72] Whether these women truly had "passions against nature" or were performing for the audience remains unknown to the historian. Lesbian activity more generally, however, does not often appear in the police documents.

That said, the Folies Bergère was actively constructed as a heterosexual space where the evidence of same-sex sexual activity was often taken either as out of place or as part of the entertainment for heterosexual viewers. For example, the report that declared the show to be "insignificant" described

67. "Rapport: Surveillance aux Folies-Bergère," December 4, 1878, JC 62, formerly BM2 7, APP. Similar pricing adjustments were used in the commercial dance halls of New York as well. See Kathy Peiss, *Cheap Amusements: Working Women and Leisure in Turn-of-the-Century New York* (Philadelphia: Temple University Press, 1986), 97.

68. "Rapport: Surveillance aux Folies-Bergère," October 29, 1876, "Rue Richer, 32," JC 62, formerly BM2 7, APP. This report contained an example: "A women told an individual yesterday to not speak to her any longer, that he was a sorcerer, and since he had fucked [*baisée*] her, she could no longer lift up a single tit [*miches*]."

69. Virmaître, *Trottoirs et lupanars,* 7.

70. "Note pour M. le Chef de la Police Municipale. Au sujet du théâtre des Folies-Bergère," February 24, 1873, "Rue Richer, 32," JC 62, formerly BM2 7, APP.

71. "Rapport: Surveillance aux Folies-Bergère," November 11, 1876, "Rue Richer, 32," JC 62, formerly BM2 7, APP.

72. "Rapport: Surveillance aux Folies-Bergère," November 8, 1876, "Rue Richer, 32," JC 62, formerly BM2 7, APP.

the liberties the male clientele took with the women who frequented the establishment: "The exit is as always too narrow . . . [and] the men take hold of the women in their arms under the pretext of protecting them from the jostling and take the opportunity to touch them."[73] The report concludes by describing "a gentleman crying out 'what a charming whorehouse,' who found himself in the crowd holding before him a woman who did not have the appearance of a prostitute, struggling as well as she could, and his friend, indicating to him the young men in the corridor of the gallery, responded in a loud voice: 'surprised there are so many fairies [*tantes*]; we will come back.'"[74] The report thus highlights at one and the same time how male pederasts interacted with other men in the Folies Bergère but also how they could become an obstacle to heterosexual pleasure and power. By making itself into a new kind of brothel premised on heterosexual relations, even as its entertainments relied on mixing various kinds of people, the indeterminacies of the street were simultaneously evoked and disavowed. Men who sought sex with other men may have been able to access the Folies Bergère, but they had become essentially out of place.

In making the music hall into a brothel, the managers created an imaginary space predicated on the sexual availability of women but one where the prostitutes could not unexpectedly "assault" men as on the streets. The making of sexual commerce into spectacle, then, involved the domestication of street solicitation by providing men with the ability to publicly demonstrate sexual power. For example, on the evening of October 3, 1877, a thirty-nine-year-old paper maker named Pierre Kintzinger was arrested during a night out with two friends. The police report from the night describes how "an individual who was wandering the *promenoir* with affectation, was calling out to women with a loud voice while addressing the most licentious remarks at them."[75] Ordinarily the report would stop there and not describe the actual remarks, because no arrest would have followed. At around 10:30 in the evening on this night, however, the police stepped in after a woman named Eugènie Ricard crossed Kintzinger's path. He "touched her hair from behind while telling her, in a manner that ensured that the people who occupied the loges could hear, that she had a nice pussy [*un beau chat*]," and then "he put his hand on her dress, and touched her lower-abdomen in the area of her

---

73. "Rapport: Surveillance exercée aux Folies-Bergère," September 16, 1877, "Rue Richer, 32."

74. Ibid.

75. "Rapport: Surveillance aux Folies-Bergère," October 4, 1877, "Rue Richer, 32," JC 62, formerly BM2 7, APP; and "Procès-Verbal, Kintzinger," October 3, 1877, "Rue Richer, 32," JC 62, formerly BM2 7, APP.

womb."[76] Kintzinger was then taken before the police and the director of the Folies Bergère.

The extant archival documents from the period detail the intense surveillance of the Folies Bergère by the morals police but only rarely refer to the behavior of the men who visited. Kintzinger seemed to have been surprised that his behavior attracted any note at all. When his two friends refrained from joining in on the fun, he "encouraged his friends to imitate him, assuring them that they had nothing to fear [because] the Folies Bergère was known to all Parisians to be a brothel."[77] When brought before the police, he claimed that he "did not believe he was committing an infraction by slinging the insults which had been overheard by Monsieur Clément, Commissaire of Police."[78] Kintzinger's excuses, alongside his allusion to what all Parisians supposedly knew, reveals how the tourist discourse analyzed above constructed spaces of heterosexual power. His actions constituted an attempt to reduce Ricard to her sex and made her into his own object, a silence almost confirmed by her own interview with the police, which simply acknowledges the facts as reported by the observing officer.[79] Kintzinger did so because he believed that he had entered a space explicitly designed to encourage him to engage his sexual fantasies, even to the extent of condoning sexual assault. Indeed, he had paid the entry fee for the privilege. The ordinary rules of social comportment were not meant to apply here. Institutions such as the Folies Bergère were thus intended, like the brothels before them, to channel male sexual privilege and provide opportunities for its enactment in public. The association of certain entertainment spaces with sex multiplied the available venues for the exercise of male sexual power.

And yet within this story lay other possibilities. Kintzinger, after all, ran into trouble not because he had approached the wrong woman—a later description of the night by the police superintendent describes her as a registered prostitute—but rather because he overstepped certain unnamed expectations. "The most serious problem," the same report concluded, "is that, sadly, good fathers, unfamiliar with Parisian habits, may yet bring to the Folies Bergère their wives and their children, who would then witness

---

76. The French slang for "pussy" is translated in the feminine form of the word for "cat" (*une chatte*), but the context leaves little doubt that this is what Kintzinger meant. "Rapport: Surveillance aux Folies-Bergère," October 4, 1877, "Rue Richer, 32," JC 62, formerly BM2 7, APP; and "Procès-Verbal, Kintzinger," October 3, 1877, "Rue Richer, 32," JC 62, formerly BM2 7, APP.

77. "Procès-Verbal, Kintzinger."

78. "Rapport: Surveillance aux Folies-Bergère," October 4, 1877.

79. "Procès-Verbal: Déclaration de la Mademoiselle Ricard," October 3, 1877, "Rue Richer, 32," JC 62, formerly BM2 7, APP.

all of these scandals."[80] The moralizing tone of the report certainly complements the various discourses described thus far. In its concern for the safety and moral security of innocent women, it reinforces the gendered hierarchy that Kintzinger himself attempted to take advantage of. The worst possible thing is not that a prostitute had been assaulted, but rather that an honest woman could have been as well. The implication, then, is that this venue was no space for them.

And yet one cannot help but recognize another possibility: that in providing an interior space where one could safely witness the spectacle of the street, the institution could actually attract "wives and daughters." In a later scene in *Bel-Ami,* Duroy returns to the Folies Bergère, with his first mistress, Clotilde, in tow. As they enjoyed the space, Clotilde "scarcely looked at the stage, for she was utterly engrossed by the prostitutes parading round behind her back; and she turned to watch them, wanting to touch them, to feel their breasts, their cheeks, their hair, to discover what those creatures were made of."[81] Clotilde was not a potential client, but she was a member of the prostitutes' public, a willing member no less. As she repeatedly turns around for another look, she enjoys the imagined tactile experience of perhaps more fully joining them in their escapades. At the same time, however, she was able to enter this space only insofar as it remained a scene of ordinary consumption as well and so long as she was accompanied by a man. The intersection of a public of consumption and a public sexual culture thus allowed bourgeois women a momentary instance of a supposedly forbidden pleasure, even as they had to defend themselves against the very violence that so attracted at least some of the clientele.

The provision of heterosexual pleasure was therefore not absolute in these new entertainments. Rather, some venues offered the public the opportunity to purchase more ambiguous experiences than even those of the Folies Bergère. Although *bals publics* (public dances) often participated in a heterosexual economy through "the commodification of female bodies under the guise of entertainment," they also commodified indeterminate sexual desires through the obfuscation of gender identity.[82] Like the other venues examined here, public dances took on a variety of forms, but most were surrounded by moral suspicion. By the Second Empire, bals publics were increasingly associated with the possibility of vice, especially the masked balls that mostly

---

80. Commissaire de Police Clément to Préfet de Police, "Surveillance aux Folies Bergère," October 14, 1877, "Rue Richer, 32," JC 62, formerly BM2 7, APP.

81. Maupassant, *Bel-Ami* (1885), 128. Translation is from Maupassant, *Bel-Ami* (2008), 84.

82. Lela Kerley, *Uncovering Paris: Scandals and Nude Spectacles in the Belle Époque* (Baton Rouge: Louisiana State University Press, 2017), 13.

concern us here.[83] Félix Carlier believed that young prostitutes often entered the profession at the dances at the *bals de barrières*—institutions on the outskirts of Paris—and, after finding their first lovers there, then moved to those in the interior of Paris, where they became "living merchandise."[84] "Instead of being a space of distraction, a salutary exercise for the health, a relaxation from life's preoccupations," Carlier declared, "these dances are the school for the corruption of youth, bazaars of prostitutes, a nursery for pimps."[85] Rejecting all the justifications for the pleasures of Paris, Carlier argued that these establishments were blights on society, corrupting its youth when it was most vulnerable. The police often agreed: in 1883 they declared, for instance, that the bal Bruckner on the Left Bank, not too far from the Invalides, attracted the worst people in the neighborhood of Grenelle—"prowlers from the barriers, prostitutes, pimps, a great number of young men and of young girls, almost children, already depraved."[86]

Police surveillance of dance halls for prostitution should not be surprising in light of their broader interest in the use of public space for solicitation. The Salle Valentino—directed by a supposed pederast—appeared relatively frequently during the late Second Republic and early Second Empire.[87] In 1852 the police received a denunciation from someone claiming that he had met one of "the men exciting young men to the most horrible debauchery and attracting them to their homes in order to corrupt them" at the Valentino.[88] They also arrested several men "cross-dressed as women and whose looks indicated that they were pederasts" at the Valentino in 1876.[89] The police also noted that pederasts went to the bal Favié and the bal de la porte Saint Martin during the Second Empire.[90] In addition, one 1880 report on the bal de la Reine Blanche did note "some women wearing masculine costume."[91]

---

83. On the "moral crisis" of public dancing in the 1850s, see François Gasnault, *Guinguettes et lorettes: Bals publics et danse sociale à Paris entre 1830 et 1870* (Paris: Aubier, 1986), 233–243.

84. Carlier, *Les deux prostitutions,* 23.

85. Ibid., 269.

86. "Rapport: Au sujet du Bal Bruckner sis Rue Cambronne, 4," March 17, 1883, DA 138, doc. 133, APP.

87. "Pédés," n.d., 113, BB 4, APP.

88. Anonymous to Préfet de Police, February 28, 1852, DA 230, doc. 220, APP.

89. "Rapport: Au sujet des pédérastes qui fréquent le bal Valentino," March 24, 1876, DA 230, doc. 387, APP.

90. "Pédés," BB4, 1–3; "Note pour M. le Chef de la Police Municipale: Sodomite à surveiller," January 18, 1858, DA 230, doc. 272, APP. See also Revenin, *Homosexualité et prostitution masculines,* 58–60; Jean-Claude Féray, *"Pédés:" Le premier registre infamant de la préfecture de police de Paris au XIXe siècle suvi d'un dictionnaire des noms propres et noms communs les plus significatifs du register et d'annexes* (Paris: Quintes-feuilles, 2012), 29.

91. "Rapport: Surveillance exercée au bal de la Reine Blanche," February 11, 1880, DA 138, doc. 53, APP.

Men who sought sex with other men, some who dressed as women and some who did not, could be seen throughout the bals publics of the second half of the nineteenth century, and people continued to go to these sites despite that fact. In fact, they may have gone precisely to witness them. If this rendered men who sought sex with other men into a spectacle rather than participants in a public culture, then that was precisely the point of this kind of commercialization.

Public dances served as a way of constructing shared social values.[92] As such, they allowed Parisians to incorporate elements of nineteenth-century public sexual culture into their leisure time while also evacuating it of its threatening elements, notably its spontaneity. These entertainments took on a variety of forms—from the working-class dances of the outskirts to the bohemian venues of Montmartre—but here I conclude with the masked dances of "the most notorious *bal public,* the bal de l'Opéra."[93] Several other historians have discussed the importance of the Opera Ball as a space for interaction between gentlemen and courtesans or prostitutes. Charles Bernheimer, for instance, has described it as a "carnival event, where classes and sexes mixed in a mad transgressive medley, [it] was notorious as a stage for the alluring exhibition of bodies actually or potentially for sale (uncertainty was part of the intrigue)."[94] Similarly, Linda Nochlin, referring to Édouard Manet's depiction of the Opera Ball (Figure 6.1), has argued that "the women, in their provocative anonymity, are the point of the picture—or rather, the point is in some sense the nascent act of physical intimacy growing up everywhere among the hidden but patently attractive women and the (theoretically) identifiable men of the world who surround them."[95] Both scholars have emphasized the masked ball as a space where gentlemen came to sexually interact with women of other classes, just as those class identifications were ultimately obscured by the mask. They recognized how heterosexual desire was inciting men precisely through the ambiguous identities of its objects.

However, the mask could also veil the gender of the person who bore it, confusing the very promise of heterosexual liaison. As Carlier described it, "There, these strange beings of vice, some in men's clothes, others disguised as women, dance together, caress one another, flirt and cover one another in repugnant kisses."[96] Thus, while Manet's depiction featured no masked

---

92. Kerley, *Uncovering Paris,* 14.
93. Ibid.
94. Charles Bernheimer, *Figures of Ill Repute: Representing Prostitution in Nineteenth-Century France* (Cambridge, Mass: Harvard University Press, 1989), 40.
95. Linda Nochlin, "A Thoroughly Modern Masked Ball," *Art in America* 71, no. 10 (1983): 196.
96. Carlier, *Les deux prostitutions,* 361.

FIGURE 6.1. Édouard Manet, *Bal masqué à l'opéra* (Masked Ball at the Opera), 1873, oil on canvas. (Courtesy National Gallery of Art, Washington, D.C.)

"man," it is possible that at least one of the masked "women" was not a woman at all. For instance, the veiled woman in the foreground, whose face we cannot distinguish, leans in to talk to another masked lady even as an interested suitor appraises her charms. Is that the excitement the man sought? Not the titillation of deciding whether a particular female body was for sale or not, but whether a particular female body was, in fact, a female body? Perhaps the conscious turn of her head away from the man was a way of ensuring that his look always hit from the side, continuing the façade. Interestingly, drawing one's eyes down the length of the three figures reveals them to all bleed into one another, the man's legs lost amid the two women's dominoes. The three—one woman, one man, one probable woman, perhaps man—become one mixed gender figure at the Opera Ball: the femme-homme come to life.

This reading of Manet's painting rests on associations of gender indeterminacy with the crowds of the Opera Ball. On December 28, 1854, for instance, a young man named O. Doulay was "accosted by a woman who invited [him] to dance." She insisted that they leave and that he sleep at her place. "Having arrived at her/his domicile," he later wrote to the police, "I discovered that this woman was nothing other than one of those men who the police seek so actively."[97] The newly revealed man attempted to force the writer to stay with him, but the writer managed to escape. This particular young man, seeking the more overt sexual titillation of a public liaison, found himself embroiled in another type entirely. Indeed, the sexual excitement lay with the deceiver who risked their safety and reputation in order to trick or otherwise entice young men into having sex with them. Perhaps the dancer knew that the likelihood of consummating such a relationship was not high—though probably far from impossible—but that the pleasure in the deception outweighed both the risk and the lack of sexual consummation. Moreover, the writer's willingness to sign his name and address attests to two convictions: first, that he would be believed, and, second, that there was no shame in admitting falling for the deception, one so real that the letter shifts from the feminine gender to the masculine once the revelation occurred.

The play of gender and sexual desire attendant with the masked ball of the opera was a source of anxiety and amusement. For example, in *La corruption à Paris,* Ali Coffignon describes seeing a striking woman enter the hall "who audaciously flirted with a middle-age man." Noticing "a highly ranked civil servant who had since become prefect of police" also looking at the couple, Coffignon approached "to ask the name of the young woman."[98] Instead of responding, the civil servant invited him to visit his office another day. When Coffignon did so, the functionary showed Coffignon a photograph of the "young woman from the Opera": "The photograph showed a young woman leaning her elbows on a window, her head covered by a mantilla [a silk scarf] and resting on her nervous and sharpened hands, her eyebrows well-arched, her nose fine and her lips smiling in order to allows us to see her superbly aligned teeth."[99] Coffignon was then given another picture, this one of "a young man of between sixteen and eighteen years old, with a hardy complexion, having entirely the look of a precocious pimp." Goaded into a comparison between the two photos, Coffignon became "struck" by the resemblance: "Brother and sister?" he asked. "I learned then that the young woman who attracted with so much *coqueterie* the attention of the corridors of the Opéra was nothing other than a celebrity pederast," he explained and then concluded, "The Opéra, during the nights of the masked balls, is perhaps the only area where pederasty holds court openly for the initiated, invisible for everyone else."[100]

---

97. O. Doulay to Préfet de Police, December 29, 1854, DA 230, doc. 252, APP.

98. Ali Coffignon, *Paris-vivant: La corruption à Paris* (Paris: Librairie Illustrée, 1888), 338–339.

99. Ibid., 340.

100. Ibid., 341.

It is interesting that Coffignon's story does not reveal much repugnance at his own deception but rather mild amusement, even as he laments that these men continued to practice their trade at the opera. His evident attraction to the woman remained clear, despite his surprise by his inability to tell the difference between man and woman. The gender play at the opera was less threatening than it was part of the show. The masked ball therefore was not simply a space of either hetero- or homosexual pleasure. It also enabled elite Parisians to purchase the unexpected pleasure of sliding between the two. If heterosexual relations, especially as they allowed middle- and upper-class men to demonstrate their power over women, remained the more overt draw, they also always served as an enabling excuse for other encounters. Indeed, the men who cross-dressed as they sought sex or flirted with unsuspecting men effectively used the presumption of heterosexuality to their own advantage. That neither other guests, the police, nor moral commenters were always able to successfully distinguish between women and men dressed as women highlights how spaces such as the Opera Ball sold the experience of engaging with public sex, if not the sexual act itself.

Conclusion

These cafés, music halls, dance halls, and bars were not the only places where men and occasionally women could seek out a culture of public sex in nineteenth-century Paris, but they were the most prominent.[101] The spaces may have been different, but the goal was the same: to express and experience sexual pleasure in public alongside one's compatriots and neighbors. Ironically, although the consummation of such activity often took place through obfuscation, the fact that what one really desired was sex rather than, say, a beer or a show was not so hidden. In other words, the serving girls who plied their bodies as well as drinks may have used their employment as a cover for sexual solicitation, but that cover was a thin veil. All of this is to say that public sex did cause anxiety among experts and certain segments of the population, but it also served as a central source of the pleasures of the city.

The moralizing tone of the discourse serves to hide the fact that many Parisians quite enjoyed these experiences. However, although many kinds of

---

101. Boutiques, *cremeries,* and gambling houses were all also mentioned as sites of debauchery or pleasure, depending on your point of view. On boutiques and gambling houses, see Léo Taxil, *La prostitution contemporaine: Étude d'une question sociale* (Paris: Librairie Populaire), 214; Coffignon, *La corruption à Paris,* 86–89. For a case of a glove shop accused of actually being a clandestine brothel, see the dossier on Elise Bruyere and Anna Philibert Montré in D2U6 35, AP. For an example of a cremerie, see "Rapport: Au sujet du passage Raguinot, 8," April 19, 1880, "Passage Raguinot. Dossier général," JC 74, formerly BM2 14, APP.

Parisians—those who desired the opposite sex, those who desired the same sex, men, women—could and did enjoy these spaces, they did so through the common assumption that they placed women at the mercy of men. Even drinking establishments that catered to same-sex sexual desire relied on the prevailing assumption that to sell sex was to sell women. Although women—as both customers and employees—could find ways of locating agency and pleasure within those limitations, the fundamental structure remains the same.

That such constraints emerged through environments that often set about isolating and categorizing elements of the public sexual culture, selling the temporary experience of indecipherability to those who could pay, underscores a tense relationship between the preservation of patriarchy and emerging forms of sexual commerce, both "gay" and "straight." If men who sought sex with other men relied on spaces like brasseries à femmes and the Folies Bergère to protect their own use of commercial space to locate sexual partners, they did so by collaborating with the construction of new brothels for men to seek sex with women as well. That many of those women either enjoyed the play or were paid for it does nothing to remove how they became a tool for the protection and preservation of male-male desire in new ways. The prostitute became increasingly subordinate not just to men who sought sex with women but also to those who sought sex with other men. At the same time, this process relied on the presence of working-class women to the emergence of both an early mass consumer culture and the creation of same-sex sexual spaces. In this respect, even as the female prostitute remained constrained, she was also absolutely essential to the emergence of both modern sexual life and modern urban existence more broadly.

CONCLUSION

In 1903, under pressure from abolitionists, the French Republic convened an Extraparliamentary Commission to study the regulationist regime. At its very first meeting, the *procureur général* of the Cour d'appel, Léon Bulot, stood up and, after dismissing out of hand the idea of making female prostitution a crime, asked whether they should not consider male prostitution, which is "a true offense because it is against nature: it is a stain that must be purged from great cities." In response, the abolitionist Louis Fiaux declared himself in agreement with Bulot's first point but against the second: "Recognizing that inversion is, like female prostitution, very often a source of shameful profits, was it not also frequently pathological?" In response, the commission recommended forming a subcommission on the subject while their own continued to address the initial problem of female prostitution.[1] Fiaux's declaration showcases how understandings of male same-sex sexual activity had changed by the early twentieth century. No longer falling under the category of prostitution, no longer a set of desires and practices to which all men—by virtue of need, greed, or immorality—were susceptible, now it became a state of being, a sickness, distinguished and distinguishable from the act of female prostitution.

---

1. Louis Fiaux, *La police des mœurs devant la Commission Extraparlementaire du Régime des Mœurs* (Paris: Félix Alcan, 1907), 1:7–11. See also *Commission Extraparlementaire du Régime des Mœurs: Procès-verbaux des séances* (Melun, France: Imprimerie Administrative, 1909), 8–10.

This distinction would fundamentally alter the ways that sex circulated about the twentieth-century city as modern sexual politics reshaped the meaning of same-sex sexual activity, even as regulationist understandings of female prostitution lingered in France until World War II. Perhaps no two early twentieth-century thinkers represent these shifts as well as Marcel Proust and André Gide, both of whom came to prominence at precisely the moment when men began to speak in the name of modern homosexuality. In 1911 Gide began privately circulating parts of his "defense" of homosexuality in a book titled *Corydon* (1924).[2] *Corydon* consists of four dialogues between the title character and an unnamed friend who confronts Corydon about rumors of his homosexuality. The book stands as an almost too perfect example of a "reverse discourse"; it took up the language of science and history to argue that pederasty—and Gide did mean pederasty in its more classical sense—signified cultural efflorescence, martial values, and social health rather than cultural degradation, effeminacy, and degeneration.[3] Gide's book came perilously close to breaking his friend Proust's dictum that "you can tell anything, but on the condition that you never say 'I.'"[4] Gide's ability to do so rested on the fundamentally conservative politics of the book, as he argued that homosexuality could play a role in the preservation of French masculinity.[5] Homosexuality had begun to speak for itself, but it did so not in terms of a public sexual culture that so disturbed Parisians as they were included in it. Rather, it spoke in the name of those who complained about it. In other words, Gide sought to separate his own sexual practices from those condemned as deviant and pathological. Thus, by distinguishing homosexuality from the disturbing practices of the street, he presaged the dominant strategy of what would become known as "gay rights" by emphasizing homosexuality as natural, normal, and complementary to an idealized set of bourgeois values.[6]

---

2. André Gide, *Corydon* (Paris: 1924).

3. Michel Foucault, *The History of Sexuality,* vol. 1, *An Introduction,* trans. Robert Hurley (New York: Vintage, 1990), 100–102.

4. Michael Lucey, *Never Say I: Sexuality and the First Person in Colette, Gide, and Proust* (Durham, N.C.: Duke University Press, 2006), 1.

5. Martha Hanna, "Natalism, Homosexuality, and the Controversy over *Corydon,*" in *Homosexuality in Modern France,* ed. Jeffrey Merrick and Bryant T. Ragan Jr. (New York: Oxford University Press, 1996), 207–209.

6. Often associated with the "homophile" movements of the postwar period, this strategy both predates and postdates that movement. On the homophile movement in France, see esp. Julian Jackson, *Living in Arcadia: Homosexuality, Politics, and Morality in France from the Liberation to AIDS* (Chicago: University of Chicago Press, 2009). On twentieth-century gay politics in France, see Frédéric Martel, *Le rose et le noir: Les homosexuels en France depuis 1968* (Paris: Seuil, 1996); Florence Tamagne, *Histoire de l'homosexualité en Europe: Berlin, Londres, Paris, 1919–1939* (Paris: Seuil, 2000); Scott Gunther, *The Elastic Closet: A History of Homosexuality*

Gide's move contributed to a climate of cultural reaction in early twentieth-century France that emphasized traditional gender roles, condemned so-called individualist sexual practices, and subjected female prostitutes to continued police oppression.[7] By accepting certain assumptions about masculinity and femininity, Gide equally condemned effeminate men and female prostitutes—as moralists before him had—just as homosexuality was becoming increasingly distinct from other forms of sexual deviance. At the same time, new forms of women's self-presentation—represented first by the "new woman" and then by the early twentieth-century "modern woman"—provided avenues for women's public participation in urban life outside the terms of sexual exchange elaborated within the public sexual culture.[8] This development, empowering for some, further marginalized those who sold sex, even as the image of the sexual culture remained central to practices of consumption in modern dancing and theater.[9]

The isolation of public sexual practices thus occurred on a dual plane. First, bourgeois men interested in sex with other men began to disavow certain activities in the hope of domesticating their own identities. Second, and relatedly, female prostitutes within the urban milieu found themselves increasingly isolated by both the old moralists and feminists. The early twentieth century has often been seen as a period of efflorescence of madcap

in France, 1942–Present (New York: Palgrave Macmillan, 2009). On some of these themes in other locations, see John d'Emilio, *Sexual Politics, Sexual Communities: The Making of a Homosexual Minority in the United States, 1940–1970*, 2nd ed. (Chicago: University of Chicago Press, 1998); Harry Oosterhuis, "Homosexual Emancipation in Germany before 1933: Two Traditions," in *Homosexuality and Male Bonding in Pre-Nazi Germany*, ed. Harry Oosterhuis (New York: Haworth Press, 1991), 1–27; Marc Stein, *City of Sisterly and Brotherly Loves: Lesbian and Gay Philadelphia, 1945–1972* (Philadelphia: Temple University Press, 2004).

7. On these themes, see esp. Alain Corbin, *Les filles de noce: Misère sexuelle et prostitution au XIXe siècle* (Paris: Flammarion, 1982), 474–480; Mary Louise Roberts, *Civilization without Sexes: Reconstructing Gender in Postwar France, 1917–1927* (Chicago: University of Chicago Press, 1994), esp. chap 1; Carolyn J. Dean, *The Frail Social Body: Pornography Homosexuality, and Other Fantasies in Interwar France* (Berkeley: University of California Press, 2000); Judith Surkis, *Sexing the Citizen: Morality and Masculinity in France, 1870–1920* (Ithaca, N.Y.: Cornell University Press, 2006), esp. chap 7.

8. Mary Louise Roberts, *Disruptive Acts: The New Woman in Fin-de-Siècle France* (Chicago: University of Chicago Press, 2002); Roberts, *Civilization without Sexes*, pt. 1.

9. Some considerations of sex and sexuality in early twentieth-century dance, theater, and popular culture include Adrian Rifkin, *Street Noises: Parisian Pleasure, 1900–40* (Manchester, U.K.: Manchester University Press, 1993); Kelley Conway, *Chanteuse in the City: The Realist Singer in French Film* (Berkeley: University of California Press, 2004); Lela F. Kerley, *Uncovering Paris: Scandals and Nude Spectacles in the Belle Époque* (Baton Rouge: Louisiana State University Press, 2017); Allison Abra, *Dancing in the English Style: Consumption, Americanisation, and National Identity in Britain, 1918–50* (Manchester, U.K.: Manchester University Press, 2017), chap. 4.

urban pleasures; the roaring twenties were the *années folles* for a reason. Gilles Barbedette and Michel Carassou, for instance, contrasted the "diversity" of the 1920s with the "uncertain embryo of the 'underground' of the Belle Époque. . . . The *Années folles* contributed, moreover, to the birth of a climate, an ambiance, without any comparison to the first decades of the century."[10] While certainly a moment of self-discovery for many, the interwar period must also be seen as a period where sexual practices became more restricted. The sexual categories that so confounded nineteenth-century moral commentators hardened. As elsewhere, prostitutes symbolized cultural crisis and remained outcast, while middle-class homosexuals began to divorce their sexual identity from the pursuit of sex in public.[11] More and more, the pursuit of pleasure in public required actively avoiding evidence of public sexuality for both those who otherwise sought out illicit pleasure and those who never would have done so.

And yet it remains the case that people used the city in the pursuit of pleasure in ways that contrasted with its prescribed uses. Men continued to seek sex with other men in public, even if their former compatriots began heaping opprobrium on them. Prostitutes continued to act as a central feature of the urban sexual economy, reaching a new height as participants in "the brothel of Europe" during World War II.[12] New technologies and spaces radically transformed how people enjoyed the city and also provided opportunities for subverting the city in new ways. The Métro, first appearing in 1900, radically compressed distance, lessened the importance of the street, and rendered "local" the entirety of Paris but also entailed new underground spaces of encounter.[13] The cinema encouraged audiences to watch a screen rather than each other, but also brought about new ways of visualizing sexu-

---

10. Gilles Barbedette and Michel Carassou, *Paris Gay 1925* (Paris: Presses de la Renaissance, 1981), 15.

11. See, for instance, Dorothy Rowe, *Representing Berlin: Sexuality and the City in Imperial and Weimar Germany* (Aldershot, U.K.: Ashgate, 2003), chap. 3; George Chauncey, *Gay New York: Gender, Urban Culture, and the Making of the Gay Male World, 1890–1940* (New York: Basic Books, 1994), chap. 4.

12. Mary Louise Roberts, *What Soldiers Do: Sex and the American GI in World War II France* (Chicago: University of Chicago Press, 2013), 133–134.

13. Marcel Proust, for instance, described the Métro as follows: "Some of these Pompeians upon whom the fire of Heaven was already pouring, descended into the Métro passages which were dark as catacombs. They knew, of course, that they would not be alone there. And the darkness which bathes everything as in a new element had the effect, an irresistibly tempting one for certain people, of eliminating the first phase of lust and enabling them to enter, without further ado the domain of caresses which as a rule demands preliminaries." Marcel Proust, *Remembrance of Things Past*, trans. C. K. Moncrieff and Stephen Hudson, 2 vols. (London: Wordsworth Editions, 2006), 2:1122. See also Christopher Prendergast, *Paris and the Nineteenth Century* (Oxford, U.K.: Blackwell, 1992), 99–101.

ality in public.[14] These technologies reshaped the public sexual culture of the nineteenth century into a faster but perhaps less personalized and more identitarian form, culminating the rise of twenty-first-century technologies, such as global hookup apps and online personals.[15]

The terms of the relationship between management and sexual practice I have described in this book may have shifted, therefore, but the fundamental tension remained. In the nineteenth century, public sex stood as an important point on which urban managers sought to exert control over the urban population. The effective management of sexual activity signified the stability of social order and physical health. However, such stability never actually solidified, because authorities found themselves incapable of effectively regulating the public spaces they built and encouraged. This difficulty rendered it exceedingly hard to separate the proper from the improper pleasures of the city. The appropriation of the city for sexual solicitation rendered all who entered public space complicit in the public sexual culture. No one could escape the possibility of becoming a member of a public sexual culture predicated on addressing both those who sought it out and those who did not. By encouraging interaction between strangers in sites of pleasure, the very nature of the modern city rendered this mixing inevitable.

Faced with this result, Parisians found themselves torn between two possibilities. First, they could react negatively and encourage authorities to make sure the city remained the purified, regularized environment they had been promised. These Parisians found themselves unable to escape evidence of public sex, even in their supposedly private homes. This failure deeply threatened elite faith in their own place within urban culture. By encouraging the authorities to clean the city, they also invited them to violate the division between private and public, thus revealing how arbitrary that line actually was. Second, ordinary people could find ways of enjoying the mixing of the proper and the improper. Whether in a brasserie à femmes or in a dance hall, men and women enjoyed the sexual possibilities of modern Paris but only when carefully curated by proprietors and the police. And yet this pursuit of pleasure still put into question some of the gendered and classed assumptions of the nineteenth-century city as men fell under the sway of the working-class server or were tricked by a cross-dresser and as women found new objects of their own gaze and imagined pleasures of prostitution. In a constant repeti-

---

14. Conway, *Chanteuse in the City,* chap. 5.

15. The relationship between American, global, and local LGBTQ language and practices in France is explored in Denis Provencher, *Queer French: Globalization, Language, and Sexual Citizenship in France* (New York: Routledge, 2007). See also Mehammed Amadeus Mack, *Sexagon: Muslims, France, and the Sexualization of National Culture* (New York: Fordham University Press, 2017), 67–68.

rion that crafted modern urban life, women and men moved about the city and repeatedly chose between these two poles, neither decision restraining their ability to choose differently later, neither remaining absolute.

We should remain aware of the possibilities of subversion within commercial entertainments and their deployment of sex that characterize the world of today, even as those strategies remain more circumspect. At the same time, an emphasis on the commercial has made other sexual spaces seem even more incongruous. It is indeed in the unexpected that some appropriations continue to showcase the power of public sex. The use of urinals by men seeking sex with other men forced experts to reconceptualize the possibilities of the city by challenging their attempt to make the city more commercially available in the first place. By using facilities of public hygiene for sexual pleasure, pederasts forced commentators to confront their inability to distinguish between those who sought sex with other men and those who did not. Their failure to separate the proper from the improper users of public urinals showcased the most powerful effect of the use of the city for public sex. Public sex disrupted received wisdom, forced reactions among those who believed they already understood the urban environment, and ultimately affected the meaning of the city for all who inhabited it.

Public sexual activity outside the commercial realm has been almost entirely removed from public view. Rather than spreading out the availability of venal sex via the tolerated brothel, red-light districts are occasionally permitted while Craigslist.fr was once used to provide new ways of purchasing sex.[16] Whether the rise of new clubs in the Marais or the closure of the Parisian public urinals, new urban developments have been far more successful than their forebearers at eliminating illicit sexuality from public space.[17] A key part of this success, however, remains the active collaboration of certain segments of sexual activists who, in an effort to secure the rights to partici-

---

16. In 2018, in response to anti-trafficking legislation then making its way through the U.S. Congress, Craigslist removed personal ads from its global suite of websites. This decision reflects ongoing controversies that date to the late nineteenth century over the relationship between anti–sex trafficking efforts and the regulation of consensual sex, both paid and unpaid. Lisa Bonos, "Goodbye, Craigslist personal ads. Those seeking casual sex will miss you," *Washington Post,* March 23, 2018, available at https://www.washingtonpost.com/news/soloish/wp/2018/03/23/goodbye-craigslist-personal-ads-those-seeking-casual-sex-will-miss-you, accessed June 27, 2018. On these debates in the late nineteenth-century context, see esp. Judith R. Walkowitz, "Male Vice and Feminist Virtue: Feminism and the Politics of Prostitution in Nineteenth-Century Britain." *History Workshop,* no. 13 (1982): 79–93.

17. On the rise of the Marais as a gay space, see Michael Sibalis, "Urban Space and Homosexuality: The Example of the Marais, Paris' 'Gay Ghetto,'" *Urban Studies* 41, no. 9 (2004): 1739–1758. See also David Caron, *My Father and I: The Marais and the Queerness of Community* (Ithaca, N.Y.: Cornell University Press, 2009).

pate in bourgeois society, have abandoned the most radical possibilities of their own activism. This abandonment has certainly not remained uncontested, but it is difficult to dispute the relative success of those who seek to hide sex from public view. The urban culture of the nineteenth century was a moment when the appropriate pleasures of urban life slid easily into the inappropriate pleasures of illicit sex. Through the course of the twentieth century, that moment came to a close. But the movement between the proper and the improper, the licit and the illicit remains a powerful example of the ability of everyday life, ordinary activity, to powerfully affect the environment in which it takes place.

BIBLIOGRAPHY

ARCHIVAL SOURCES

Archives Nationales (France) (AN)

Series F7—Police général:
F7 4338: Rapports de délégués du ministère de la police (1814–1828)
F7 9305: Filles publiques (an IX-1846)

Series F21—Beaux-arts:
F21 1046: Préfecture de Police. Réglementation de l'affichage à l'intérieur et à l'extérieur des théâtres de Paris (1830–1868)
F21 1338: Rapports du bureau des théâtres avec la Préfecture de Police, notamment en ce qui concerne la surveillance des cafés-concerts (1845–1904)

Archives de Paris (AP)

Series D2U6—Tribunal correctionnel de la Seine: dossiers de procédure correctionnelle (1828–1940):
D2U6 35: Dossier on Bruyère, Elisa, and Montre, Anna Philiberte; excitation habituelle de mineurs à la débauche, vagabondage, March 2, 1876.
D2U6 37: Dossier on Duval, Henri Joseph; outrage à la pudeur, June 15, 1876

Series Pérotin 10653—Travaux d'aménagement (1860–1930):
Pérotin 10653 39: Chalets de nécessité—Boulogne (bois de)

Series V.O3—Eaux, canaux, égouts:
V.O3 419: Voie publique; service des concessions; urinoirs
V.O3 425: Urinoirs: plans, jurisprudence

Archives de la Préfecture de Police (APP)

Series BB: Cabinet du préfet, affaires réservées, affaires de mœurs (fin du XIXe siècle):
BB 4: Pédés
BB 5: Pédés
BB 6: Péderastes et divers

Series BM2: Brigade mondaine:
(Series BM2 is currently being reclassified as Series JC. I provide both sets of locators as of July 2018, but they may change. In the process of researching this book, all 65 of the original BM2 cartons were reviewed. Only those cited are listed here.)
BM2 7 (JC 62): Rue Richer, 32
BM2 10 (JC 61): Rue Pigalle, 63
BM2 14 (JC 74): Passage Raguinot. Dossier général
BM2 15 (JC 42): Quai de l'Hôtel de Ville, 16
BM2 15 (JC 86): Boulevard Barbès. Dossier général
BM2 16 (JC 46): Boulevard St. Germain, 166
BM2 16 (JC 60): Boulevard de la Madeleine. Dossier général
BM2 17 (JC 49): Rue Mazarine, 68
BM2 19 (JC 76): Boulevard Edgar-Quinet. Dossier général
BM2 20 (JC 40): Boulevard Beaumarchais. Dossier général
BM2 24 (JC 50): Rue Racine, 3
BM2 28 (JC 44): Rue des Tournelles, 32
BM2 28 (JC 71): Rue de Villejuif, 15
BM2 31 (JC 48): Rue Bréda, 29
BM2 32 (JC 33): Palais-Royal. Dossier général
BM2 32 (JC 61): Rue de Provence. Dossier général
BM2 32 (JC 85): Avenue de Wagram. Dossier général
BM2 33 (JC 34): Rue du Plat d'Etain, 3
BM2 33 (JC 66): Rue de la Fidélité, 3
BM2 34 (JC 35): Rue St. Denis, 71
BM2 34 (JC 88): Boulevard de la Chapelle, 88
BM2 37 (JC 95): Boulevard de la Villette. Dossier général
BM2 42 (JC 82): Bois de Boulogne. Dossier général
BM2 45 (JC 49): Rue Monsieur-le-Prince, 65
BM2 45 (JC 64): Passage Brady, 74
BM2 47 (JC 38): Rue St. Denis, 289
BM2 58 (JC 95): Boulevard de la Villette, 123bis
BM2 60 (JC 54): Gare St. Lazare. Dossier général
BM2 60 (JC 208): Champs-Élysées. Dossier général
BM2 63 (JC 70): Rue Rampon, 14
BM2 65 (JC 59): Passage Jouffroy. Dossier général
BM2 65 (JC 87): Boulevard de la Chapelle, 74

Series DA: Réglementation et vie quotidienne (1810–1980):
DA 138: Salle. 4, rue de Cambronne
DA 220: Mœurs.

DA 221: Mœurs
DA 222: Mœurs
DA 223: Mœurs
DA 226: Mœurs, 5
DA 230: Mœurs
DA 231: Mœurs
DA 851: Prostitution

Series DB: Préfecture de Police. Documents administratifs et coupures de presse (1800–2000):
DB 407: Prostitution
DB 408: Prostitution

PERIODICALS

The Independent
Le Nouveau Journal
Le Petit Parisien
Washington Post

PUBLISHED PRIMARY SOURCES

"À MM. les Députés. Projet de pétition sur la liberté individuelle, par un spartiate, de ceux que vulgairement on nomme voleurs: et a l'appui de la pétition des filles publiques." Paris: Marchands de Nouveautés: 1830.

Auguez, Paul. *Les marchands de plaisir.* Paris: Dentu, 1856.

"Aux Ministres!!! Nouvelle pétition des filles publiques de Paris, tendant à obtenir de LL. EE. la révocation de l'ordonnance attentatoire à leurs liberté, rendue contre elles." Paris: Libraires du Palais-Royal, 1830.

Baudelaire, Charles. *Œuvres complètes.* Vol. 1. Paris: Gallimard, 1975.

———. *The Painter of Modern Life and Other Essays.* Translated and edited by Jonathan Mayne. London: Phaidon Press, 1965.

Becquerel, Alfred. *Traité élémentaire d'hygiène privée et publique.* 6th ed. Paris: Asselin, 1877.

Béraud, F.F.A. *Les filles publiques de Paris et la police qui les régit.* 2 vols. Paris: Desforges, 1839.

Bérenger, René. "Proposition de loi: Sur la prostitution et les outrages aux bonnes mœurs." *Sénat Session 1894.* Paris: P. Mouillot, 1894.

———. *Rapport fait au nom de la commission chargée d'examiner la proposition de loi de M. Bérenger, sur la prostitution et les outrages aux bonnes mœurs.* Paris: Imprimerie du sénat, 1895.

Butler, Joséphine, Aimé Humbert, and Armand Després. *La police des mœurs et la morale: Discours prononcés à Paris, en Janvier et Février 1877 par Mme Joséphine Butler et MM. A. Humbert, Butler, Donat Sautter, et le Dr. Després avec un appendice contenant le compte rendu sommaire des études du Conseil Municipal de Paris sur le Service des Mœurs.* Paris: Sandoz et Fischbacher, 1877.

Canler, Louis. *Mémoirs de Canler, Ancien chef du service de sûreté.* 2nd ed. Paris: J. Hetzel, 1862.

Carlier, Félix. *Études de pathologie sociale: Les deux prostitutions (1860–1870).* Paris: E. Dentu, 1887.

———. "Étude statistique sur la prostitution clandestine à Paris de 1855 à 1870." *Annales d'hygiène publique et de médecine légale* 2, no. 36 (1871): 292–308.

Caufeynon, Dr. [Jean Fauconney]. *La pédérastie: Historique, causes, la prostitution pédéraste, mœurs des pédérastes, observations médico-légales.* Paris: Offenstadt, 1902.

———. *La prostitution: La débauche à Paris—les maisons de tolérance—la prostitution clandestine—règlements de police—caractère des prostituées.* Paris: Offenstadt, 1902.

César. "Pétition d'un souteneur à M. le préfet de police de Paris, à l'occasion de l'ordonnance qu'il vient de rendre contre les filles publiques, appuyée d'une lettre d'un fruitier de la rue Froidmanteau." Paris: Principaux Libraires au Palais-Royal, 1830.

Charcot, Jean-Martin, and Valentin Magnan. "Inversion du sens génital et autres perversions génitales." *Archives de neurologie* 3 (1882): 53–60 and 4 (1882): 296–332.

Chevallier, A. "Notice historique sur la conservation, la désinfection et l'utilisation des urines." *Journal de chimie médicale, de pharmacie et de toxicologie et revue des nouvelles scientifiques nationales et étrangères* 2 (1856): 364–384, 416–430.

Chevallier, M. A. "Note sur la nécessité de multiplier et d'améliorer les urinoirs publics." *Annales d'hygiène publique et de médecine légale* 2, no. 36 (1871): 285–291.

Code pénal, suivi d'une table alphabétique et raisonnée des matières. Paris: P. Didot l'Aîné et Firmin Didot, 1810.

Coffignon, Ali. *Paris-Vivant: La corruption à Paris.* Paris: Librairie Illustrée, 1888.

Commenge, O. *Hygiène sociale: La prostitution clandestine à Paris.* Paris: Schleicher Frères, 1897.

Commission extraparlementaire du régime des mœurs: Procès-verbaux des séances. Melun, France: Imprimerie Administrative, 1909.

"Complainte authentique, originale et seule véritable, sur la grande catastrophe des filles de Paris." Paris: Marchands de Nouveautés, 1830.

Condorcet, Jean-Antoine-Nicolas de Caritat, marquis de. *Œuvres complètes.* Vol. 7. Brunswick, Germany: Vieweg, 1804.

Conseil Municipal de Paris. *Année 1872 Procès-Verbaux.* Paris: Imprimerie Municipale, 1873.

———. "Rapport présenté par M. L. Fiaux, au nom de la Commission Spéciale de la Police des Mœurs." No. 26 (1883).

Corlieu, Auguste. *La prostitution à Paris.* Paris: J.-B. Baillière, 1887.

Cox-Algit, Dr. *Anthropophilie, ou étude sur la prostitution masculine à notre époque.* Nantes, France: Morel, 1881.

d'Aurevilly, J. Barbey. *Memoranda.* Paris: Rouveyre et G. Blond, 1883.

Davray, Jules. *L'amour à Paris.* Paris: J.-B. Ferreyrol, 1890.

de Balzac, Honoré. *La comédie humaine.* Vol. 6. Edited by Pierre-Georges Castex. Paris: Garnier, 1977.

Delcourt, Pierre. *Le vice à Paris.* Paris: Alphonse Piaget, 1887.

Delvau, Alfred. *Les plaisirs de Paris: Guide pratique et illustré.* Paris: Achille Faure, 1867.

Devergie, Alphonse. *Médecine légale, théorique et pratique.* 3rd ed. Vol. 1. Paris: Germer-Baillière, 1852.

"Doléances des filles de joie de Paris, à l'occasion de l'ordonnance qui leur défend de se montrer en public, arrangées en complainte par l'une d'elles, enrichies de notes et adressées aux nymphes." Paris: Libraires du Palais-Royal, 1830.

Du Camp, Maxime. *Paris: Ses organs, ses fonctions et sa vie dans la second moitié du XIXe siècle.* 5th ed. 6 vols. Paris: Hachette, 1875.

d'Urville, Flévy. *Les ordures de Paris.* Paris: Librairie Sartorius, 1874.

Engin. "Réponse de M. Engin, aux pétitions des filles publiques suivie de deux scènes historiques de révolte occasionnées par la nouvelle ordonnance de police." Paris: Libraires du Palais-Royal, 1830.

Fiaux, Louis. *La police des mœurs devant la Commission Extraparlementaire du Régime des Mœurs.* 3 vols. Paris: Félix Alcan, 1907–1910.

Fonssagrives, J.-B. *Hygiène et assainissement des villes.* Paris: J.-B. Baillière, 1874.

Gide, André. *Corydon.* Paris: 1924.

"Grande, véritable et lamentable complainte romantique de ces demoiselles, écrite sous la dictée d'une ci-devant nymphe du No 113, accompagnée de notes et commentaires." Paris: Gaultier-Laguionie, 1830.

Granveau, A. *La prostitution dans Paris.* Paris: 1868.

Guide complet des plaisirs mondains et des plaisirs secrets à Paris. Paris: André Hall, n.d.

Guide des plaisirs à Paris. Paris: Édition Photographique, n.d. [1899].

Guide secret de l'étranger célibataire à Paris. Paris: L. Gabillaud, n.d. [1889].

Guyot, Yves. *La police.* Paris: G. Charpentier, 1884.

———. *La police des mœurs: Lettres adressées au journal* La Lanterne *par un ex-agent des mœurs et un médecin.* Paris: Administration du Journal La Lanterne, 1879.

Hayès, Dr. *La pédérastie: Historique, conséquences funestes de ce vice honteux.* Paris: Librairie des Publications Modernes, 1891.

Hugo, Victor. *Les misérables.* Paris: Gallimard, 1951.

———. *Les misérables.* Translated by Charles E. Wilbour. New York: Modern Library, 1992.

Instruction sur la police des cafés, cabarets, auberges et de tous les lieux publics: Avec la jurisprudence de la Cour de cassation sur tous les cas particuliers. Paris: Léautey, 1896.

Lacassagne, Alexandre. *Précis de médecine judiciaire.* Paris: G. Masson, 1878.

"La Paulinade, grande conspiration de la fameuse Pauline et des 20.000 filles publiques de Paris, contre M. Mangin et ses agens. Poème romantique, en trois chants dans le genre adapté par l'auteur d'Hernani." Paris: Chez les Marchands de Nouveautés, 1830.

Laugier, Maurice. "Du rôle de l'expertise médico-légale dans certains cas d'outrage public à la pudeur." *Annales d'hygiène publique et médecine légale* 2, no. 50 (1878): 164–173.

Laure. "Prière romantique de Laure, dite la Séduisante, à tous les amateurs des prêtresses de Vénus et aux augustes défenseurs de Thémis, au sujet de l'ordonnance qui défend aux charmantes déesses de Paphos de sortir de leurs temples, publiée par un amoureux en délire." Paris: Marchands de Nouveautés, 1830.

Laurent, Armand. *De la fréquence des maladies vénériennes.* Paris: J.-B. Baillière, 1893.

Lecour, C. J. *La prostitution à Paris et à Londres, 1789–1870.* Paris: P. Asselin, 1870.

"Le Tocsin de ces demoiselles, ou Mémoire à consulter adressé à tous les barreaux de France, et dénonciation aux cours royales, au sujet d'un arrêté de M. Mangin, contre les filles publiques, suivi de plusieurs lettres édifiantes et curieuses." Paris: Marchands de Nouveautés, 1830.

Legrand du Saulle, Henri. *Étude médico-légale sur la séparation de corps.* Paris: F. Savy, 1866.

"Les filles en cage ou Déguerpissons! Par un abonné au cachet des maisons de plaisir de la capitale." Paris: Peytieux, 1830.

"Le vrai motif de la captivité des femmes soumises, et leurs plus grands ennemis dévoilés." Paris: Marchands de Nouveautés, 1830.

Macé, Gustave. *La police parisienne: Mes lundis en prison.* Paris: G. Charpentier, 1889.

Martineau, Louis. "Leçons sur la sodomie." *L'union médicale* 31 (1881): 616–619, 625–629, 697–702, 721–727.

———. *La prostitution clandestine.* Paris: Delahaye et Lecrosnier, 1885.

Masson, Louis. *Les "Conveniences" à Londres.* Paris: Ch. Schlaeber, 1892.

Mathieu, Émile. *Les cafés-concerts.* Paris: 1863.

Maupassant, Guy de. *Bel-Ami.* Paris: Victor-Havard, 1885.

———. *Bel-Ami.* Translated by Margaret Mauldon. New York: Oxford University Press, 2008.

Michelet, Jules. *La femme.* Paris: Hachette, 1860.

M.J.M. "Épitre à M. Mangin au sujet de l'ordonnance attentatoire à la liberté des femmes." Paris: 1830.

"No. 3481. Décret sur les Cafés, Cabarets, et Débits de boissons." In *Bulletin des lois de la République française* 8, no. 475. Paris: Imprimerie Nationale, 1851.

Parent-Duchâtelet, Alexandre. *De la prostitution dans la ville de Paris, considérée sous le rapport de l'hygiène publique, de la morale et de l'administration.* 2 vols. Paris: J.-B. Baillière, 1836.

———. *De la prostitution dans la ville de Paris, considérée sous le rapport de l'hygiène publique, de la morale et de l'administration.* 3rd ed. 2 vols. Paris: J.-B. Baillière, 1857.

Pauline. "Pétition des filles publiques de Paris à M. le Préfet de police, au sujet de l'ordonnance qu'il vient de rendre contre elles." Paris: 1830.

Pierrot, Alfred-Jean-Marie. *Essai d'étude sur l'atténuation de l'alcoolisme et de la prostitution par la modification de la loi du 17 juillet 1880 sur les cafés, cabarets et débits de boissons.* Montmédy, France: P. Pierrot, 1895.

"Plainte et révélations nouvellement adressées par les filles de joie de Paris à la congrégation, contre l'ordonnance de M. Mangin, qui leur défend de circuler dans les rues pour offrir leurs charmes aux passans." Paris: Garnier, 1830.

"Projet d'un nouveau règlement concernant les filles publiques et les maisons de prostitution, tendant à en diminuer le nombre, sans employer la rigueur, et sans attenter à la liberté des prostituées. Soumis à M. le Préfet de Police. Par un Ami de la Charte, Dans l'intérêt du Commerce et des Mœurs." Paris: Libraires du Palais-Royal, 1830.

"Prospectus." *Annales d'hygiène publique et de médecine légale* 1, no. 1 (1829): v–viii.

Proust, A. *Traité d'hygiène.* 2nd ed. Paris: G. Masson, 1881.

Proust, Marcel. *Remembrance of Things Past.* Translated by C. K. Scott Moncrieff and Stephen Hudson. 2 vols. London: Wordsworth Editions, 2006.

Raffalovich, Marc-André. *Uranisme et unisexualité: Étude sur différentes manifestations de l'instinct sexuel.* Lyon: A. Storck, 1896.

"Réponse de M. le Préfet à toutes les pétitions et réclamations des filles publiques de Paris." Paris: 1830.

Reuss, L. *La prostitution au point de vue de l'hygiène et de l'administration en France et à l'étranger.* Paris: J. B. Baillière, 1889.

Rigaud, Lucien. *Dictionnaire d'argot moderne.* Paris: Paul Ollendorff, 1881.

Rosine. "Observations soumises par une fille de joie à M. le Préfet de police, Sur les dangers que les hommes et les honnêtes femmes ont à craindre des effets de son ordonnance qui défend aux filles prostituées de sortir de chez elles; le tort qu'elle fait au commerce, et sur les moyens de réparer tant de maux sans nuire aux bonnes mœurs." Paris: Marchands de Nouveautés, 1830.

"Salubrité publique—ordinance." *Annales d'hygiène publique et médecine légale* 1, no. 44 (1850): 470–471.

Seul et véritable guide secret des étrangers à Paris. Sceaux, France: Charaire, n.d.

Tardieu, Ambroise. *Dictionnaire d'hygiène publique et de salubrité, ou répertoire de toutes les questions relatives à la santé publique, considérées dans leurs rapports avec les subsistances, les épidémies, les professions, les établissements et institutions d'hygiène et de salubrité.* 2nd ed. 4 vols. Paris: J.-B. Baillière, 1862.

———. *Étude médico-légale sur les attentats aux mœurs.* Paris: J.-B. Baillière, 1857.

———. *Étude médico-légale sur les attentats aux mœurs.* 3rd ed. Paris: J.-B. Baillière, 1859.

Taxil, Léo. *La prostitution contemporaine: Étude d'une question sociale.* Paris: Librairie Populaire, 1884.

Théodore. "50,000 voleurs de plus à Paris, ou réclamations des anciens marlous de la capitale contre l'ordonnance de M. le Préfet de Police, concernant les filles publiques." Paris: Marchands de Nouveautés, 1830.

Vidocq, Eugène François. *Les voleurs: Physiologie de leurs mœurs et de leur langage.* 2 vols. Paris: 1837.

Virginie. "Deuxième pétition adressée à M. Le Préfet de Police, par les filles publiques de Paris, la première, a cause de sa nullité, étant restée sans réponse, suivie de lettres de condoléance de leurs consœurs des départements." Paris: Marchands de Nouveautés, 1830.

Virmaître, Charles. *Trottoirs et lupanars.* Vol. 4. *Paris documentaire (Mœurs).* Paris: Henri Perrot, 1893.

W, Arthur. "Confidences et aveux d'un Parisien: La comtesse, Paris (1850–1861)." In *Notes et observations de médecine légal: Attentats aux mœurs,* edited by Henri Legludic, 237–349. Paris: G. Masson, 1896.

———. "Secret Confessions of a Parisian." In *Queer Lives: Men's Autobiographies from Nineteenth-Century France,* edited and translated by William A. Peniston and Nancy Erber, 7–72. Lincoln: University of Nebraska Press, 2007.

Westphal, Carl. "Die Konträre Sexualempfindung, Symptom Eines Neuropathischen (psychopathischen) Zustandes," *Archiv für psychiatrie und nervenkrankheiten* 2 (1870): 73–108.

Zola, Émile. *Au bonheur des dames (The Ladies' Delight).* Edited and translated by Robin Buss. London: Penguin, 2001.

———. *Nana.* Translated by George Holden. New York: Penguin, 1972.

———. *Les Rougon-Macquart: Histoire naturelle et sociale d'une famille sous le Second Empire.* 5 vols. Paris: Gallimard, 1961.

SECONDARY SOURCES

Abra, Allison. *Dancing in the English Style: Consumption, Americanisation, and National Identity in Britain, 1918–50*. Manchester, U.K.: Manchester University Press, 2017.

Abraham, Julie. *Metropolitan Lovers: The Homosexuality of Cities*. Minneapolis: University of Minnesota Press, 2009.

Adler, Laure. *Les maisons closes, 1830–1930*. Paris: Fayard/Pluriel, 2010.

———. *Secrets d'alcôve: Histoire du couple de 1830 à 1930*. Paris: Hachette Littératures, 1983.

Ahearn, Edward J. 2013. "A Café in the High Time of Haussmannization: Baudelaire's Confrontation with the Eyes of the Poor." In *The Thinking Space: The Café as a Cultural Institution in Paris, Italy, and Vienna,* edited by Leona Rittner, W. Scott Haine, and Jeffrey H. Jackson, 93–100. Farnham, U.K.: Ashgate, 2013.

Ahmed, Sara. *Queer Phenomenology: Orientations, Objects, Others*. Durham, N.C.: Duke University Press, 2006.

Aisenberg, Andrew R. *Contagion: Disease, Government, and the "Social Question" in Nineteenth-Century France*. Stanford, Calif.: Stanford University Press, 1999.

Albert, Nicole G. "De la topographie invisible à l'espace public et littéraire: Les lieux de plaisir lesbien dans le Paris de la Belle Époque." *Revue d'histoire moderne et contemporaine* 4 nos. 53–54 (2006): 87–105.

———. *Lesbian Decadence: Representations in Art and Literature of Fin-de-Siècle France*. Translated by Nancy Erber and William Peniston. New York: Harrington Park Press, 2016.

Anderson, Malcolm. *In Thrall to Political Change: Police and Gendarmerie in France*. Oxford: Oxford University Press, 2011.

Balducci, Temma. "Aller à pied: Bourgeois Women on the Streets of Paris." In *Women, Femininity, and Public Space in European Visual Culture, 1789–1914,* edited by Temma Balducci and Heather Belnap Jensen, 151–166. Burlington, Vt.: Ashgate, 2014.

———. *Gender, Space, and the Gaze in Post-Haussmann Visual Culture: Beyond the Flâneur*. London: Routledge, 2017.

Baldwin, Peter. *Contagion and the State in Europe, 1830–1930*. Cambridge: Cambridge University Press, 1999.

Barbedette, Gilles, and Michel Carassou. *Paris Gay 1925*. Paris: Presses de la Renaissance, 1981.

Barnes, David S. *The Great Stink of Paris and the Nineteenth-Century Struggle against Filth and Germs*. Baltimore: Johns Hopkins University Press, 2006.

Barrows, Susanna. "'Parliaments of the People': The Political Culture of Cafés in the Early Third Republic." In *Drinking: Behavior and Belief in Modern History,* edited by Susanna Barrows and Robin Room, 87–97. Berkeley: University of California Press, 1991.

Bauer, Heike. "Theorizing Female Inversion: Sexology, Discipline, and Gender at the Fin de Siècle." *Journal of the History of Sexuality* 18, no. 1 (2009): 84–102.

Beachy, Robert. *Gay Berlin: Birthplace of a Modern Identity*. New York: Vintage, 2014.

Beccalossi, Chiara. *Female Sexual Inversion: Same-Sex Desires in Italian and British Sexology, c. 1870–1920*. New York: Palgrave Macmillan, 2012.

Bech, Henning. *When Men Meet: Homosexuality and Modernity.* Translated by Teresa Mesquit and Tim Davies. Chicago: University of Chicago Press, 1997.

Belenky, Masha. "From Transit to *Transitoire*: The Omnibus and Modernity." *Nineteenth-Century French Studies* 35, no. 2 (2007): 408–421.

Benjamin, Walter. *The Arcades Project.* Edited by Rolf Tiedemann. Translated by Howard Eiland and Kevin McLaughlin. Cambridge, Mass: Belknap Press, 1999.

Berlanstein, Lenard R. *Daughters of Eve: A Cultural History of French Theater Women from the Old Regime to the Fin de Siècle.* Cambridge, Mass.: Harvard University Press, 2001.

Berlant, Lauren, and Michael Warner. "Sex in Public." *Critical Inquiry* 24, no. 2 (1998): 547–566.

Berlière, Jean-Marc. *Le monde des polices en France: XIXe–XXe siècles.* Paris: Éditions Complexe, 1996.

———. *La police des mœurs sous la IIIe République.* Paris: Seuil, 1992.

Berman, Marshall. *All That Is Solid Melts into Air: The Experience of Modernity.* New York: Penguin, 1988.

Bernheimer, Charles. *Figures of Ill Repute: Representing Prostitution in Nineteenth-Century France.* Cambridge, Mass: Harvard University Press, 1989.

Boutin, Aimée. *City of Noise: Sound and Nineteenth-Century Paris.* Urbana: University of Illinois Press, 2015.

Bowie, Karen, ed. *La modernité avant Haussmann: Formes de l'espace urbain à Paris, 1801–1853.* Paris: Éditions Recherches, 2001.

Bravmann, Scott. *Queer Fictions of the Past: History, Culture, and Difference.* Cambridge: Cambridge University Press, 1997.

Brigstocke, Julian. *The Life of the City: Space, Humour, and the Experience of Truth in Fin-de-Siècle Montmartre.* Farnham, U.K.: Ashgate, 2014.

Brown-May, Andrew, and Peg Fraser. "Gender, Respectability, and Public Convenience in Melbourne, Australia, 1859–1902." In *Ladies and Gents: Public Toilets and Gender,* edited by Olga Gershenson and Barbara Penner, 75–89. Philadelphia: Temple University Press, 2009.

Buck-Morss, Susan. "The Flâneur, the Sandwichman, and the Whore: The Politics of Loitering." *New German Critique,* no. 39 (1986): 99–140.

Burney, Ian A. *Bodies of Evidence: Medicine and the Politics of the English Inquest, 1830–1926.* Baltimore: Johns Hopkins University Press, 2000.

Calhoun, Craig. "Introduction: Habermas and the Public Sphere." In *Habermas and the Public Sphere,* edited by Craig Calhoun, 1–48. Cambridge, Mass: MIT Press, 1992.

Cannon, James. *The Paris Zone: A Cultural History, 1840–1944.* Farnham, U.K.: Ashgate, 2015.

Carmona, Michel. *Haussmann: His Life and Times, and the Making of Modern Paris.* Translated by Patrick Camiller. Chicago: Ivan R. Dee, 2002.

Caron, David. *My Father and I: The Marais and the Queerness of Community.* Ithaca, N.Y.: Cornell University Press, 2009.

Carter, Karen L. "Unfit for Public Display: Female Sexuality and the Censorship of Fin-de-Siècle Publicity Posters." *Early Popular Visual Culture* 8, no. 2 (2010): 107–124.

Cavanagh, Sheila L. *Queering Bathrooms: Gender, Sexuality, and the Hygienic Imagination.* Toronto: University of Toronto Press, 2010.

Chaperon, Sylvie. *Les origines de la sexologie (1850–1900)*. Paris: Payot and Rivages, 2012.

Chauncey, George. "From Sexual Inversion to Homosexuality: Medicine and the Changing Conceptualization of Female Deviance." *Salmagundi*, nos. 58–59 (1982–1983): 114–146.

———. *Gay New York: Gender, Urban Culture, and the Making of the Gay Male World, 1890–1940*. New York: Basic Books, 1994.

Chevalier, Louis. *Laboring Classes and Dangerous Classes in Paris during the First Half of the Nineteenth Century*. Translated by Frank Jellinek. New York: H. Fertig, 1973.

Chisholm, Dianne. *Queer Constellations: Subcultural Space in the Wake of the City*. Minneapolis: Minnesota University Press, 2005.

Choquette, Leslie. "Degenerate or Degendered? Images of Prostitution and Homosexuality in the French Third Republic." *Historical Reflections/Réflexions Historiques* 23, no. 2 (1997): 205–228.

———. "Gay Paree: The Origins of Lesbian and Gay Commercial Culture in the French Third Republic." *Contemporary French Civilization* 41, no. 1 (2016): 1–24.

———. "Homosexuals in the City: Representations of Lesbian and Gay Space in Nineteenth-Century Paris." *Journal of Homosexuality* 41, nos. 3–4 (2002): 149–167.

Clark, T. J. *The Painting of Modern Life: Paris in the Art of Manet and His Followers*. Rev. ed. Princeton, N.J.: Princeton University Press, 1999.

Clark-Huckstep, Andrew E. "*The History of Sexuality* and Historical Methodology." *Cultural History* 5, no. 2 (2016): 179–199.

Clayson, Hollis. *Painted Love: Prostitution in French Art of the Impressionist Era*. Los Angeles: Getty Publications, 2003.

Clayson, Hollis, and André Dombrowski, eds. *Is Paris Still the Capital of the Nineteenth Century? Essays on Art and Modernity, 1850–1900*. London: Routledge, 2016.

Cole, Joshua. *The Power of Large Numbers: Population, Politics, and Gender in Nineteenth-Century France*. Ithaca, N.Y.: Cornell University Press, 2000.

Conner, Susan. "Life in the Streets: Policing Prostitution in Revolutionary Paris, 1789–1794." *Proceedings of the Consortium on Revolutionary Europe, 1750–1850* 16 (1986): 156–167.

Conway, Kelley. *Chanteuse in the City: The Realist Singer in French Film*. Berkeley: University of California Press, 2004.

Copley, Antony R. H. *Sexual Moralities in France, 1780–1980: New Ideas on the Family, Divorce, and Homosexuality*. London: Routledge, 1989.

Corbin, Alain. *Les filles de noce: Misère sexuelle et prostitution au XIXe siècle*. Paris: Flammarion, 1982.

———. *The Foul and the Fragrant: Odor and the French Social Imagination*. Cambridge, Mass: Harvard University Press, 1986.

———. *Le miasme et la jonquille: L'odorat et l'imaginaire social, XVIIIe–XIXe siècles*. Paris: Flammarion, 1986.

———. *Women for Hire: Prostitution and Sexuality in France after 1850*. Translated by Alan Sheridan. Cambridge, Mass: Harvard University Press, 1990.

Counter, Andrew J. *The Amorous Restoration: Love, Sex, and Politics in Early Nineteenth-Century France*. Oxford: Oxford University Press, 2016.

Coviello, Peter. *Tomorrow's Parties: Sex and the Untimely in Nineteenth-Century America*. New York: New York University Press, 2013.

Davidson, Arnold I. *The Emergence of Sexuality: Historical Epistemology and the Formation of Concepts.* Cambridge, Mass.: Harvard University Press, 2001.

Davidson, Denise Z. *France after Revolution: Urban Life, Gender, and the New Social Order.* Cambridge, Mass: Harvard University Press, 2007.

Dean, Carolyn J. *The Frail Social Body: Pornography Homosexuality, and Other Fantasies in Interwar France.* Berkeley: University of California Press, 2000.

de Certeau, Michel. *The Practice of Everyday Life.* Translated by Steven Rendall. Berkeley: University of California Press, 1984.

de la Carrera, Rosalina. "History's Unconscious in Victor Hugo's *Les Misérables.*" *MLN* 96, no. 4 (1981): 839–855.

Delattre, Simone. *Les douze heures noirs: La nuit à Paris aux XIXe siècle.* Paris: Albin Michel, 2003.

Deluermoz, Quentin. "Police Forces and Political Crises: Revolutions, Policing Alternatives, and Institutional Resilience in Paris, 1848–1871." *Urban History* 43, no. 2 (2016): 232–248.

———. *Policiers dans la ville: La construction d'un ordre public à Paris (1854–1914).* Paris: Publications de la Sorbonne, 2012.

d'Emilio, John. "Capitalism and Gay Identity." In *Powers of Desire: The Politics of Sexuality,* edited by Ann Snitow, Christine Stansell, and Sharon Thompson, 100–113. New York: Monthly Review Press, 1983.

———. *Sexual Politics, Sexual Communities: The Making of a Homosexual Minority in the United States, 1940–1972.* 2nd ed. Chicago: University of Chicago Press, 1998.

Deutsch, Sarah. *Women and the City: Gender, Space, and Power in Boston, 1870–1940.* New York: Oxford University Press, 2000.

Doan, Laura. *Disturbing Practices: History, Sexuality, and Women's Experience of Modern War.* Chicago: University of Chicago Press, 2013.

Dowbiggin, Ian. *Inheriting Madness: Professionalization and Psychiatric Knowledge in Nineteenth-Century France.* Berkeley: University of California Press, 1991.

D'Souza, Aruna, and Tom McDonough, eds. *The Invisible* Flâneuse? *Gender, Public Space, and Visual Culture in Nineteenth-Century Paris.* Manchester, U.K.: Manchester University Press, 2006.

Edelman, Lee. *Homographesis: Essays in Gay Literary and Cultural Theory.* New York: Routledge, 1994.

Emsley, Clive. "Policing the Streets of Early Nineteenth-Century Paris." *French History* 1, no. 2 (1987): 257–282.

Erber, Nancy, and William A. Peniston, trans. *Marc-André Raffalovich's "Uranism and Unisexuality: A Study of Different Manifestations of the Sexual Instinct,"* edited by Philip Healy and Frederick S. Roden. New York: Palgrave Macmillan, 2016.

Evans, Richard J. "Prostitution, State, and Society in Imperial Germany." *Past and Present,* no. 70 (1976): 106–129.

Faderman, Lillian. *Surpassing the Love of Men: Romantic Friendship and Love between Women from the Renaissance to the Present.* New York: Morrow, 1981.

Farge, Arlette. *The Allure of the Archives.* Translated by Thomas Scott-Railton. New Haven, Conn.: Yale University Press, 2013.

Felski, Rita. *The Gender of Modernity.* Cambridge, Mass: Harvard University Press, 1995.

Féray, Jean-Claude. *Grecques, les mœurs du hanneton? Histoire du mot* pédérastie *et de ses dérivés en langue française.* Paris: Quintes-feuilles, 2004.

———. *"Pédés:" Le premier registre infamant de la préfecture de police de Paris au XIXe siècle suivi d'un dictionnaire des noms propres et noms communs les plus significatifs du registre, et d'annexes.* Paris: Quintes-feuilles, 2012.

Ferguson, Eliza. "The Cosmos of the Paris Apartment: Working-Class Family Life in the Nineteenth Century." *Journal of Urban History* 37, no. 1 (2011): 59–67.

Ferguson, Priscilla Parkhurst. *Paris as Revolution: Writing the Nineteenth-Century City.* Berkeley: University of California Press, 1994.

Foucault, Michel. *Discipline and Punish: The Birth of the Prison.* Translated by Alan Sheridan. New York: Vintage, 1979.

———. *The History of Sexuality.* Vol. 1, *An Introduction.* Translated by Robert Hurley. New York: Vintage, 1990.

———. "Of Other Spaces." *Diacritics* 16, no. 1 (1986): 22–27.

Fournier, Eric. *Paris en ruines: Du Paris haussmannien au Paris communard.* Paris: Éditions Imago, 2008.

Frankis, Jamie S., and Paul Flowers. "Public Sexual Cultures: A Systematic Review of Qualitative Research Investigating Men's Sexual Behaviors with Men in Public Spaces." *Journal of Homosexuality* 56, no. 7 (2009): 861–893.

Gandy, Matthew. *The Fabric of Space: Water, Modernity, and the Urban Imagination.* Cambridge, Mass: MIT Press, 2014.

Gasnault, François. *Guinguettes et lorettes: Bals publics et danse sociale à Paris entre 1830 et 1870.* Paris: Aubier, 1986.

Gibson, Mary. *Prostitution and the State in Italy, 1860–1915.* 2nd ed. Columbus: Ohio State University Press, 1999.

Giles, Geoffrey J. "Legislating Homophobia in the Third Reich: The Radicalization of Prosecution against Homosexuality by the Legal Profession." *German History* 23, no. 3 (2005): 339–354.

Gilfoyle, Timothy J. *City of Eros: New York City, Prostitution, and the Commercialization of Sex, 1790–1920.* New York: W. W. Norton, 1992.

Gluck, Mary. *Popular Bohemia: Modernism and Urban Culture in Nineteenth-Century Paris.* Cambridge, Mass: Harvard University Press, 2005.

Goldstein, Jan. *Console and Classify: The French Psychiatric Profession in the Nineteenth Century.* Cambridge: Cambridge University Press, 1987.

Gonzalez-Quijano, Lola. *Capitale de l'amour: Filles et lieux de plaisir à Paris aux XIXe siècle.* Paris: Vendémiaire, 2015.

———. "Entre désir sexuel et sentiments: L'apprentissage amoureux des étudiants du quartier latin du second XIXe siècle." In *Les jeunes et la sexualité: Initiations, interdits, identités (XIXe–XXIe siècle),* edited by Véronique Blanchard, Régis Revenin, and Jean-Jacques Yvorel, 180–188. Paris: Éditions Autrement, 2010.

Gronberg, Theresa Ann. "Femmes de Brasseries." *Art History* 7, no. 3 (1984): 329–344.

Grosz, Elizabeth. "Bodies-Cities." In *Sexuality and Space,* edited by Beatriz Colomina, 241–253. Princeton, N.J.: Princeton Architectural Press, 1992.

Grout, Holly. *The Force of Beauty: Transforming French Ideas of Femininity in the Third Republic.* Baton Rouge: Louisiana State University Press, 2015.

Gunther, Scott. *The Elastic Closet: A History of Homosexuality in France, 1942–Present* New York: Palgrave Macmillan, 2009.

Habermas, Jürgen. *The Structural Transformation of the Public Sphere: An Inquiry into a Category of Bourgeois Society.* Translated by Thomas Burger. Cambridge, Mass: MIT Press, 1991.

Hahn, H. Hazel. *Scenes of Parisian Modernity: Culture and Consumption in the Nineteenth Century.* New York: Palgrave Macmillan, 2009.

Hahn, Pierre. *Nos ancêtres les pervers: La vie des homosexuels sous le Second Empire.* Béziers, France: H and O Éditions, 2006.

Haine, W. Scott. *The World of the Paris Café: Sociability among the French Working Class, 1789–1914.* Baltimore: Johns Hopkins University Press, 1996.

Halperin, David M. *How to Do the History of Homosexuality.* Chicago: University of Chicago Press, 2002.

Hanna, Martha. "Natalism, Homosexuality, and the Controversy over *Corydon.*" In Merrick and Ragan, *Homosexuality in Modern France,* 202–224.

Hansen, Karen V. "'No Kisses Is Like Youres': An Erotic Friendship between Two African-American Women during the Mid-Nineteenth Century." *Gender and History* 7, no. 2 (1995): 153–182.

Harris, Ruth. *Murders and Madness: Medicine, Law, and Society in the Fin de Siècle.* Oxford, U.K.: Clarendon Press, 1989.

Harsin, Jill. *Policing Prostitution in Nineteenth-Century Paris.* Princeton, N.J.: Princeton University Press, 1985.

Harvey, David. *Paris, Capital of Modernity.* New York: Routledge, 2006.

Harvey, Elizabeth D. "The Portal of Touch." *American Historical Review* 116, no. 2 (2011): 385–400.

Hekma, Gert. "'A Female Soul in a Male Body': Sexual Inversion as Gender Inversion in Nineteenth-Century Sexology." In *Third Sex, Third Gender: Beyond Sexual Dimorphism in Culture and History,* edited by Gilbert Herdt, 213–239. New York: Zone Books, 1994.

Herring, Scott. *Another Country: Queer Anti-Urbanism.* New York: New York University Press, 2010.

———. *Queering the Underworld: Slumming, Literature, and the Undoing of Lesbian and Gay History.* Chicago: University of Chicago Press, 2007.

Herzog, Dagmar. *Sex after Fascism: Memory and Morality in Twentieth-Century Germany.* Princeton, N.J.: Princeton University Press, 2005.

Hopkins, Richard S. *Planning the Greenspaces of Nineteenth-Century Paris.* Baton Rouge: Louisiana State University Press, 2015.

Horowitz, Sarah. "Policing and the Problem of Privacy in Restoration-Era France, 1815–30." *French History* 27, no. 1 (2013): 45–68.

Houbre, Gabrielle. *Le livre des courtisanes: Archives secrètes de la police des mœurs, 1861–1876.* Paris: Tallandier, 2006.

Houlbrook, Matt. "The Private World of Public Urinals: London 1918–57." *London Journal* 25, no. 1 (2000): 52–70.

———. *Queer London: Perils and Pleasures in the Sexual Metropolis, 1918–1957.* Chicago: University of Chicago Press, 2005.

Howard, John. *Men Like That: A Southern Queer History.* Chicago: University of Chicago Press, 1999.

Howell, Philip. "Prostitution and Racialised Sexuality: The Regulation of Prostitution in Britain and the British Empire before the Contagious Diseases Acts." *Environment and Planning D: Society and Space* 18, no. 3 (2000): 321–339.

Hubbard, Phil. *Sex and the City: Geographies of Prostitution in the Urban West*. Aldershot, U.K.: Ashgate, 1999.

Hubbard, Phil, and Teela Sanders. "Making Space for Sex Work: Female Street Prostitution and the Production of Urban Space." *International Journal of Urban and Regional Research* 27, no. 1 (2003): 75–89.

Humphreys, Laud. *Tearoom Trade: Impersonal Sex in Public Places*. New York: Aldine, 1970.

Hunt, Alan. "Regulating Heterosocial Space: Sexual Politics in the Early Twentieth Century." *Journal of Historical Sociology* 15, no. 1 (2002): 1–34.

Iacub, Marcela. *Through the Keyhole: A History of Sex, Space, and Public Modesty in Modern France*. Translated by Vinay Swamy. Manchester, U.K.: Manchester University Press, 2016.

Iskin, Ruth E. *Modern Women and Parisian Consumer Culture in Impressionist Painting*. Cambridge: Cambridge University Press, 2007.

———. "Selling, Seduction, and Soliciting the Eye: Manet's Bar at the Folies-Bergère." *Art Bulletin* 77, no. 1 (1995): 25–44.

Jackson, Julian. *Living in Arcadia: Homosexuality, Politics, and Morality in France from the Liberation to AIDS*. Chicago: University of Chicago Press, 2009.

Jacquemet, Gérard. "Urbanisme parisien: La bataille du tout-à-l'égout à la fin du XIXe siècle." *Revue d'histoire moderne et contemporaine* 26, no. 4 (1979): 505–548.

Jenner, Mark S. R. "Follow Your Nose? Smell, Smelling, and Their Histories." *American Historical Review* 116, no. 2 (2011): 335–351.

Johnson, Colin R. *Just Queer Folks: Gender and Sexuality in Rural America*. Philadelphia: Temple University Press, 2013.

Jones, Colin. *Paris: Biography of a City*. New York: Penguin, 2004.

Jordan, David P. *Transforming Paris: The Life and Labors of Baron Haussmann*. New York: Free Press, 1995.

Kenney, Moira Rachel. *Mapping Gay L.A.: The Intersection of Place and Politics*. Philadelphia: Temple University Press, 2001.

Kerley, Lela F. *Uncovering Paris: Scandals and Nude Spectacles in the Belle Époque*. Baton Rouge: Louisiana State University Press, 2017.

Kingston, Ralph. "Capitalism in the Streets: Paris Shopkeepers, *Passages Couverts*, and the Production of the Early Nineteenth-Century City." *Radical History Review* 2012, no. 114 (2012): 39–65.

Kirkland, Stephane. *Paris Reborn: Napoléon III, Baron Haussmann, and the Quest to Build a Modern City*. New York: St. Martin's Press, 2013.

Knopp, Lawrence. "Sexuality and the Spatial Dynamics of Capitalism." *Environment and Planning D: Society and Space* 10, no. 6 (1992): 651–669.

Koshar, Rudy. "'What Ought to Be Seen': Tourists' Guidebooks and National Identities in Modern Germany and Europe." *Journal of Contemporary History* 33, no. 3 (1998): 323–340.

Koven, Seth. *Slumming: Sexual and Social Politics in Victorian London*. Princeton, N.J.: Princeton University Press, 2004.

Kudlick, Catherine J. *Cholera in Post-Revolutionary Paris: A Cultural History*. Berkeley: University of California Press, 1996.

Kushner, Nina. *Erotic Exchanges: The World of Elite Prostitution in Eighteenth-Century France*. Ithaca, N.Y.: Cornell University Press, 2013.

La Berge, Ann F. *Mission and Method: The Early Nineteenth-Century French Public Health Movement.* Cambridge: Cambridge University Press, 1992.

Lacan, Jacques. *Écrits: A Selection.* Translated by Alan Sheridan. New York: W. W. Norton, 1977.

Laite, Julia. *Common Prostitutes and Ordinary Citizens: Commercial Sex in London, 1885–1960.* Houndmills, U.K.: Palgrave Macmillan, 2012.

Lefebvre, Henri. *The Production of Space.* Translated by Donald Nicholson-Smith. Oxford, U.K.: Blackwell, 1991.

Legg, Stephen. *Prostitution and the Ends of Empire: Scale, Governmentalities, and Interwar India.* Durham, N.C.: Duke University Press, 2014.

Lehning, James R. *To Be a Citizen: The Political Culture of the Early French Third Republic.* Ithaca, N.Y.: Cornell University Press, 2001.

Levine, Philippa. "Modernity, Medicine, and Colonialism: The Contagious Diseases Ordinances in Hong Kong and the Straits Settlements." In *Gender, Sexuality, and Colonial Modernities,* edited by Antoinette Burton, 35–48. London: Routledge, 1999.

Lewis, Briana. "The Sewer and the Prostitute in *Les Misérables*: From Regulation to Redemption." *Nineteenth-Century French Studies* 44, nos. 3–4 (2016): 266–278.

Long, Scott. "When Doctors Torture: The Anus and the State in Egypt and Beyond." *Health and Human Rights* 7, no. 2 (2004): 114–140.

Loyer, François. *Paris Nineteenth Century: Architecture and Urbanism.* Translated by Charles Lynn Clark. New York: Abbeville Press, 1988.

Lucey, Michael. *Never Say I: Sexuality and the First Person in Colette, Gide, and Proust.* Durham, N.C.: Duke University Press, 2006.

Mack, Mehammed Amadeus. *Sexagon: Muslims, France, and the Sexualization of National Culture.* New York: Fordham University Press, 2017.

Mah, Harold. "Phantasies of the Public Sphere: Rethinking the Habermas of Historians." *Journal of Modern History* 72, no. 1 (2000): 153–182.

Manin, Lise. "Perverses promiscuités? Bains publics et cafés-concerts parisiens au second XIXe siècle," *Genre, sexualité et société* 10 (2013). http://journals.openedition.org/gss/2955. Accessed April 9, 2018.

Mansker, Andrea. *Sex, Honor, and Citizenship in Early Third Republic France.* New York: Palgrave Macmillan, 2011.

Marcus, Sharon. *Apartment Stories: City and Home in Nineteenth-Century Paris and London.* Berkeley: University of California Press, 1999.

———. *Between Women: Friendship, Desire, and Marriage in Victorian England.* Princeton, N.J.: Princeton University Press, 2007.

Marhoefer, Laurie. *Sex and the Weimar Republic: German Homosexual Emancipation and the Rise of the Nazis.* Toronto: University of Toronto Press, 2015.

Martel, Frédéric. *Le rose et le noir: Les homosexuels en France depuis 1968.* Paris: Seuil, 1996.

Martin, Biddy. "Extraordinary Homosexuals and the Fear of Being Ordinary." *differences* 6, nos. 2–3 (1994): 100–125.

Martin, Brian Joseph. *Napoleonic Friendship: Military Fraternity, Intimacy and Sexuality in Nineteenth-Century France.* Durham, NH: University of New Hampshire Press, 2011.

Martin, Lowry Gene. "Desire, Fantasy, and the Writing of Lesbos-sur-Seine, 1880–1939." Ph.D. diss., University of California, Berkeley, 2010.

Martínez, Elena María. "Archives, Bodies, and Imagination: The Case of Juana Aguilar and Queer Approaches to History, Sexuality, and Politics." *Radical History Review* 2014, no. 120 (2014): 159–182.

Matlock, Jann. *Scenes of Seduction: Prostitution, Hysteria, and Reading Difference in Nineteenth-Century France.* New York: Columbia University Press, 1994.

McLaren, Angus. *Sexual Blackmail: A Modern History.* Cambridge, Mass: Harvard University Press, 2002.

Merrick, Jeffrey. "Commissioner Foucault, Inspector Noël, and the 'Pederasts' of Paris, 1780–3." *Journal of Social History* 32, no. 2 (1998): 287–307.

———. "New Sources and Questions for Research on Sexual Relations between Men in Eighteenth-Century France." *Gender and History* 30, no. 1 (2018): 9–29.

Merrick, Jeffrey, and Bryant T. Ragan Jr., eds. *Homosexuality in Modern France.* New York: Oxford University Press, 1996.

Merriman, John. *Police Stories: Building the French State, 1815–1851.* Oxford: Oxford University Press, 2006.

Miller, D. A. *The Novel and the Police.* Berkeley: University of California Press, 1988.

Miller, Michael B. *The Bon Marché: Bourgeois Culture and the Department Store, 1869–1920.* Princeton, N.J.: Princeton University Press, 1981.

Mort, Frank. *Dangerous Sexualities: Medico-moral Politics in England since 1830.* 2nd ed. London: Routledge, 2000.

Mumford, Kevin J. *Interzones: Black/White Sex Districts in Chicago and New York in the Early Twentieth Century.* New York: Columbia University Press, 1997.

Murat, Laure. *La loi du genre: Une histoire culturelle du "troisième sexe."* Paris: Fayard, 2006.

———. "La tante, le policier et l'écrivain: Pour une protosexologie de commissariats et de romans." *Revue d'histoire des sciences humaines* 2, no. 17 (2007): 47–59.

Nead, Lynda. *Victorian Babylon: People, Streets, and Images in Nineteenth-Century London.* New Haven, Conn.: Yale University Press, 2000.

Nesci, Catherine. *Le flâneur et les flâneuses: Les femmes et la ville à l'époque romantique.* Grenoble, France: Ellug, 2007.

Nochlin, Linda. "A Thoroughly Modern Masked Ball," *Art in America* 71, no. 10 (1983): 188–201.

Nord, Philip G. *Paris Shopkeepers and the Politics of Resentment.* Princeton, N.J.: Princeton University Press, 1986.

Nye, Robert A. *Crime, Madness, and Politics in Modern France: The Medical Concept of National Decline.* Princeton, N.J.: Princeton University Press, 1984.

———. "The History of Sexuality in Context: National Sexological Traditions." *Science in Context* 4, no. 2 (1991): 387–406.

———. *Masculinity and Male Codes of Honor in Modern France.* Berkeley: University of California Press, 1998.

———. "Sex Difference and Male Homosexuality in French Medical Discourse, 1830–1930." *Bulletin of the History of Medicine* 63, no. 1 (1989): 32–51.

Offen, Karen. "Depopulation, Nationalism, and Feminism in Fin-de-Siècle France." *American Historical Review* 89, no. 3 (1984): 648–676.

———. "Madame Ghénia Avril de Sainte-Croix, the Josephine Butler of France." *Women's History Review* 17, no. 2 (2008): 239–255.

Oosterhuis, Harry. "Homosexual Emancipation in Germany before 1933: Two Traditions." In *Homosexuality and Male Bonding in Pre-Nazi Germany,* edited by Harry Oosterhuis, 1–27. New York: Haworth Press, 1991.

———. *Stepchildren of Nature: Krafft-Ebing, Psychiatry, and the Making of Sexual Identity.* Chicago: University of Chicago Press, 2000.

Palmowski, Jan. "Travels with Baedeker: The Guidebook and the Middle Classes in Victorian and Edwardian England." In *Histories of Leisure,* edited by Rudy Koshar, 105–130. Oxford, U.K.: Berg, 2002.

Papayanis, Nicholas. *Horse-Drawn Cabs and Omnibuses in Paris: The Idea of Circulation and the Business of Public Transit.* Baton Rouge: Louisiana State University Press, 1996.

———. *Planning Paris before Haussmann.* Baltimore: Johns Hopkins University Press, 2004.

Park, Sun-Young. *Ideals of the Body: Architecture, Urbanism and Hygiene in Postrevolutionary Paris.* Pittsburgh: University of Pittsburgh Press, 2018.

Parsons, Deborah. *Streetwalking the Metropolis.* Oxford: Oxford University Press, 2000.

Pastorello, Thierry. "L'abolition du crime de sodomie en 1791: Un long processus social, répressif et pénal." *Cahiers d'histoire: Revue d'histoire critique* 112–113 (2010): 197–208.

Payne, Howard. *The Police State of Louis Napoleon Bonaparte, 1851–1860.* Seattle: University of Washington Press, 1966.

Pedersen, Jean Elisabeth. "Regulating Abortion and Birth Control: Gender, Medicine, and Republican Politics in France, 1870–1920." *French Historical Studies* 19, no. 3 (1996): 673–698.

Peiss, Kathy. *Cheap Amusements: Women and Leisure in Turn-of-the-Century New York.* Philadelphia: Temple University Press, 1986.

Peniston, William A. *Pederasts and Others: Urban Culture and Sexual Identity in Nineteenth-Century Paris.* New York: Harrington Park Press, 2004.

———. "A Public Offense against Decency: The Trial of the Count de Germiny and the 'Moral Order' of the Third Republic." In *Disorder in the Court: Trials and Sexual Conflict at the Turn of the Century,* edited by George Robb and Nancy Erber, 12–32. New York: New York University Press, 1999.

Peniston, William A., and Nancy Erber, eds. *Queer Lives: Men's Autobiographies from Nineteenth-Century France.* Lincoln: University of Nebraska Press, 2007.

Perreau, Bruno. *Queer Theory: The French Response.* Stanford, Calif.: Stanford University Press, 2016.

Pillet, Elisabeth. "Cafés-concerts et cabarets." *Romantisme,* no. 75 (1992): 43–50.

Pinkney, David H. *Napoleon III and the Rebuilding of Paris.* Princeton, N.J.: Princeton University Press, 1958.

Plott, Michèle. "The Rules of the Game: Respectability, Sexuality, and the *Femme Mondaine* in Late-Nineteenth-Century Paris." *French Historical Studies* 25, no. 3 (2002): 531–556.

Plumauzille, Clyde. *Prostitution et révolution: Les femmes publiques dans la cité républicaine (1789–1804).* Ceyzérieu, France: Champ Vallon, 2016.

Pollock, Griselda. *Vision and Difference: Femininity, Feminism, and Histories of Art.* London: Routledge, 1988.

Potofsky, Allan. *Constructing Paris in the Age of Revolution.* New York: Palgrave Macmillan, 2009.

Prendergast, Christopher. *Paris and the Nineteenth Century.* Oxford, U.K.: Blackwell, 1992.

Procacci, Giovanna. *Gouverner la misère: La question sociale en France, 1789–1848.* Paris: Seuil, 1993.

Provencher, Denis M. *Queer French: Globalization, Language, and Sexual Citizenship in France.* New York: Routledge, 2007.

Quinlan, Sean M. *The Great Nation in Decline: Sex, Modernity, and Health Crises in Revolutionary France, c. 1750–1850.* Aldershot, U.K.: Ashgate, 2007.

Rabinow, Paul. *French Modern: Norms and Forms of the Social Environment.* Chicago: University of Chicago Press, 1995.

Ragan, Bryant T., Jr. "The Enlightenment Confronts Homosexuality." In Merrick and Ragan, *Homosexuality in Modern France,* 8–29.

Rappaport, Erika Diane. *Shopping for Pleasure: Women in the Making of London's West End.* Princeton, N.J.: Princeton University Press, 2000.

Ratcliffe, Barrie M. "Cities and Environmental Decline: Elites and the Sewage Problem in Paris from the Mid-Eighteenth to the Mid-Nineteenth Century." *Planning Perspectives* 5 (1990): 189–222.

———. "Classes laborieuses et classes dangereuses à Paris pendant la première moitié du XIXe siècle? The Chevalier Thesis Reexamined." *French Historical Studies* 17, no. 2 (1991): 542–574.

Rearick, Charles. *Pleasures of the Belle Époque: Entertainment and Festivity in Turn-of-the-Century France.* New Haven, Conn.: Yale University Press, 1985.

Reid, Donald. *Paris Sewers and Sewermen: Realities and Representations.* Cambridge, Mass: Harvard University Press, 1991.

Revenin, Régis. *Homosexualité et prostitution masculines à Paris, 1870–1918.* Paris: L'Harmattan, 2005.

Rey, Michel. "Police et sodomie à Paris au XVIIIe siècle: Du péché au désordre." *Revue d'histoire moderne et contemporaine* 29, no. 1 (1982): 113–124.

Rifkin, Adrian. *Street Noises: Parisian Pleasure, 1900–40.* Manchester, U.K.: Manchester University Press, 1993.

Roberts, Mary Louise. *Civilization without Sexes: Reconstructing Gender in Postwar France, 1917–1927.* Chicago: University of Chicago Press, 1994.

———. *Disruptive Acts: The New Woman in Fin-de-Siècle France.* Chicago: University of Chicago Press, 2002.

———. *What Soldiers Do: Sex and the American GI in World War II France.* Chicago: University of Chicago Press, 2013.

Rosario, Vernon A. *The Erotic Imagination: French Histories of Perversity.* Oxford: Oxford University Press, 1997.

———. "Pointy Penises, Fashion Crimes, and Hysterical Mollies: The Pederasts' Inversions." In Merrick and Ragan, *Homosexuality in Modern France,* 146–176.

Ross, Andrew Israel. "Dirty Desire: The Uses and Misuses of Public Urinals in Nineteenth-Century Paris." *Berkeley Journal of Sociology* 53 (2009): 62–88.

———. "Serving Sex: Playing with Prostitution in the *Brasseries à femmes* of Late Nineteenth-Century Paris." *Journal of the History of Sexuality* 24, no. 2 (2015): 288–313.

———. "Sex in the Archives: Homosexuality, Prostitution, and the Archives de la Préfecture de Police de Paris." *French Historical Studies* 40, no. 2 (2017): 267–290.

Rowe, Dorothy. *Representing Berlin: Sexuality and the City in Imperial and Weimar Germany.* Aldershot, U.K.: Ashgate, 2003.

Rupp, Leila J. "Sexual Fluidity 'Before Sex.'" *Signs* 37, no. 4 (2012): 849–856.

Sante, Luc. *The Other Paris.* New York: Farrar, Straus, and Giroux, 2015.

Sautman, Francesca Canadé. "Invisible Women: Lesbian Working-Class Culture in France, 1880–1930." In Merrick and Ragan, *Homosexuality in Modern France,* 177–201.

Schultz, Gretchen. *Sapphic Fathers: Discourses of Same-Sex Desire from Nineteenth-Century France.* Toronto: University of Toronto Press, 2015.

Schwartz, Vanessa R. *Spectacular Realities: Early Mass Culture in Fin-de-Siècle Paris.* Berkeley: University of California Press, 1998.

Scott, Joan Wallach. *Only Paradoxes to Offer: French Feminists and the Rights of Man.* Cambridge, Mass: Harvard University Press, 1996.

Sedgwick, Eve Kosofsky. *Between Men: English Literature and Male Homosocial Desire.* New York: Columbia University Press, 1985.

———. *Epistemology of the Closet.* Berkeley: University of California Press, 1990.

Shapira, Michal. "Indecently Exposed: The Male Body and Vagrancy in Metropolitan London before the Fin de Siècle." *Gender and History* 30, no. 1 (2018): 52–69.

Shapiro, Ann-Louise. *Housing the Poor of Paris, 1850–1902.* Madison: University of Wisconsin Press, 1985.

Shaya, Gregory. "The Flâneur, the Badaud, and the Making of a Mass Public in France, circa 1860–1910." *American Historical Review* 109, no. 1 (2004): 41–77.

Sibalis, Michael. "The Palais-Royal and the Homosexual Subculture of Nineteenth-Century Paris." *Journal of Homosexuality* 41, nos. 3–4 (2001): 117–129.

———. "Paris-Babylone/Paris-Sodome: Images of Homosexuality in the Nineteenth-Century City." In *Images of the City in Nineteenth-Century France,* edited by John West-Sooby, 13–22. Moorooka, Queensland, Australia: Boombana Publications, 1998.

———. "The Regulation of Male Homosexuality in Revolutionary and Napoleonic France, 1789–1815." In Merrick and Ragan, *Homosexuality in Modern France,* 80–101.

———. "Urban Space and Homosexuality: The Example of the Marais, Paris' 'Gay Ghetto.'" *Urban Studies* 41, no. 9 (2004): 1739–1758.

Sohn, Anne-Marie. "The Golden Age of Male Adultery: The Third Republic." *Journal of Social History* 28, no. 3 (1995): 469–490.

———. *"Sois un homme!" La construction de la masculinité au XIXe siècle.* Paris: Seuil, 2009.

Soppelsa, Peter. "The Fragility of Modernity: Infrastructure and Everyday Life in Paris, 1870–1914." Ph.D. diss., University of Michigan, 2009. https://deepblue.lib.umich.edu/handle/2027.42/6237.

Sowerwine, Charles. "The Sexual Contract(s) of the Third Republic." *French History and Civilizations* 1 (2005): 245–253.

Spector, Scott. *Violent Sensations: Sex, Crime, and Utopia in Vienna and Berlin, 1860–1914.* Chicago: University of Chicago Press, 2016.

Stansell, Christine. *City of Women: Sex and Class in New York, 1789–1860.* Urbana: University of Illinois, 1987.

Stauter-Halsted, Keely. *The Devil's Chain: Prostitution and Social Control in Partitioned Poland*. Ithaca, N.Y.: Cornell University Press, 2015.

Stein, Marc. *City of Sisterly and Brotherly Loves: Lesbian and Gay Philadelphia, 1945–1972*. Chicago: University of Chicago Press, 2004.

Stovall, Tyler. *The Rise of the Paris Red Belt*. Berkeley: University of California Press, 1990.

Surkis, Judith. *Sexing the Citizen: Morality and Masculinity in France, 1870–1920*. Ithaca, N.Y.: Cornell University Press, 2006.

Tamagne, Florence. *Histoire de l'homosexualité en Europe: Berlin, Londres, Paris, 1919–1939*. Paris: Seuil, 2000.

Tanner, Jessica. "Turning Tricks, Turning the Tables: Plotting the *Brasserie à Femmes* in Tabarant's *Virus d'Amour.*" *Nineteenth-Century French Studies* 41, nos. 3–4 (2013): 255–271.

Terni, Jennifer. "The Omnibus and the Shaping of the Urban Quotidian: Paris, 1828–60." *Cultural and Social History* 11, no. 2 (2014): 217–242.

Tester, Keith, ed. *The* Flâneur. New York: Routledge, 1994.

Thomas, Greg M. "Women in Public: The Display of Femininity in the Parks of Paris." In *The Invisible* Flâneuse? *Gender, Public Space, and Visual Culture in Nineteenth-Century Paris,* edited by Aruna D'Souza and Tom McDonough, 32–48. Manchester, U.K.: Manchester University Press, 2006.

Thompson, Victoria. "Creating Boundaries: Homosexuality and the Changing Social Order in France, 1830–1870." In Merrick and Ragan, *Homosexuality in Modern France,* 102–127.

———. "Urban Renovation, Moral Regeneration: Domesticating the Halles in Second-Empire Paris." *French Historical Studies* 20, no. 1 (1997): 87–109.

———. *The Virtuous Marketplace: Women and Men, Money and Politics in Paris, 1830–1870*. Baltimore: Johns Hopkins University Press, 2000.

Tiersten, Lisa. *Marianne in the Market: Envisioning Consumer Society in Fin-de-Siècle France*. Berkeley: University of California Press, 2001.

Tulard, Jean. "1800–1815, L'organisation de la police." In *Histoire et dictionnaire de la police: Du moyen âge à nos jours,* edited by Michel Aubouin, Arnaud Teyssier, and Jean Tulard, 268–330. Paris: Robert Laffont, 2005.

Turner, Mark W. *Backward Glances: Cruising the Queer Streets of New York and London*. New York: Reaktion Books, 2003.

Van Casselaer, Catherine. *Lot's Wife: Lesbian Paris, 1890–1914*. Liverpool: Janus Press, 1986.

Vicinus, Martha. *Intimate Friends: Women Who Loved Women, 1778–1928*. Chicago: University of Chicago Press, 2004.

Wakeman, Rosemary. *The Heroic City: Paris, 1945–1958*. Chicago: University of Chicago Press, 2009.

Walkowitz, Judith R. *City of Dreadful Delight: Narratives of Sexual Danger in Late-Victorian London*. Chicago: University of Chicago Press, 1992.

———. "Male Vice and Feminist Virtue: Feminism and the Politics of Prostitution in Nineteenth-Century Britain." *History Workshop,* no. 13 (1982): 79–93.

———. *Prostitution and Victorian Society: Women, Class, and the State*. Cambridge: Cambridge University Press, 1980.

Warner, Michael. *Publics and Counterpublics.* New York: Zone Books, 2002.

Watson, Katherine D. *Forensic Medicine in Western Society: A History.* London: Routledge, 2011.

Weeks, Jeffrey. "Inverts, Perverts, and Mary-Annes: Male Prostitution and the Regulation of Homosexuality in England in the Nineteenth and Early Twentieth Centuries." In *Hidden from History: Reclaiming the Gay and Lesbian Past,* edited by Martin Bauml Duberman, Martha Vicinus, and George Chauncey, 195–211. New York: New American Library, 1989.

Weisz, George. "The Politics of Medical Professionalization in France, 1845–1848." *Journal of Social History* 12, no. 1 (1978): 3–30.

Willemin, Véronique. *La mondaine: Histoire et archives de la police des mœurs.* Paris: Éditions Hoëbeke, 2009.

Williams, Rosalind. *Dream Worlds: Mass Consumption in Late Nineteenth-Century France.* Berkeley: University of California Press, 1982.

Wilson, Colette E. *Paris and the Commune, 1871–78: The Politics of Forgetting.* Manchester, U.K.: Manchester University Press, 2007.

Wilson, Elizabeth. *The Sphinx in the City: Urban Life, the Control of Disorder, and Women.* Berkeley: University of California Press, 1992.

Wolff, Janet. "The Invisible *Flâneuse*: Women and the Literature of Modernity." *Theory, Culture, and Society* 2, no. 3 (1985): 37–46.

Yates, Alexia M. *Selling Paris: Property and Commercial Culture in the Fin-de-Siècle Capital.* Cambridge, Mass: Harvard University Press, 2015.

INDEX

Page numbers in italics refer to illustrations.

ANDREW ISRAEL ROSS is an Assistant Professor of History at Loyola University Maryland.